INTRODUCTION TO NON-WILDERNESS SEARCH AND RESCUE

JOSEPH THOMAS BOBOT
WEMT/NASAR SAR TECH I/MLPI

Joseph Thomas Bobot started his professional public service career in 1990 upon graduation from the Ohio Peace Officer Training Academy at Central Ohio Technical College in 1990 where after he served as a police officer for five years prior to entering the field of Emergency Medical Services. It was in 1993 that Mr. Bobot became an Emergency Medical Technician - Basic and later in 1996 obtained his Paramedic certification and in 2010 became a Wilderness EMT. It was during his career in public safety that he found an interest in Search & Rescue and in 2000 became a certified Search & Rescue Technician - Level II by the National Association for Search & Rescue.

Mr. Bobot has had extensive disaster response experience. He was a first responder during Hurricane Fran ('96) and Floyd ('99). He was also a FEMA Disaster Assistant Employee and the FEMA Logistics Chief at the DAE Processing Center in Atlanta, GA for Hurricanes' Charlie, Frances, Ivan, and Jeanne in 2004. Mr. Bobot also led a team of disaster volunteers to Mobile, Alabama after Hurricane Katrina where he and other volunteers assisted in the recovery efforts in 2005. Mr. Bobot found himself at "ground zero" 11 hours after the World Trade Center towers fell on September 11, 2001. After 9/11 Mr. Bobot, along with others in the public safety community saw the need for better prepared communities and assisted in the development of the CERT program in Ohio and became one of initial state-wide CERT development committee members and one of only two Nationally recognized CERT Program Managers in Ohio upon completion of the T4 CERT Manager course in Los Angeles, CA. In 2010 received his SAR Technician / Crew Leader – Level I and completed the Managing the Lost Person Incident (MLPI) Course.

He has also numerous certifications in Hazardous Materials Operations, Weapons of Mass Destruction Response, Mass casualty care, triage, and response as well as the recipient of the FEMA Independent Study Professional Development Course in addition to over 20 other FEMA courses. Mr. Bobot received his certification as a NASAR SAR Technician - Level 1 / Crew Leader in October of 2010 and graduated from the Air Force Rescue Coordination Center Basic Inland Search & Rescue School in 2011. Mr. Bobot.

As a recipient of the President's Volunteer Service Award, Gold level, on numerous occasions earned him the President's Call To Service Award for over 4,000 volunteer hours from 2001 - 2004. Mr. Bobot has been recognized by the State of Ohio Senate, House of Representatives, Ohio Auditor of State, US Dept. of Homeland Security, Ohio Emergency Management Agency, and other public and private entities for outstanding professional volunteer service.

Mr. Bobot is also a first responder instructor for the New Mexico Tech, Energetic Materials Research & Testing Center (EMRTC) "Incident Response to Terrorist Bombing" and "Prevention and Response to Suicide Bombing Incidents" mobile awareness course. Additionally, he is a first responder instructor for the Center for Radiological Nuclear Training (CTOS) "Radiological/Nuclear Awareness" mobile course. Mr. Bobot was Unit 6 Captain for the Ohio Special Response Team from 2020 – 2023. Mr. Bobot has been an Adjunct Faculty at Columbus State Community College, Department of EMS Education where he is the primary instructor for the EMS1107 Wilderness SAR elective course and Preceptor for EMT basic classes since 2004. He also is the Manager of the Emergency Medical Services Team at the Columbus Zoo and Aquarium and Zoombezi Bay Water Park since 2003.

INTRODUCTION TO NON-WILDERNESS SEARCH AND RESCUE

Joseph Thomas Bobot

The National Association For Search And Rescue, Inc.

The National Association For Search And Rescue, Inc.
PO Box 6930
Williamsburg, VA 23188
info@nasar.org

Copyright 2025 by The National Association For Search And Rescue, Inc.

All rights reserved. No part of the material protected by this copyright may be reproduced or utilized in any form, electronic, mechanical, including photocopying, recording, or by any information storage and retrieval system, without permission of the copyright owner.

The content, statements, views, and opinions herein are the sole expression of the respective authors and not that of The National Association For Search And Rescue, Inc. (NASAR). Reference herein to any commercial product, process, or service by trade name, trademark, manufacturer, or otherwise does not constitute or imply its endorsement or recommendation by NASAR. Any such reference shall not be used to for advertising or marketing for product placement purposes. All trademarks displayed are the trademarks of the parties noted herein. The *Introduction to Non-Wilderness Search And Rescue* is an independent publication and has not been authorized, sponsored, or otherwise approved by the owners of the trademarks or service marks referenced in this publication.

There may be images and photos in this publication that feature models; these models do not necessarily endorse, represent, or participate in the activities in the images. Any screenshots in this publication are for educational and instructive purposes only. Any individuals and scenarios featured in the case studies throughout this publication may be real or fictitious and are used for education purposes only.

The procedures, protocols and processes in this publication are based on the most current recommendations of responsible SAR and medical sources. NASAR, however, makes no guarantee as to, and assume no responsibility for, the correctness, sufficiency, or completeness of such information or recommendations. Other additional safety measures may be required under particular circumstances.

This publication is intended solely as a guide to the appropriate procedures to be employed when rendering emergency care in the location of a missing person. It is not intended as a statement of the standards of care required in any particular situation, because the risk, circumstances, resources, environment, and the missing persons medical and mental condition can vary widely from one emergency to another. Nor is it intended that this publication shall in any way advise emergency responders concerning legal authority to perform the activities, processes, or procedures discussed. Such local determination should be made only with the aid of legal counsel.

Library of Congress
Names: Bobet, Joseph, author
Title: Introduction to Non-Wilderness Search And Rescue
Identifier: 978-0-9864440-7-4 (paperback)

Joseph dedicates this text to all the SAR responders in our communities. They place their lives on hold and take extraordinary risk to search for and rescue those in need.

Joseph expresses many thanks to:

Ohio Special Response Team

Mark Sexton

Jerry Whaley

Fernando Moreira

Dale Thompson

for their contributions to the SAR community and the publication of this book.

Table of Contents

Chapter	Title	Page
1	**Unit 1** SAR Basics	02
2	**Unit 2** Legal & Ethical Issues	16
3	**Unit 3** ICS	26
4	**Unit 4** SAR Resources	45
5	**Unit 5** SAR Communications	59
6	**Unit 6** Personal Safety	70
7	**Unit 7** 24-Hour SAR Pack	89
8	**Unit 8** Incident & Scene Safety	102
9	**Unit 9** Land Navigation	125
10	**Unit 10** Clues & Tracking	163
11	**Unit 11** Search Tactics	180
12	**Unit 12** Rescue & Recovery	198
13	**Unit 13** Lost Person Behavior	216

UNIT 1 | SAR BASICS

1.1 The SAR Motto
1.2 SAR Defined
1.3 Life Cycle of a SAR Event
1.4 Four Components of a SAR Incident
1.5 Specialty Search and Rescue
1.6 The Scope of Search & Rescue
1.7 The National SAR Plan
1.8 USCG, CAP & FEMA
1.9 The AFRCC
1.10 International SAR System
1.11 Getting Involved in SAR

Upon completion of this chapter and the related course activities, the student will be able to meet the following objectives:

- Origin of the SAR motto
- Life cycle of a SAR event
- LAST
- The "Classic Mystery"
- The AFRCC
- The NRF & ESF #9
- Define "Search" and "Rescue"
- Mission of the INSARG
- Define the "PHACKS"

1.1 The Search And Rescue Motto

The search and rescue (SAR) motto **"That others may live"** has origins from an officer's report on the rescue by Cape Hatteras Life Saving Station, North Carolina, of survivors of the wreck of the barquentine vessel *Ephraim Williams* on December 22, 1884. On December 22, 1884, Keeper Benjamin B. Dailey of Cape Hatteras Station and his crew took their surfboat into the huge breakers crashing ashore and through immense seas to the wreck of the Ephraim Williams. An entry in the journal stated the following: "I do not believe that a greater act of heroism is recorded than that of Dailey and his crew on that momentous occasion. These poor, plain men, dwellers upon lonely sands of Hatteras, took their lives in their hands and, at the most imminent risk, crossed the most tumultuous sea that any boat within memory of living men had ever attempted on that bleak coast, and all for what? *That others might live* to see home and friends." [1]

Most recently, the quote was prominent in the movie, *The Guardian*, portraying U.S. Coast Guard rescue swimmers. This motto has been adopted by search and rescue (SAR) teams of all types to signify the core values of those who, at times, risk their own lives to save the lives of others.

The oldest recorded SAR response comes from the Vergulde Draeck (Gilded Dragon) incident. This vessel was a Dutch merchant ship in the seventeenth century. The vessel set sail from Texel bound for Batavia (now Jakarta), but on April 28, 1656 was wrecked off Ledge Point, 107 kilometers north of what is now Perth, Western Australia. It was reported that 75 survivors (of 193 originally on board) made it to shore and dispatched a small boat to Batavia to call for help. Despite three search and rescue missions to locate them, the remaining survivors were never found. [2]

1.2 Search And Rescue Defined

The general field of search and rescue includes many specialty subfields, mostly based upon terrain considerations. These include mountain rescue; ground search and rescue, including the use of search and rescue dogs; urban search and rescue in cities; combat search and rescue on the battlefield and air-sea rescue over water.

There are many definitions surrounding "search and rescue" as well as many forms of responses. The Canadian Forces define SAR as: "The search for, and provision of aid to, persons, ships or other craft which are, or are feared to be, in distress or imminent danger." The United States Coast Guard defines SAR as: "The use of available resources to assist persons or property in potential or actual distress."

The United States Defense Department's definition of Search as "An operation normally coordinated by a Rescue Coordination Center (RCC) or rescue subcenter, using available personnel and facilities to locate persons in distress." and Rescue as "An operation to retrieve persons in distress, provide for their initial medical or other needs, and deliver them to a place of safety."

The "Missing vs. Lost" Perspective

Search management courses have traditionally assumed the subject being sought is "lost." This can establish a mindset that ignores the other possibilities, such as simply being overdue, purposefully hiding, victim of an accident, etc. There are four types of subjects considered in search planning. [3]

A **Lost Person** is a person who is temporarily disorientated and wishes to be found (someone who has been out walking in the woods, taken a wrong turn and no longer knows where they are).

A **Voluntarily Missing Person** is someone who has control over their actions and who has decided upon a course of action (wishes to leave home, unauthorized absence from a Care Home, or to commit suicide).

An **Influenced Missing Person** is missing against their will (possible abduction, or murder victim).

An **Incapacitated Missing Person** is someone who has met with a sudden illness such as a stroke, someone wandering off due to a mental condition such as dementia, or a person injured from an accident such as broken leg from falling down an embankment.

1.3 Life Cycle of a SAR Event

The life cycle of a SAR event *(Fig. 1-1)* doesn't start with the call for help. It is continuously evolving in a cyclic manner. It starts when a searcher begins the training or as a department begins writing SAR into their procedures. The incident that requires SAR intervention is in the middle of this cycle.

At the beginning is constant improvement, training, researching new technology and equipment, writing policy and procedures, getting ready for the call. At the end of this cycle is the critique, or discussion about how the team did during the incident, identifying lessons learned and using that feedback in pre-planning. The life cycle of a SAR event has six major phases:

- **Planning** or "Preplanning" is a term applied to the overall planning which occurs before an incident and addresses all phases of likely situations. Good preplanning means being ready in terms of equipment, organization, management, and training.

- **Notification** is the moment in time that an incident is made known to SAR personnel. There are two phases of notification: first the notification of a SAR mission (usually the call to 911) and the notification of SAR resources to respond.

- **Strategy** asks the question "What actions can be carried out?" As each SAR phase begins, situation-specific planning and strategy development arises from completed pre-planning efforts. During this phase, the details are developed regarding how the current incident will be managed.

- **Tactics** are those plans that are physically carried out. Tactical assignments may include either passive and/or active search techniques.

- **Suspension** happens at the end of a search along with demobilization. If the subject has been found, the search is suspended, and the access phase can commence. However, if the subject has not been found, the decision to discontinue active search efforts is a necessary, but difficult decision.

- **Critique** is <u>VERY IMPORTANT!</u> Within 48 hours of returning from the incident and After Action Review (AAR) should take place with all the responders. The results of the AAR should be used to develop the Corrective Action Plan (CAP). Both the AAR and CAP are part of the Incident Command System (ICS).

1.4 Four Components of a SAR Incident

There is one thing that all search and rescue incidents have in common. Search and rescue operations must have a beginning, a middle and an end. Each mission has a different timeline **(Fig. 1-2)**, however, each component, or phase must be completed before the next phase can begin.

There are the four phases to every search and rescue incident and they are best known by the acronym: LAST. [4]

- **LOCATE:** This phase represents the act of looking for and determining the subject's location. This is the most difficult and crucial component of the search function.

- **ACCESS:** This phase requires that we be able to reach the subject once located. It may still yet be several hours until SAR personnel can physically reach the subject due to their location, difficulty accessing them or technical resources required.

- **STABILIZE:** This phase requires that SAR personnel assess and maintain the subject's medical and physical wellbeing until they are ready to be moved to a safe environment.

- **TRANSPORT:** This phase represents the physical removal from the location found to the safe environment.

(Fig 1-2) Dynamic LAST Example

In the above example, (top) the majority of searches will consist of a long period looking for the subject. (Bottom) it took a rescue team considerable time to access the patient once found while the other phases were relatively equal in length of time. Image courtesy of J. Bobot.

Each of the four phases of a search and rescue operation must be allowed to evolve on its own. You cannot skip a component as the next is dependent upon the one before it. For example, you can't access someone you have not yet located.

1.5 Specialty Search and Rescue

Search and rescue skills are diverse and cover many areas, including the following specialized areas of response. Search and rescue services, in general, may be provided by paid or volunteer professionals. However, the labor-intensive and occasional nature of mountain rescue, along with the specific techniques and local knowledge required for some environments, means that mountain and wilderness rescue is often undertaken by volunteer teams. These are frequently made up of local climbers, guides or other specially trained persons. Mountain and wilderness search and rescue are often free **(Fig. 1-3)**, although in some parts of the world rescue organizations may charge for their services.

There are exceptions, e.g. Switzerland, where mountain rescue is highly expensive (ranging from $2,000 to $4,000) and charged to the patient. In more remote or less-developed parts of the world, organized mountain rescue services are often negligible or nonexistent. In the United States, mountain rescue is handled by professional teams within some national parks and by volunteer teams elsewhere and operate under the authority of the local sheriff's department or National Park Service.

Ground Search and Rescue - Ground search and rescue refer to activities that occur on land in a mountainous, wilderness, rural, suburban or urban environment. Traditionally associated with wilderness zones, ground search and rescue services are often required in urban and suburban areas to locate persons with Alzheimer's disease, autism, dementia, or other conditions that lead to wandering behavior. Ground search and rescue missions that occur in urban areas should not be confused with "Urban SAR" or "US&R", which in many jurisdictions refers to the location and extraction of people from disaster environments.

(Fig. 1-3) Members of the Ohio Special Response Team pose by their response vehicle. OSRT is a volunteer team that does not charge for their services. Image courtesy of Harry Mains.

Mountain Rescue - Mountain rescue relates to search and rescue operations specifically in rugged and mountainous terrain. In the United States, mountain rescue is handled by professional teams within national parks or by volunteer teams. Parks with professional teams include Denali National Park, Yosemite National Park, Grand Teton National Park, and Mount Rainier National Park. Volunteer teams are part of the Mountain Rescue Association (MRA) and operate under the authority of the local sheriff's department.

Urban Search and Rescue - Urban search and rescue (USAR), also referred to as Heavy Urban Search and Rescue (HUSAR), is the location and rescue of persons in collapsed buildings or other urban and industrial entrapments. Because of the specialized nature of the work, most teams are multi-disciplinary and include personnel from fire, structural engineering, and emergency medical services. Unlike traditional ground search and rescue workers, most USAR responders also have basic training in structural collapse and are professional firefighters with hazardous materials training. While earthquakes have traditionally been the cause of USAR operations, terrorist attacks and extreme weather such as tornadoes and hurricanes have also resulted in the deployment of these resources.

Air-Sea Rescue - (ASR) refers to the combined use of aircraft and surface vessels to search for and recover survivors of aircraft downed at sea as well as sailors and passengers of sea vessels in distress.

Combat Search and Rescue - Combat search and rescue refers to search and rescue operations that are carried out during war or are within or near combat zones.

1.6 The Scope of Search And Rescue

The term "Search and Rescue" or "SAR" is often looked at or categorized as one function. In actuality it is two very distinct and separate functions with a third area referred to as "support." These functions outline the three major skill areas of a SAR Response. The following is a description of the three required skill areas of a SAR response that makes up its scope. **(Fig. 1-4)**.

(Fig 1-4) Where the volunteer fits within the scope of SAR. Image courtesy J. Bobot.

- **Search:** All activities associated with the discovery of an individual or individuals missing or reported lost. This activity is also known as **"The Classic Mystery!"** This is because as searchers we do not search for subjects, we search for "clues" first. These clues will lead to the subject. We do this because the subject may be mobile, unresponsive, evasive, elusive, or dead! Clues will always be there, unless destroyed by weather or contamination.

- **Rescue:** All activities directed towards and requiring the utilization of trained personnel to access and extricate persons trapped in damaged buildings, vehicles, woodlands, waterways, high angle or underground locations; and to provide emergency medical treatment of such persons.

- **Support:** All activities directed toward the planning and operational aspects of the search mission. This can include, but are not limited to logistics, finance, planning and operational readiness in support of the overall mission.

As a SAR responder, you may be needed to perform all three of these functions as the incident dictates. No one function is more important than the others as all three must work in concert for the incident to be safe and a success.

Search and rescue uses established processes and procedures. Responsibility for situational assessment and determination of resource needs rests with the incident commander in coordination with local, state, and federal Emergency Operating Centers (EOCs) and appropriate Emergency Support Functions (ESF).

Government Coordination

In January 2008, the United States Department of Homeland Security (DHS) released the National Response Framework (NRF), which serves as a general guide to how the nation conducts an all-hazards incident response. It also provides a comprehensive approach to local or large-scale domestic incident response.

The NRF is built on flexible, scalable, and adaptable coordinating structures to align key roles and responsibilities, linking all levels of government and private sector businesses and nongovernmental organizations.

In support of the NRF, there are 15 annexes **(Table 1-1)** relating to Emergency Support Functions (ESF). These annexes describe the roles and responsibilities of federal departments and agencies as ESF Coordinators, primary agencies, or support agencies. Search and Rescue is included as ESF-9 and divides SAR into four primary elements, while assigning a federal agency with the lead role for each of the four elements:

TABLE 1-1	
ESF #1	Transportation
ESF #2	Communications
ESF #3	Public Works and Engineering
ESF #4	Firefighting
ESF #5	Emergency Management
ESF #6	Mass Care, Assistance, and Human Services
ESF #7	Logistics Management and Resource Support
ESF #8	Public Health and Medical Services
ESF #9	Search and Rescue
ESF #10	Oil and Hazardous Materials Response
ESF #11	Agriculture and Natural Resources
ESF #12	Energy
ESF #13	Public Safety and Security
ESF #14	Long-Term Community Recovery
ESF #15	External Affairs

- **Waterborne:** United States Coast Guard and the United States Coast Guard Auxiliary.

- **Structural Collapse-USAR:** Department of Homeland Security Federal Emergency Management Agency.

- **Inland-wilderness:** United States Department of Interior, the National Park Service, and the Federal Emergency Management Agency.

- **Aeronautical:** United States Air Force Rescue Coordination Center, the Civil Air Patrol and the United States Air Force Aerospace Rescue and Recovery Service.

The NRF describes events beyond the simple missing or lost person incident. There are many different instances during which SAR personnel can be used. For example, law enforcement may need help looking for a key piece of evidence that was abandoned by the perpetrator. Or the coroner and the NTSB (National Transportation & Safety Bureau) may need help searching for parts of an aircraft that crashed in the woods.

SAR personnel may be called upon to supplement public safety forces during a large-scale disaster that impacts an entire town or city. These events are called catastrophic incidents.

1.7 The National SAR Plan

The National Search and Rescue Plan, signed by the Departments of Homeland Security, Defense, Interior, Transportation and Commerce, the National Aeronautics and Space Administration and the Federal Communications Commission, supports Federal efforts in the response to catastrophic incidents as described in the National Response Framework (2008) and Emergency Support Function #9, Search and Rescue.

A **catastrophic incident** is any natural or manmade incident, including terrorism, which results in extraordinary levels of mass causalities, damage, or disruption severely affecting the population, infrastructure, environment, economy, national morale, and/or government functions.

The National SAR Plan was developed by an interagency Committee on Search and Rescue (NSARC) to delegate SAR responsibilities at the Federal, State, and local level **(Fig. 1-5)**. NSARC Members include:

(Fig. 1-5) Members of the interagency Committee on Search & Rescue (NSARC). Dept. of Defense (DOD), Dept. of Commerce (DOC), Dept. of Transportation (DOT), Dept. of the Interior (DOI), Dept. of Homeland Security (DHS), Federal Communications Commission (FCC) and The National Aeronautics and Space Administration (NASA). Image courtesy of the USCG.

- **US Air Force (USAF):** Monitors the Air Force Rescue Coordination Center (AFRCC) at Tyndall AFB, Florida and coordinates Federal resources used for SAR.

- **US Coast Guard (USCG):** Searches any navigable waterway in the U.S. and up to 3 miles inland.

- **Federal Aviation Administration (FAA):** Provides search information for all downed aircraft.

- **Civil Air Patrol (CAP):** Civilian auxiliary of the USAF who flies more than 85 percent of inland SAR missions as directed by the USAF.

- **Local Authorities:** SAR missions in the United States are usually under the direction of law enforcement - "missing person" cases are deemed "criminal" until proven otherwise.

The NRF can be found at the following web address:
https://www.dco.uscg.mil/Portals/9/CG-5R/manuals/National_SAR_Plan_2016.pdf

Catastrophic Incident SAR (CIS) consists of civil SAR operations carried out as all or part of the response to an emergency or disaster declared by the President, under provisions of the National Response Framework and its Emergency Support Function-9, Search and Rescue.

This is most often used during a large-scale natural disaster such as a tornado or hurricane. A major disaster or civil emergency may generate conditions that vary widely in scope, urgency, and degree of devastation. Substantial numbers of people could be in life-threatening situations requiring prompt rescue and medical care. Depending on the nature of a catastrophic incident (i.e., earthquake, hurricane, terrorist attack, etc.), CIS operations may or may not be necessary; if CIS operations are conducted, operations may be minor, or a major aspect of the overall incident response. Also, State, local, and tribal authorities may or may not be able to conduct CIS operations with their own resources.

An effective response to a major catastrophic incident typically requires immediate, well-planned, and closely coordinated large-scale actions and use of resources from multiple organizations. For an incident to be deemed a wide area search incident, the following conditions must apply:

- The situation taxes all available, local resources.
- Due to the scope of the incident requires various types of resources and areas of expertise.
- There are an unknown number of subjects involved.
- There is a large geographical area involved.

1.8 USCG, CAP & FEMA

The United States Coast Guard

Before the 1900s, searches were carried out when ships were wrecked, but people who got lost in the back country were often never rescued or were found only by chance. For many of these incidents at sea, volunteer sailors formed organized groups. This happed in many countries. They later were known as the "coast guard."

In the United States, the U.S. Coast Guard (USCG) is one of the country's si armed services and a unique agency of the federal government. The USCG can trace their history back to August 4, 1790, when the first Congress authorized the construction of 10 vessels to enforce tariff and trade laws and to prevent smuggling.

The USCG received its present name in 1915 under an act of Congress when the Revenue Cutter Service merged with the Life-Saving Service. The nation then had a single maritime service dedicated to saving life at sea and enforcing the nation's maritime laws. The Coast Guard began to maintain the country's aids to maritime navigation, including operating the nation's lighthouses, when President Franklin Roosevelt ordered the transfer of the Lighthouse Service to the Coast Guard in 1939.

(Fig. 1-6) NEW ORLEANS (Aug. 30, 2005) - Coast Guard Petty Officer 2nd Class Scott D. Rady, 34, of Tampa, Florida, pulls a pregnant woman from her flooded New Orleans home here today. Rady is a rescue swimmer sent from Clearwater, Florida, to help aid in search and rescue efforts in the wake of Hurricane Katrina. U.S. Coast Guard photo courtesy of Petty Officer 2nd Class Nyxo Lyno Cangemi.

The Coast Guard is one of the oldest organizations of the federal government and, until the Navy Department was established in 1798, served as the nation's only armed force afloat. They continued to protect the nation throughout our long history and have served proudly in every one of the nation's conflicts. Our national defense remains one of the most important functions of the USCG even today. In times of peace they operate as part of the Department of Homeland Security.

Civil Air Patrol (CAP)

The Civil Air Patrol is a Congressionally chartered, federally supported, non-profit corporation that serves as the official civilian auxiliary of the United States Air Force (USAF). CAP is a volunteer organization with an aviation-minded membership that includes people from all backgrounds, lifestyles, and occupations.

Membership in the organization consists of cadets ranging from 12 to just under 21 years of age, and senior members 18 years of age and up. These two groups each can participate in a wide variety of pursuits; the cadet program contributes to the development of youth with a structured syllabus and organization based upon United States Air Force ranks and pay grades, while the older members serve as instructors, supervisors, and operators. All members wear uniforms while performing their duties.

Nationwide, CAP is a major operator of single-engine general aviation aircraft, used in the execution of its various missions, including orientation flights for cadets and the provision of significant emergency services capabilities. Because of these extensive flying opportunities, many CAP members become licensed pilots.

The Civil Air Patrol is well known for its search activities in conjunction with search and rescue (SAR) operations. CAP is involved with approximately three-quarters of all aerial inland SAR missions directed by the United States Air Force Rescue Coordination Center. CAP is credited with saving an average of 100 lives per year. [5]

Federal Emergency Management Agency (FEMA)

FEMA established the National Urban Search and Rescue (USAR) Response System in 1989 as a framework for structuring local emergency services personnel into integrated disaster response task forces. Events such as the 1995 bombing of the Alfred P. Murrah building in Oklahoma City, the Northridge (CA) earthquake, the Kansas grain elevator explosion in 1998 and earthquakes in Turkey and Greece in 1999 underscore the need for highly skilled teams to rescue trapped victims. The terrorist attacks on the World Trade Center and the Pentagon on September 11, 2001, thrust FEMA's Urban Search and Rescue (US&R) teams into the spotlight as well as major natural disasters **(Fig. 1-7)**.

FEMA Urban Search and Rescue Team, Virginia Task Force 2, prepare to enter a badly damaged beachfront building on Orange Beach, Ala. Image courtesy of Butch Kinerney.

While on-the-ground support of disaster recovery efforts is a major part of FEMA's charter, the agency also provides state and local governments with experts efforts and relief funds for infrastructure, in conjunction with the Small Business Administration.

In addition to this, FEMA provides funds for training of response personnel throughout the United States and its territories as part of the agency's preparedness effort.

FEMA USAR Teams

Federal Emergency Management (FEMA) Urban Search and Rescue Task Force (USAR-TF) is a team of individuals specializing in urban search and rescue, disaster recovery, and emergency triage and medicine. The teams are deployed to emergency and disaster sites within six hours of notification.

There are 28 Task Forces in the United States, each sponsored by a local fire agency. The role of these task forces is to support state and local emergency responders' efforts to locate subjects and manage rescue operations. Each task force consists of trained personnel, canines, and a comprehensive equipment cache.

USAR task force members work in four areas of specialization:

- Search, to find victims trapped after a disaster.
- Rescue, which includes safely digging victims out of tons of collapsed concrete and metal.
- Technical, made up of structural specialists who make rescues safe for the rescuers.
- Medical, which cares for the victims before and after a rescue.

In the event of a disaster in the United States, the nearest three Task Forces are typically activated and sent to the site of the disaster.

1.9 The AFRCC

As the United States' inland search and rescue coordinator, the Air Force Rescue Coordination Center serves as the single agency responsible for coordinating on-land federal SAR activities in the 48 contiguous United States, Mexico, and Canada.

The AFRCC operates 24 hours a day, seven days a week. The center directly ties into the Federal Aviation Administration's alerting system and the U.S. Mission Control Center. In addition to the Search and Rescue Satellite Aided Tracking information, the AFRCC computer system contains resource files that list federal and state organizations, which can conduct or assist in SAR efforts throughout North America. The AFRCC is located at Tyndall Air Force Base, Florida. The center directly ties into the Federal Aviation Administration's alerting system and the United States Mission Control Center **(Fig. 1-8)**.

(Fig. 1-8) Search and Rescue coordinators Maj. Bill Kennedy and Staff Sgt. Diane Brown monitor ongoing SAR operations. Image courtesy of U.S. Air Force / Capt. Jared Scott.

During ongoing SAR missions, the center serves as the communications hub and provides coordination and assistance to on-scene commanders or mission coordinators to accomplish the mission's objective in the safest and most effective manner possible.

When a distress call is received, the center investigates the request, coordinates with federal, state, and local officials, and determines the type and scope of response necessary. Once verified as an actual distress situation, the AFRCC requests support from the appropriate federal SAR force. This may include Civil Air Patrol, United States Coast Guard, or other Department of Defense assets, as needed. State agencies can be contacted for state, local, or civil SAR resource assistance within their jurisdiction.

The AFRCC also formulates and manages SAR plans, agreements and policies throughout the continental United States. Additionally, it presents a mobile Search Management Course to Civil Air Patrol wings throughout the United States to produce qualified incident commanders thus improving national SAR capability.

1.10 International Search And Rescue System

Search and rescue is an international system. After an earthquake in Armenia in 1988, the German, Swiss and Austrian SAR Units founded in 1991 the International Search And Rescue Advisory Group (INSARAG). INSARAG is a global network of more than 80 countries and disaster response organizations under the United Nations umbrella.

The INSARAG's primary mission is to facilitate coordination between the various international USAR teams who make themselves available for deployment to countries experiencing devastating events of structural collapse due primarily to earthquakes. The group works on coordination by facilitating opportunities for communication between these groups ahead of such events.

The INSARAG Guidelines provide guidance for the preparation and deployment of search and rescue teams for international disaster response operations to earthquake-prone countries as well as checklists for the minimum requirements of USAR teams envisaged to deploy in international response operations.

The INSARAG Guidelines define coordination and cooperation procedures for international and national responders in major disasters. The standards that our US&R teams utilize are the same as those around the world. In addition, the Guidelines focus on topics of concern to any organization that deploys to international emergency response operations. These include background information about the international humanitarian environment and an explanation of the role of the United Nations system under the Office for the Coordination of Humanitarian Affairs.

1.11 Getting Involved in SAR

In most of the country, search and rescue is made up of volunteers. SAR volunteers are often vital to the safe return of a loved one. Volunteer SAR teams are often made up of a wide range of demographics from professional fire/EMS workers, college students, retired professionals, and those from any other profession. Physical ability usually is the only factor when it comes to SAR field work. SAR personnel exhibit various qualities that make them "professional" as they are volunteering.

Search and Rescue operations function day and night. (top & center). Volunteer searchers at Ground Zero, Kyle Wimer (left) and author, Joseph Bobot (right) September 2001. Photo courtesy J. Bobot.

The **qualities of a good searcher**, also known as the **PHACKS**:

- **Proficient** in their duties and skills.
- **Humble** in their character.
- **Able** in their performance.
- **Compassionate** in their manner.
- **Knowledgeable** through experience & study.
- **Safety-minded** in their operations.

Weak Link Theory

Sequence of events or objects dependent on the support of the whole. The whole is only as reliable as the weakest member or link. A SAR team is dependent upon each other and work together to make the incident outcome the best possible.

There are many roles and responsibilities aside from the searchers and rescuers in the field or the team members who are filmed as they carry the child to an awaiting ambulance. It takes people behind the scenes as well, such as those in command, those getting sandwiches and those who provide the training every month. The only time that the team comes first is when safety is concerned. The first priority is your personal safety, then the safety of your teammates and then the subject.

FOOTNOTES

(1) Unknown, (1884) Excerpt from an officer's report on the rescue by Cape Hatteras Life Saving Station, North Carolina, of survivors of the wreck of the barquentine vessel Ephraim Williams. US Coast Guard Historian's Office.

(2) Henderson, James A. (1982). Marooned: The Wreck of the Vergulde Draeck and the Abandonment and Escape from the Southland of Abraham Leeman in 1658. St. George Books.

(3) Dougher, Hugh. (2010). "Search Management Systems, A Practical Approach to Initiating and Directing Efforts to Resolve Missing Person Incidents".

(4) Bannerman, Foster, Hill, Hood, Thrasher & Wolf, (1999). Introduction to Search & Rescue. National Association for Search & Rescue.

(5) Emergency Services". Civil Air Patrol. Archived from the original on 25 April 2006.

VITAL VOCABULARY

Catastrophic Incident SAR (CIS): Civil SAR operations carried out as all or part of the response to an emergency or disaster declared by the President, under provisions of the National Response Framework and its Emergency Support Function-9, Search and Rescue (ESF-9).

Catastrophic Incident: Is any natural or manmade incident, including terrorism, which results in extraordinary levels of mass causalities, damage, or disruption severely affecting the population, infrastructure, environment, economy, national morale, and/or government functions.

Emergency Support Functions (ESF): Federal agencies that contain resources or expertise to support an emergency response or disaster declaration.

International Search & Rescue Advisory Group (INSARAG): A global network of more than 80 countries and disaster response organizations under the United Nations umbrella that addresses issues in urban search and rescue and disaster response.

National Response Framework (NRF): This is a document which serves as a general guide to how the nation conducts an all-hazards incident response.

Rescue: This is an operation to retrieve persons in distress, provide for their initial medical or other needs, and deliver them to a place of safety.

Search: This is an operation normally coordinated by a Rescue Coordination Center (RCC) or rescue sub-center, using available personnel and facilities to locate persons in distress.

Wide Area Search: A situation that has affected a large geographical area where there are an unknown number of subjects and where local resources are overwhelmed. This type of incident will require resources from both the urban and inland SAR communities.

UNIT 2 | LEGAL & ETHICAL ISSUES

2.1 Morals & Ethics

2.2 The Law and You

2.3 Minimizing Risk

2.4 Laws Protecting Volunteers

2.5 Scope of Practice

2.6 Consent and Refusal of Care

2.7 Legal Fundamentals & Privacy

2.8 Trespassing

2.9 Documentation

2.10 Liability Insurance

> Upon completion of this chapter and the related course activities, the student will be able to meet the following objectives:
> - Explain the difference between "morals" and "ethics"
> - Identify the five elements needed to prove negligence in a court of law
> - Explain the various types of "consent"
> - Explain the various trespass laws
> - Explain the purpose of the SAR Mission Log

2.1 Morals & Ethics

The fundamental responsibilities of the emergency provider, be they fire, law enforcement, EMTs or search and rescue personnel, are to conserve life, to alleviate suffering, to promote health, to do no harm, and to encourage the quality and equal availability of emergency care. The SAR responder provides services based on human need, with respect for human dignity, unrestricted by consideration of nationality, race, creed, color, or status. The SAR provider must refuse to participate in unethical procedures and assumes the responsibility to expose incompetence or unethical conduct of others to the appropriate authority in a proper and professional manner.

Morals are the social, religious, or personal standards of right and wrong. While ethics are the rules or standards that govern the conduct of members of a particular group or profession. Dutiful attention to virtue, teamwork, beneficence, justice, and respect for patient autonomy provides a coherent approach to addressing many ethical dilemmas in the out-of-hospital setting.

2.2 The Law and You

This unit will introduce some of the basic concepts and definitions of the law and how they apply to SAR responders. All rescue personnel know the basic rule of emergency care is to "do no further harm." However, despite our good intentions and best efforts, accidents and mistakes happen. When someone "suffers" at the hand of another person, including rescue workers, they can sue, go to court, and collect financial compensation for their injuries or emotional trauma. A tort (originally from the French, meaning "wrong") is a wrong that involves a breach of a civil duty owed to someone else. An intentional tort is a category of torts that describes a civil wrong resulting from an intentional act on the part of another person.

An unintentional tort is called negligence. Negligence is a type of tort (also known as a civil wrong) where a person is harmed unintentionally through the failure to provide care equal to the standard of care expected of the rescuer who is a reasonable person, fully trained, and is acting under similar circumstances **(Table 2-1)**. One can minimize the possibility of being sued for negligence through setting one's personal and professional standards high and following accepted industry and professional standards.

TABLE 2-1
Five Elements Needed to Prove Negligence in a Court of Law
Legal causation or remoteness
Factual causation (Direct Cause)
Breach of Duty
Duty of Care
Harm

2.3 Minimizing Risk

The following are a few of the main ways to minimize the risk of a lawsuit while performing your duties:

- Learning and refreshing your skills and following the training standards of your department.
- Perform each act in the best and safest way.
- Practice, practice and practice your skills. Especially the skills that are not used very often.
- Act with reason, compassion and focus when assisting someone in need.

- Use good judgment and don't be afraid to ask for assistance from your teammates.

2.4 Laws Protecting Volunteers

There are laws or acts protecting those who choose to serve and tend to others who are injured, ill, in peril, or otherwise incapacitated. They are intended to reduce bystanders' hesitation to assist, for fear of being sued or prosecuted for unintentional injury or wrongful death.

In some jurisdictions, Good Samaritan laws only protect those who have completed basic first aid training and are certified by health organizations, such as the American Heart Association, or American Red Cross, provided that they have acted within the scope of their training. In other jurisdictions, any rescuer is protected from liability, so long as the responder acted rationally. [1]

There are a couple of key laws that may protect the Search and Rescue Volunteer:

- **State Good Samaritan Law:** No person shall be liable in civil damages for administering emergency care or treatment at the scene of an emergency outside of a hospital, doctor's office, or other place having proper medical equipment, for acts performed at the scene of such emergency, unless such acts constitute willful or wanton misconduct.
- **42 U.S.C.S. § 14501 Federal Volunteer Protection Act:** In response to a steady decrease in volunteerism, Congress enacted the Federal Volunteer Protection Act to provide immunity for volunteers. As federal legislation, the VPA preempts less-protective state laws.

2.5 Scope of Practice

Wilderness emergency care providers, search and rescue personnel, or any other trained medical care provider must function within their individual scope of practice. Scope of Practice is a terminology used by state licensing boards for various professions that defines the procedures, actions, and processes that are permitted for the licensed individual. The scope of practice is limited to that which the law allows for specific education and experience, and specific demonstrated competency. [2]

Search and rescue personnel are not trained to provide definitive medical care, but instead focus on rapid in-field treatment and transport to higher medical providers. SAR team members work in conjunction with other medical providers such as EMTs, paramedics, nurses, and physicians, as well as with other rescue personnel. When operating in the pre-hospital environment, their actions are governed by protocols and procedures set by their system's physician medical director.

2.6 Consent and Refusal of Care

It is hard to imagine that a person needing emergency care would refuse, however this happens often for a variety of reasons. Some of these reasons stem from financial issues, where the subject thinks that it would cost too much to be treated, religious beliefs, or fear. Responders need to honor the patients wishes when they are competent to make that decision. Emergency care providers need to always make sure that the person to be taken care of grants permission to do so.

Types of Consent

Consent is granting the provider permission to render care. There are two types of consent that we need to understand. The first type of consent is expressed consent, or actual consent. This is when the subject expressly authorizes you to provide emergency care and transport.

When a subject may be hesitant on allowing you to render care, you must inform them of the potential risk, benefits and alternatives to treatment. If they decide to allow you to render care it is then known as **informed consent**. [3]

When a person is or becomes unresponsive, they are unable to give consent. This also includes subjects that are delusional, under the influence of drugs and/or alcohol, or otherwise physically or mentally unable to give expressed consent. Those who are suffering from mental illness, behavioral crisis, psychological disorders, under the influence of drugs or alcohol or who may be developmentally disabled cannot, in the eyes of the law, give informed consent.

From a legal perspective, this situation is like that of a child and consent should be obtained from the subject's legal guardian. As with children, if the legal guardian of a mentally incompetent adult is unavailable or unable to be contacted, then it would be **implied consent**.

Minors and Consent

Depending upon what state you work in, the care and treatment of children **(Fig. 2-1)** requires permission, or consent, of the parent or legal guardian.

However, in some states, a minor can give valid consent to receive medical care, depending on the minor's age and maturity. Many states also allow pregnant minors, married minors or emancipated minors to be considered adults when it comes to consent. It is always best to get permission to treat a minor; however, if a true medical emergency is present and if a parent or legal guardian is not present or able to be reached the consent is implied, just as it is with an adult.

(Fig 2-1) Group of children in a tree. Image courtesy J. Bobot.

Stopping or Ending Care

Abandonment of a patient, in medicine, occurs when a health care professional has already begun emergency treatment of a patient and then suddenly walks away while the patient is still in need, without securing the services of an adequate substitute or giving the patient adequate opportunity to find one. It is a crime in many countries and can result in the loss of one's license to practice.

Also, because of the public policy in favor of keeping people alive, the professional cannot defend himself or herself by pointing to the patient's inability to pay for services; this opens the medical professional to the possibility of exposure to malpractice liability.

However, in the realm of wilderness or remote medical care, in most jurisdictions, the stopping or the decision to not begin lifesaving medical care (such as CPR) may be granted when that care would be conducted over a very long period of time due to the distance need to be travelled by the rescue workers. This may also be enacted when rendering this type of care is not practical due to the safety of the providers.

2.7 Legal Fundamentals & Privacy

We live in a very litigious society and must safeguard ourselves from litigation and lawsuits, however, if we constantly worry about these actions, our patient care would suffer. The best way to safeguard from litigation is to be competent and compassionate. The following are some general considerations when providing emergency care:

- Don't work in constant fear of being sued.
- Know and perform your job to the best of your abilities.
- Always act in good faith to an appropriate standard of care.
- Seek professional advice when questions arise.
- Keep training and certifications current.
- Never exceed the level of training received.
- Document training, searches, and actions.

The Health Insurance Portability and Accountability Act of 1996 (HIPAA)

The Office for Civil Rights enforces the HIPAA Privacy Rule, which protects the privacy of individually identifiable health information; the HIPAA Security Rule, which sets national standards for the security of electronic protected health information; and the confidentiality provisions of the Patient Safety Rule, which protect identifiable information being used to analyze patient safety events and improve patient safety. Emergency care providers are not permitted to discuss any personal or medical information about the patient they have treated with anyone other than in the case of patient care transfer from one healthcare provider to another.

The act consists of five titles. Title I of HIPAA protects health insurance coverage for workers and their families when they change or lose their jobs. [5] Title II of HIPAA, known as the Administrative Simplification (AS) provisions, requires the establishment of national standards for electronic health care transactions and national identifiers for providers, health insurance plans, and employers. [6] Title III sets guidelines for pre-tax medical spending accounts, Title IV sets guidelines for group health plans, and Title V governs company-owned life insurance policies. When providing medical care to a subject found on a search and rescue mission, the provider is bound to follow the laws and HIPAA.

2.8 Trespass

Caution should always be used when entering anyone's land or isolated parts of state lands, tribal lands, and national parks, normally indicated by proper signage **(Fig. 2-2)**. There are some states that allow property owners to mark (or blaze) existing trees or fence post in purple paint **(Fig.2-3)**. You should always obey posted no trespassing signage until you have obtained permission from the landowner to enter and search. Any time you are out in the wilderness, you should always be aware of your surroundings.

(Fig 2-2) A properly posted "No Trespassing" sign. Image courtesy J. Bobot.

The "Trespassing" Perspective

Usually in the urban or municipal setting, such in an EMS call, when we are called to assist someone, they are granting us permission to come on to their property and knock on the door. In search and rescue situations, there may be hundreds of acres of land that needs to be searched. Not all of that land is public. We, as searchers on a search and rescue mission, must obey trespassing and property laws. [7] This is another reason why a unified command system works best for missing or lost person incidents.

(Fig 2-3) An example of a "purple" marking to delineate a property line. Image courtesy J. Bobot.

If the law enforcement representative knows where we are going to be searching, they can authorize officers to go ahead of the teams and obtain permission for teams to enter private property.

There are three trespass laws that a searcher should be aware of when dealing with private property. **Criminal Trespass** is the willful entering of property that is posted "No Trespassing." There are times when a fence may be broken or covered in underbrush and the property line isn't visible. That is called **Innocent Trespass;** where you are unaware that the land is posted "No Trespassing."

2.9 Documentation

Thorough documentation is important!!! Courts consider an action or procedure not recorded as not being performed. Keep a "Search Log" on every incident you are on! The following are some tips when it comes to documenting your actions:

- Use the correct form and write in pen.
- Include the incident number, date, and time on every entry.
- Be specific and use standard abbreviations.
- Document all actions, observations, changes, and preventive measures.

SAR Mission Logbook

SAR personnel should document their time. To facilitate the recording of training, courses, and SAR incidents for each individual on a land search and rescue team they should use a SAR Mission Log **(Fig. 2-4)**. It is a record of participation if the searcher moves to another jurisdiction. The log may be presented to the head of a team he/she wishes to join. The log is a personal record of all SAR-related activities. The log is proof of participation. It also allows the searcher to record important facts that may need to be recalled if the mission goes to court later.

(Fig 2-4) A SAR pocket mission logbook. Image courtesy J. Bobot.

2.10 Liability Insurance

SAR teams can face legal issues from providing their services, even if that service is free and with the best of intentions. General liability insurance protects your emergency organization when a person is injured, or a person's property is damaged as a result of an occurrence that's not automobile related. There are several private liability insurance providers. Here is a list of key points when looking for general liability insurance for your team:

General Liability Coverage Highlights

- Coverage for all volunteers (whether or not they are members of your organization) and employees while acting on behalf of your organization.
- Good Samaritan liability for your volunteers and employees, should they act on their own to assist someone who needs immediate help.
- Professional health care liability (often called medical malpractice liability) coverage for the acts of employees or volunteers, regardless of their level of medical training or certification.
- Operational pollution liability for incidents arising from training activities, equipment washdowns or off-premises emergency calls.
- Coverage for bodily injury or property damage arising out of the serving or selling of alcoholic beverages.
- Liability limits not eroded by the cost to defend you against covered claims.

It is important to note that volunteer drivers, while using their own cars, need to confirm that their personal auto insurance protects them appropriately.

Non-owned auto liability insurance covers liability for accidents caused by an employee or volunteer driving their own vehicle on a nonprofit's behalf. The coverage is designed to protect only the nonprofit organization, not the employee or volunteer. Coverage applies above the liability limits of the vehicle owner's personal automobile policy. There is no coverage for damage to the vehicle that is not owned by the nonprofit. To really circle the wagons and close the coverage loop, some carriers will provide an endorsement on non-owned auto policies that add the volunteer who drives his or her own car on the nonprofit's business as an additional insured under the nonprofit's non-owned auto policy. This provides coverage in excess of the volunteer's own policy limits.

Non-owned auto insurance is critical for any nonprofit that uses volunteer drivers who drive their own cars, or those nonprofits that expect employees to use their own cars for work-related transportation.

FOOTNOTES

(1) Ohio Community Service Council. (2010). Ohio Citizen Corps volunteer Handbook, Volunteer Liability. Referencing the Ohio Revised Code; ORC 2305.23.

(2) National Highway Traffic Safety Administration. (2006). National EMS Scope of Practice Model.

(3) Elsayyad, Ahmed (2014). "Informed Consent for Comparative Effectiveness Trials". New England Journal of Medicine. 370 (20): 1958–1960. doi:10.1056/NEJMc1403310.

(4) Atchinson, Brian K.; Fox, Daniel M. (May–June 1997). "The Politics Of The Health Insurance Portability And Accountability Act" (PDF). Health Affairs. 16 (3): 146–150. doi:10.1377/hlthaff.16.3.146. PMID 9141331. Archived from the original (PDF) on 2014-01-16. Retrieved 2014-01-16.

(5) "Health Plans & Benefits: Portability of Health Coverage". United States Department of Labor. 2015-12-09. Archived from the original on 2016-12-20. Retrieved 2016-11-05.

(6) "Overview". www.cms.gov. 2016-09-13. Archived from the original on 2016-11-02.

(7) https://legal-dictionary.thefreedictionary.com/Criminal+Trespass

VITAL VOCABULARY

Abandonment: In medicine, occurs when a health care professional has already begun emergency treatment of a patient and then suddenly walks away while the patient is still in need, without securing the services of an adequate substitute or giving the patient adequate opportunity to find one.

Ethics: The rules or standards that govern the conduct of members of a particular group or profession.

Expressed Consent: This is actual consent when the subject expressly authorizes you to provide emergency care and transport.

Good Samaritan Law: This is a piece of state legislature that protects a person from civil damages for administering emergency care or treatment at the scene of an emergency outside of a hospital, doctor's office, or other place.

Health Insurance Portability and Accountability Act of 1996 (HIPAA): The privacy law that protects the privacy of individually identifiable health information.

Implied Consent: This is consent which is not expressly granted by a person, but rather inferred from a person's actions and the facts and circumstances of a particular situation.

Informed Consent: This when the subject is informed of the potential risk, benefits and alternatives to treatment.

Morals: These are the social, religious, or personal standards of right and wrong.

Negligence: This is a type of tort (also known as a civil wrong) where a person is harmed unintentionally through the failure to provide care equal to the standard of care expected of the rescuer who is a reasonable person, fully trained, and is acting under similar circumstances.

Scope of Practice: This is terminology used by state licensing boards for various professions that defines the procedures, actions, and processes that are permitted for the licensed individual.

Tort: (originally from the French, meaning "wrong") is a wrong that involves a breach of a civil duty owed to someone else.

Trespassing (Criminal): *This* is the willful entering of property that is posted "No Trespassing".

Trespassing (Innocent): This is the unknown entry to private property.

Trespassing (To Save-a-Life): This is a provision for rescue personnel and can be used only when a subject is seen or heard while on private property.

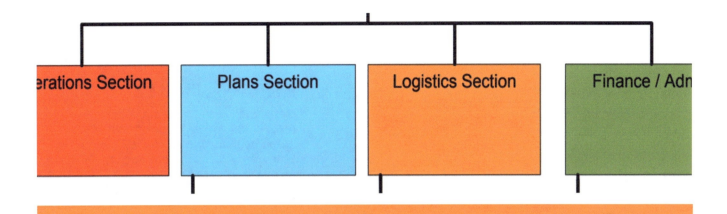

UNIT 3 | INCIDENT COMMAND SYSTEM

3.1 Incident Command and SAR
3.2 History of ICS
3.3 The Five Essential ICS Features
3.4 ICS Communications
3.5 Key Features of Unified Command
3.6 ICS Staff Positions
3.7 Incident Command and Facilities
3.8 HSPD-5 & NIMS
3.9 Subject Management
3.10 Anatomy of a Search

3.11 SAR ICS Forms
3.12 Accountability
3.13 Team Assignments

Upon completion of this chapter and the related course activities, the student will be able to meet the following objectives:

- Define "Unified Command" and "Span of Control"
- What positions make up the "General Staff" and "Command Staff"
- The purpose of a "Staging Area"
- The purpose of NIMS
- Explain the anatomy of a search
- The purpose of "accountability"
- Explain the organization structure of the Incident Command System

3.1 Incident Command and SAR

We are all willing to hit the woods and search for little Billy when he goes missing. We love the feeling of making a "save" or "rescue." But this is only one small part of the overall picture of the SAR incident. We must be able to accomplish this efficiently, effectively, and even economically. The Incident Command System (ICS) is a set of defined roles, policies, procedures, facilities, and equipment, integrated into a common organizational structure designed to improve emergency response operations of all types and complexities.

Departments, agencies and volunteer groups must look at these incidents with finances in mind. Someone is responsible for the overtime incurred, the equipment, and even the insurance. We must be fiscally aware of how we respond to any incident. Efficiency, doing things right the first time, is vital and can be accomplished by using well-trained resources. Effectively means doing things right with the right resources while utilizing the best possible tactics.

> **ADDITIONAL TRAINING**
>
> Many agencies, departments, and teams require that you take one or more FREE online courses offered by the Federal Emergency Management Agency (FEMA) for membership.
>
> **IS-100 Incident Command System**
>
> **IS-700 National Incident Management System (NIMS)**
>
> **IS-800 National Response Plan (NRP)**
>
> These courses and others can be found at the following website:
> http://training.fema.gov/IS/

But what pulls all this together and makes it run smoothly, and therefore economically, is good management. Management through a well-planned structure and organization is key to a successful outcome.

We will always agree that there is no price we can place on a human life, nor should we try to skimp on training, equipment, or supplies. The economy is not the only reason for good management on a SAR incident. The chances of successfully responding to a major situation will also be improved because good management will create opportunities and cause things to happen.

3.2 History of the Incident Command System

ICS was developed in the 1970s following a series of catastrophic fires in California's urban interface. Property damage ran into the millions, and many people died or were injured. The personnel assigned to determine the causes of these outcomes studied the case histories and discovered that response problems could rarely be attributed to lack of resources or failure of tactics. Surprisingly, studies found that response problems were far more likely to result from inadequate management than from any other single reason.

ICS is a management system designed to enable effective and efficient domestic incident management by integrating a combination of facilities, equipment, personnel, procedures, and communications operating within a common organizational structure. It is also designed to enable effective and efficient domestic incident management.

A basic premise of ICS is that it is widely applicable. It is used to organize both near-term and long-term field-level operations for a broad spectrum of emergencies, from small to complex incidents, both natural and manmade.
ICS is used by all levels of government - Federal, State, local, and tribal—as well as by many private-sector and nongovernmental organizations, no matter the complexity of the incident **(Fig.3-1)**. [1]

(Fig 3-1) Seattle, WA 10-16-07 -- FEMA and Emergency Responders work at the Region 10 Regional Response Coordination Center (RRCC) Top Officials (TOPOFF) Exercise. Marvin Nauman/FEMA photo

Incident Complexity is a term used to describe the combination of involved factors that affect the probability of control of an incident. Many factors determine the complexity of an incident, including, but not limited to: area involved, threat to life and property, political sensitivity, organizational complexity, jurisdictional boundaries, values at risk, weather, strategy and tactics, and agency policy.

3.3 The Five Essential ICS Features

The five key features that make the Incident Command System function efficiently and effectively are: [2]

1. Unity of Command
2. Common Terminology
3. Objective Management
4. Flexible and Modular Organization
5. Span-of-Control

- **Unity of Command (UC) -** This eliminates the potential for individuals to receive conflicting orders from a variety of supervisors, thus increasing accountability, preventing freelancing, improving the flow of information, helping with the coordination of operational efforts, and enhancing operational safety. This concept is fundamental to the ICS chain of command structure and is known as Unified Command.

- **Common Terminology** - Individual response agencies previously developed their protocols separately, and subsequently developed their terminology separately. This can lead to confusion as a word may have a different meaning for each organization. When different organizations are required to work together, the use of common terminology is an essential element in team cohesion and communications, both internally and with other organizations responding to the incident.

- **Objective Management** - Incident management that aims towards specific objectives. Objectives are ranked by priority, should be as specific as possible, must be attainable and if possible, given a working time-frame. Objectives are accomplished by first outlining strategies (general plans of action), then determining appropriate tactics (how the strategy will be executed) for the chosen strategy.

- **Flexible and Modular Organization** - Incident Command structure is organized in such a way as to expand and contract as needed by the incident scope, resources and hazards. Command is established in a top-down fashion, with the most important and authoritative positions established first. Only positions that are required at the time should be established. In most cases, very few positions within the command structure will need to be activated.

- **Span of Control** - To limit the number of responsibilities and resources being managed by any individual, the ICS requires that any single person's span of control should be between three and seven individuals, with **five being ideal**. In other words, one manager should have no more than seven people working under them at any given time. If more than seven resources are being managed by an individual, then they are being overloaded and the command structure needs to be expanded by delegating responsibilities (e.g. by defining new sections, divisions, or task forces). If fewer than three, then the position's authority can probably be absorbed by the next highest rung in the chain of command.

3.4 ICS Communications

One of the most recognizable features of the ICS being the use of common terminology, and we can see its importance when multiple agencies or departments arrive on the scene of an incident and start using different codes and signals. A 10-80 may mean two very different things depending on the department, agency, or team.

Common speech or syntax has always been the best practice and a communication center **(Fig. 3-2)** needs to be established early in the incident.

(Fig. 3-2) Yazoo City, MS, April 30, 2010 -- James Stewart of the FEMA Mobile Emergency Response Support Unit is set up beside the Mobile Emergency Operations Vehicle at the State/FEMA Disaster Staging Area. Photo courtesy of George Armstrong/FEMA.

Command at an Incident

Chain of command refers to the orderly line of authority within the ranks of the incident management organization. This needs to be documented and communicated early and when there are any changes. Unity of command means that every individual has a designated supervisor to whom he or she reports at the scene of the incident. These principles clarify reporting relationships and eliminate the confusion caused by multiple, conflicting directives. Incident managers at all levels must be able to control the actions of all personnel under their supervision.

3.5 Key Features of Unified Command

The term unified command is used to describe incidents involving multiple jurisdictions, a single jurisdiction with multiagency involvement, or multiple jurisdictions with multiagency involvement. Unified Command allows agencies with different legal, geographic, and functional authorities and responsibilities to work together effectively without affecting individual agency authority, responsibility, or accountability. The advantages of using Unified Command include:

- A single set of objectives is developed for the entire incident.
- A collective approach is used to develop strategies to achieve incident objectives.
- Information flow and coordination is improved between all jurisdictions and agencies involved in the incident.
- All agencies with responsibility for the incident have an understanding of joint priorities and restrictions.
- No agency's legal authorities will be compromised or neglected.
- The combined efforts of all agencies are optimized as they perform their respective assignments under a single Incident Action Plan.

Planning must also be organized, and this is done through management by objectives. This includes establishing overarching objectives; developing strategies based on incident objectives; developing and issuing assignments, plans, procedures, and protocols; establishing specific, measurable objectives for various incident management functional activities and directing efforts to attain them. The support of defined strategies and the documenting of results is required to measure performance and facilitate corrective action.

In 1980, federal officials transitioned ICS into a national program called the National Interagency Incident Management System (NIIMS), which became the basis of a response management system for all federal agencies with wildfire management responsibilities. Since then, many federal agencies have endorsed the use of ICS, and several have mandated its use.

The ICS system's ability to expand and contract as the incident dictates is designed with basic jobs or responsibilities and subordinate positions predefined to allow for the incident to grow. Position titles are universal and are used in every type of incident from a forest fire to a missing child. ICS is also applicable across disciplines (fire, EMS, law enforcement, etc.). It is structured to facilitate activities in five major functional areas: command, operations, planning, logistics, and finance and administration.

3.6 ICS Staff Positions

Incident commander (IC)

Most incidents involve a single **incident commander**. In these incidents, a single person commands the incident response and is the decision-making final authority. A Unified Command is used on larger incidents usually when multiple agencies are involved.

A Unified Command typically includes a command representative from major involved agencies and one from that group to act as the spokesman, though not designated as an Incident Commander.

The General Staff:

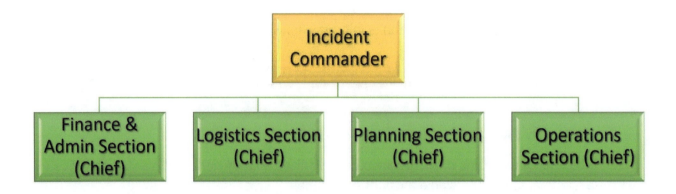

The General Staff includes Operations, Planning, Logistics, and Finance/Administrative responsibilities. These responsibilities remain with the Incident Commander (IC) until they are assigned to another individual. When the Operations, Planning, Logistics or Finance/Administrative responsibilities are established as separate functions under the IC, they are managed by a section chief and can be supported by other functional units.

The general staff can be remembered easily by their actions:

- The Planning Section (the "planners")
- The Operations Section (the "doers")
- The Logistics Section (the "getters")
- The Finance/Admin. Section (the "payers")

The following are brief descriptions of the General Staff Section Chiefs:

- **Planning Section Chief:** The Planning Section Chief is a member of the General Staff and is responsible for the collection, evaluation, dissemination and use of information about the development of the incident and the status of resources. Information is needed to understand the current situation. They predict the probable course of incident events and prepare alternative strategies for the incident. This is done by planning areas to be searched based on the missing person data collected, terrain analysis and other factors.

- **Operations Section Chief:** The Operations Section Chief activates and supervises organization elements (tactical plan) in accordance with the Incident Action Plan (IAP) and directs its execution. The Operations Section Chief also directs the preparation of unit operational plans, requests or releases resources, makes expedient changes to the IAP as necessary and reports such to the Incident Command (IC). The major responsibilities of the Operations Section Chief are to brief and assign Operations Section personnel in accordance with the IAP and supervise the Operations Section. Based on the plans developed by the Planning Chief, the OPS determine needs and request additional resources. They also assemble and disassemble strike teams assigned to the Operations Section. Operations must report information about special activities, events, and occurrences to the IC and maintain Unit/Activity Log.

- **Logistics Section Chief:** The Logistics Section Chief is a member of the General Staff and is responsible for providing facilities, services, and material in support of the incident. The Logistics Chief participates in the development and implementation of the Incident Action Plan (IAP) and activates and supervises the Branches and Units within the Logistics Section. The Logistics Section is vital to the smooth operation at an incident and providing critical supplies and support to the incident management team and the search personnel.

- **Finance/Administration Section Chief:** The Finance Section Chief is a member of the General staff and is responsible for all financial, administrative, and cost analysis aspects of the incident ensure that all personnel time records are accurately completed and transmitted to home agencies, according to policy.

The Command Staff:

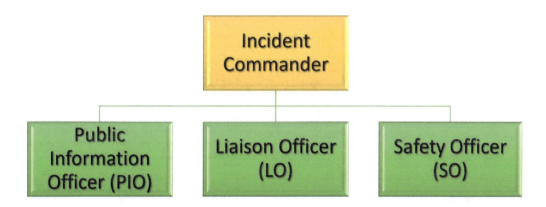

The **Command Staff** is responsible for public affairs, health and safety, and liaison activities within the incident command structure. The Incident Commander or Unified Command remains responsible for these activities or may assign individuals to carry out these responsibilities and report directly to the IC. The Incident Commander or Unified Command group fall within this section of the ICS structure.

The following is a list of Command Staff and General Staff responsibilities that either the ICS or UC of any response should perform or assign to appropriate members of the Command or General Staffs:

- Provide response direction.
- Coordinate communication with staff and media.
- Coordinate resources.
- Establish incident priorities.
- Develop mutually agreed-upon incident objectives and approve response strategies.

- Assign objectives to the response structure.
- Review and approve IAPs.
- Ensure integration of response organizations into the ICS/UC.
- Establish protocols.
- Ensure worker and public health and safety.

The following are brief descriptions of the Command Staff positions:

- **Public Information Officer (PIO):** The Public Information Officer is the communications coordinator or spokesperson for governmental organizations (i.e. city, county, school district, state government and police/fire departments) **(Fig. 3-3)**. They differ from public relations departments of private organizations in that marketing plays a more limited role. The primary responsibility of a PIO is to provide information to the media and public as required by law and according to the standards of their profession.

(Fig. 3-3) Houston, TX, September 20, 2008 -- FEMA Public Information Officer Alberto Pillot is interviewed by KXLN-TV, a Spanish station, at the Mobile Disaster Recovery Center on Chimney Rock Road. FEMA has many Spanish translators at its DRCs to accommodate the large Hispanic population affected by Hurricane Ike. Photo by Greg Henshall / FEMA

- **Safety Officer (SO):** The Safety Officer function is to develop and recommend measures for assuring personnel safety, and to monitor and/or anticipate hazardous and unsafe situations. Only one SO will be assigned for each incident. Their primary role is to continuously monitor workers for exposure to safety or health hazardous conditions. They can alter, suspend, evacuate, or terminate activities that may pose imminent safety or health danger to the workers and take appropriate action to mitigate or eliminate unsafe condition, operation, or hazard.

- **Liaison Officer (LO):** Incidents that are multi-jurisdictional, or have several agencies involved, may require the establishment of the Liaison Officer, also known as a "Family Liaison" position on the Command Staff. Only one LO will be assigned for each incident, including incidents operating under Unified Command and multi-jurisdiction incidents. The LO may have assistants as necessary, and the assistants may also represent assisting agencies or jurisdictions. In cases that involve a missing person, the LO is the only person that should make contact with the missing person's family so that a positive rapport is maintained.

There are several positions and resource definitions that fall within the incident command structure that should be known by all personnel.

- **Section:** The organization level having functional responsibility for primary segments of incident management (Operations, Planning, Logistics, Finance/Administration). The Section level is organizationally between Branch and Incident Commander and hold the ICS title of Chief.

- **Branch:** That organizational level having functional, geographical, or jurisdictional responsibility for major parts of the incident operations. The Branch level is organizationally between Section and Division/Group in the Operations Section, and between Section and Units in the Logistics Section and hold the ICS title of Director.

- **Division:** That organizational level having responsibility for operations within a defined geographic area. The Division level is organizationally between the Strike Team and the Branch and hold the ICS title of Supervisor.

- **Group:** Groups are established to divide the incident into functional areas of operation. Groups are located between Branches (when activated) and Resources in Operations and holds the ICS title of Division/Group Leader.

- **Unit:** That organization element having functional responsibility for a specific incident planning, logistics, or finance/administration activity and holds the ICS title of Unit/Team Leader.

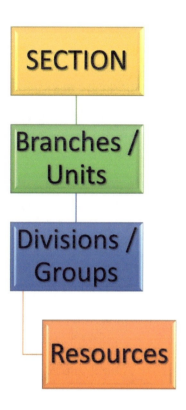

3.7 Incident Command Facilities

Various types of operational support facilities are established in the vicinity of an incident to accomplish a variety of purposes. Maintaining an accurate and up-to-date picture of resource utilization is a critical component of incident management. Response operations can form a complex structure that must be held together by response personnel working at different and often widely separated incident facilities **(Fig. 3-4)**.

(Fig. 3-5) Chino, CA, November 20, 2008 -- These wildland firefighting apparatus are staged at the Prado Staging Area. Image courtesy of Casey Deshong/FEMA.

Command facilities can include:

- A sign-in point
- An assembly area
- A camping area and parking area
- A general briefing area
- A Staging Area (Fig. 3-5)
- A mission briefing/debriefing area
- The Incident Command Post
- A communications center
- A place for logistics' supplies/storage
- A helibase and helispot

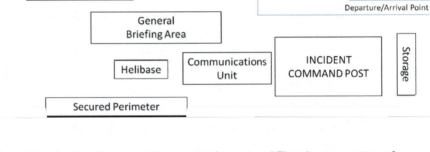

(Fig.3-4) The Incident Command Post Layout & personnel Flow. Image courtesy of J. Bobot.

Incident Command Post (ICP) is the location where the Incident Commander operates during response operations. There is only one ICP for each incident or event, but it may change locations during the event. Every incident or event must have some form of an **Incident Command Post**.

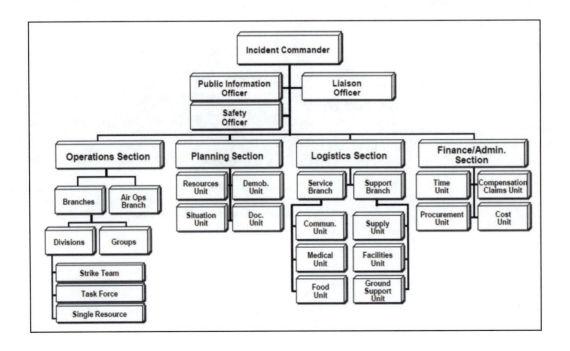

The ICS Command Structure. Image courtesy J. Bobot.

The ICP will be positioned outside of the present and potential hazard zone but close enough to the incident to maintain command. The ICP will be designated by the name of the incident, e.g., "Trail Creek ICP". As soon as practical, the following items should be considered for establishing and helping to support the command post:

1. Registration / sign in area
2. Vehicle and equipment staging area
3. Operational area for mission staff
4. External power source for mobile equipment
5. Sanitation facilities & Food Services
6. Helicopter Landing Zone(s) for air operations
7. Lighting and fuel for generators/vehicles
8. Command Post access control
9. Media briefing area

ICS Facility Identifiers

Besides having some sort of sign or flag, the official and widely recognized symbol for the command post is a green flashing light. This is a way to identify an emergency vehicle or other location being used as the incident command post.

ICS Forms are used to document an entire incident. The first form a searcher sees is the Incident Check-In Log (ICS 211). This is where a record of their participation is tracked. Many other forms are used to track and explain the tasks and assignments of the searcher such as the Team Assignment (SAR 104) form.

The following is further description of some key facility areas that can be established:

- **A Staging Area:** Can be a location at or near an incident scene where tactical response resources are stored while they await assignment. Resources in staging area are under the control of the Logistics Section and are always in available status. Staging Areas should be located close enough to the incident for a timely response, but far enough away to be out of the immediate impact zone.

- **A Helibase** is the location from which helicopter-centered air operations are conducted. Helibases are generally used on a more long-term basis and include such services as fueling and maintenance.

- **Helispots** are more temporary locations at the incident, where helicopters can safely land and take off. Multiple Helispots may be used.

- **A Base** is the location from which primary logistics and administrative functions are coordinated and administered. The Base may be co-located with the Incident Command Post. There is only one Base per incident, and it is designated by the incident name.

- **Camps** are locations, often temporary, within the general incident area that are equipped and staffed to provide sleeping, food, water, sanitation, and other services. Once these locations have been identified, they should be marked on the incident map using the proper symbols **(Fig. 3-6)**.

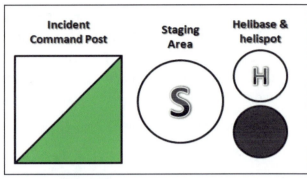

(Fig. 3-6) ICP Map Symbols. Image courtesy of J. Bobot.

3.8 HSPD-5 & NIMS

In the wake of the September 11, 2001, terrorist attacks on America **(Fig. 3-7)** and the resulting "9/11 Commission Report", the need to improve the way emergency services as well as the Federal response was identified.

On February 28, 2003, President George W. Bush, in Homeland Security Presidential Directive (HSPD)-5 Management of Domestic Incidents, directed the Secretary of Homeland Security to develop and administer the system. One aspect that relates to search and rescue personnel is the requirement that every volunteer and professional responder must complete courses on ICS and NIMS.

The National Incident Management System (NIMS) is an emergency management doctrine used nationwide to coordinate emergency preparedness and incident management and response among the public (federal, tribal, state, and local government agencies) and private sectors. NIMS is a comprehensive, national approach to incident management that is applicable at all jurisdictional levels and across functional disciplines.

(Fig. 3-7) The attacks on September 11, 2001 aided in the development of a national incident command system. Photo courtesy of the FEMA 9/11 Report.

NIMS enables us to work together to prevent, protect against, respond to, recover from, and mitigate the effects of incidents, regardless of cause, size, location, or complexity, in order to reduce the loss of life and property and harm to the environment. NIMS works hand in hand with the National Response Framework (NRF).

NIMS provides the template for the management of incidents, while the NRF provides the structure and mechanisms for national-level policy for incident management. The benefits of NIMS include a standardized approach to incident management that is scalable and flexible. It enhances cooperation and interoperability among responders from multiple jurisdictions and organizations. NIMS is applicable to all hazards.

On large or multi-level incidents, higher-level support facilities may be activated. These higher-level facilities could include:

- The **Joint Information Center (JIC)** is a temporary facility **(Fig. 3-8)** established during emergency events that provides response agencies with a means to use one communication resource and ensure that consistent and accurate information is released as quickly as possible to the general public and news media.

- A **Multiple Agency Coordination Center (MACC)**, also known as an Emergency Operations Center, is a central command and control facility responsible for the strategic, or "big picture" of the disaster. Personnel within the MACC use Multi-agency Coordination to guide their operations. The MACC coordinates activities between multiple agencies and does not normally directly control field assets but makes strategic decisions and leaves tactical decisions to agencies.

- The **Emergency Coordination Center (ECC)** is established to coordinate support for response and recovery to multi-agency and multi-jurisdictional emergencies. The common functions of all Emergency Operations Centers (EOC) is to collect, gather and analyze data; make decisions that protect life and property, maintain continuity of the government or corporation, within the scope of applicable laws; and disseminate those decisions to all con

(Fig. 3-8) Waycross, Ga., May 15, 2007 -- Public Information Officers (PIO) from different agencies work together in the Joint Information Center (JIC). Image courtesy of Mark Wolfe/FEMA

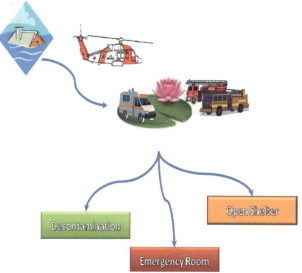

(Fig. 3-9) Example of the Lily Pad Concept of Subject management. Image courtesy of J. Bobot.

3.9 Subject Management

In New Orleans after Hurricane Katrina, areas of high ground between flooded areas served as temporary victim staging areas suitable for a drop off point during search and rescue operations. These areas were places of safety and were later called "lily pads." These are known as "Places of Safety."

A lily pad **(Fig. 3-9)** is an interim stopping point during rescue operations where survivors can be accounted for, possibly have some initial basic needs cared for, and from which they can be transported to a place of safety; certain needs of rescue personnel and their facilities might be handled at lily pads. It is not used to resupply teams in the field, this is done through logistics at the incident command post.

The International Aeronautical and Maritime Search and Rescue manual (IAMSAR) describes a place of safety as a location where:

- Rescue operations are considered to terminate because the lives of survivors are no long threatened.

- Basic human needs (such as food, shelter and medical needs) can be met; and from which transportation arrangements can be made for the survivors' next or final destination.

For large numbers of persons in distress, it may be necessary to establish a temporary safe delivery point for intermediate handling of survivors. In major aircraft or marine disasters, a short distance offshore, survivors might be transported to a suitable nearby landing area where a temporary emergency care center could be established.

The survivors should be processed, provided with emergency care, and transported to a permanently established emergency care center or a place of safety **(Fig. 3-10)**. By using a temporary delivery point, many survivors can be evacuated quickly and transferred to medical care centers. The use of lily pads can help responders remain focused more on rescue operations and less on transportation.

Lily Pad Services - The following are typical of services that may need to be provided at lily pads:

(Fig. 3-10) New Orleans, LA, August 30, 2005 -- FEMA Urban Search and Rescue workers plan operations on a bridge that is one of the areas not flooded in a neighborhood where search and rescue operations continue as a result of Hurricane Katrina. Jocelyn Augustino/FEMA

- On Scene Commander capability.

- An area for medical triage and first aid.

- Law enforcement staging resources.

- Animal containment facilities can be established.

- Communication with the SMC, SAR facilities and places of safety.

- Refueling storage or other arrangements for SAR facilities.

- Accommodations for food and rest for rescue personnel, and possibly for crew changes.

3.10 Anatomy of a Search

Within the life cycle of the SAR event, there is a flow of events that make up the anatomy of a search. This is where the participants get "plugged in" to the search.[3] The searcher will usually enter the ICS system or the search operation in the following way: **(Fig. 3-11)**

Check-In at Staging

Incident briefing

Receive Assignment

Mission Briefing

Deploy on Assignment

Mission Debriefing

Return to Staging

Check-out

Return to Service

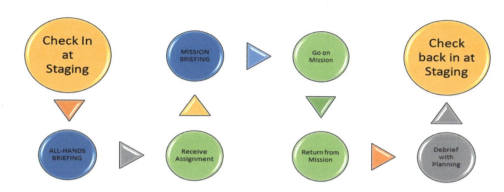

(Fig. 3-11) Flow chart showing the process of a searcher through the mission process. Image courtesy of J. Bobot.

- **Check-in:** All SAR personnel must travel to the incident site and check in. A standard ICS-211 form is used at check-in. The complexity and size of incident determines if check-in is formal or informal / on-site or off-site. No matter how check in set-up is, insist that your presence be documented and tracked.

- **Incident Briefing:** This is a summary of the situation, past and present. There are two basic briefings that occur. The first type is an "all-hands" briefing where everyone responding is gathered and vital information is shared. This usually occurs once a day. The other type of briefing is a pre-mission briefing. This is where you get your individual team's mission outline and incident update.

- **Assignment:** Assignments are necessary for all personnel at the incident to outline individual or group/team roles and responsibilities. These are vital for the incident to run smoothly. These positions can be within the incident command post or an "on the ground" mission that teams or individuals are responsible for completing that is outlined in the Incident Action Plan.

- **Mission Debriefing:** This is the transfer of information from field personnel to the search management team. When a team returns from completing their assigned mission, they are debriefed. During this debriefing they are asked various questions such as "How well do you think you searched your area?" Or "Does your area need further search efforts?"

- **Check-out:** Just as important as checking in is checking out. This is part of the overall accountability for the command team. The check-out is also part of the management function called "demobilization."

- **Return to service:** This is when the searcher returns home or to their respective stations. The most important thing in this phase is that everyone cleans, restocks, and readies their equipment for the next search incident.

3.11 SAR ICS Forms

There are many ICS forms (**Table 3-1**) used during an incident. Management forms are used to aid in the planning and organization of the incident while other forms are used by search crews. All the forms are designed and cross-referenced to provide structured Organization, Management, Operations and Planning functions within the standard ICS framework.

The forms are broken down into four main groups:

- Initial Response - Four to six forms are typically used for a hasty-search incident.
- Extended Response - A complete set of forms for managing extended SAR incidents.
- Close - Final documentation at conclusion of the incident.
- Information - Planning data, maps, interviews, etc.

The forms are designed to provide an overview of the ICS organizational structure, clear ICS section responsibility for each form, linking of information between forms and incorporation of the latest SAR mathematics into the development of an effective Operations Plan. [4]

ICS and SAR forms can be handwritten or typed. They can even simply be jotted down in a notebook if the search is just beginning and you are getting organized. Never let search crews stand around and wait for you to gather and start filling out forms during the initial moments of a search.

3.12 Accountability

The term **accountability** is the state of being accountable; liability to be called on to render an account; responsible for; answerable for. This is certainly the case when it comes to personnel at an incident. The incident commander or the unified command is ultimately responsible or "accountable" for all the personnel on the scene, but every person there must be accountable for themselves and others in their charge. Many fire and rescue agencies are now acknowledging the necessity of having a way to track and account for their

TABLE 3-1
ICS 201 Incident Briefing
ICS 202 Incident Objectives
ICS 203 Assignment List
ICS 205 Communications Plan
ICS 206 Medical Plan
ICS 208 Safety Briefing
ICS 211 Check-In Log
ICS 214 Unit Log
SAR 99 Remote Medical Care Form
SAR 300 General Briefing – Missing Person
SAR 101 Search Urgency Analysis
SAR 102A Scenario Worksheet
SAR 102B Evaluator Worksheet – Scenario
SAR 102C Scenario Consensus
SAR 103 AMDR/Spacing Worksheet
SAR 104 Team Assignment
SAR 105A Segment Area Worksheet
SAR 105B Evaluator Worksheet - Area
SAR 105C Segment Consensus
SAR 106 Resource Allocation Worksheet
SAR 107 Urban Interview Log
SAR 110 Debriefing (Ground)
SAR 111 Debriefing (K9)
SAR 133 Radio Log
SAR 134 Clue Log
SAR 135 Clue Report
SAR 136 Primary Print Report
SAR 302 Missing Person Questionnaire
SAR 401 Segment POS Worksheet

personnel.

Essentially, personnel accountability is an effort to improve the safety of emergency responders by keeping track of their locations and assignments when operating at the scene of an incident. Accountability can be maintained in many different ways. Irrespective of the type of **Personnel Accountability System (PAS)** implemented, the goals are generally similar.

A properly implemented PAS will help to ensure that the incident command staff knows the exact number and identity of personnel working at an incident, their approximate locations, and whether they are in distress. In some form or another, regardless of size or nature, personnel accountability is a part of every incident to which search and rescue personnel may respond.

3.13 Team Assignments

As teams prepare to go out into the field, the planning section will identify high probability areas to search. When a team is formed, they will report to the Briefing area and receive a form (SAR 104 Team Assignment Form) that will be taken with them out into the field and returned to the Debriefing area after they complete their mission.

FOOTNOTES

(1) ICS Review Document EXTRACTED FROM -E/L/G0300INTERMEDIATE INCIDENT COMMAND SYSTEM FOR EXPANDING INCIDENTS, ICS300

(2) "Glossary: Simplified Guide to the Incident Command System for Transportation Professionals". Federal Highway Administration, Office of Operations. Retrieved 24 October 2018.

(3) Bannerman, Foster, Hill, Hood, Thrasher & Wolf, (1999). Introduction to Search & Rescue. National Association for Search & Rescue.

(4) "Standardized Emergency Management System (SEMS) Guidelines". State of California, Office of Emergency Services. Archived from the original on 5 April 2009. Retrieved 16 July 2009.

VITAL VOCABULARY

Accountability: This is an effort to improve the safety of emergency responders by keeping track of their locations and assignments when operating at the scene of an incident.

Command Staff: Consists of the Public Information Officer, Safety Officer, and Liaison Officer who report directly to the Incident Commander.

General Staff: Consists of the Operations Chief, Planning Chief, Logistics Chief and Finance and Administrative Chief within the Incident Command System.

Helibase: A location from which helicopter-centered air operations are conducted.

Helispots: Temporary locations at the incident, where helicopters can safely land and take off.

Incident Action Plan (IAP): This formally documents incident goals (known as control objectives in NIMS), operational period objectives, and the response strategy defined by incident command during response planning.

Incident Command Post (ICP): A location where the Incident Commander operates during response operations.

Incident Command System (ICS): This is a set of personnel, policies, procedures, facilities, and equipment, integrated into a common organizational structure designed to improve emergency response operations of all types and complexities.

Incident Commander (IC): This person is responsible for all aspects of the response, including developing incident objectives and managing all incident operations.

Incident Complexity: This is a term used to describe the combination of involved factors that affect the probability of control of an incident.

Lily Pad: This is an interim stopping point during rescue operations where survivors can be accounted for, possibly have some initial basic needs cared for, and from which they can be transported to a place of safety; certain needs of rescue personnel and their facilities might be handled at lily pads.

National Incident Management System (NIMS): The structured framework used nationwide for both governmental and non-governmental agencies to respond to natural disasters and or terrorist attacks at the local, state, and federal levels of government.

Personnel Accountability System (PAS): This is a personnel tracking system in place at all incidents to track the personnel involved in the incident to promote safety.

Span of Control: A term originating in military organization theory, but now used more commonly in incident management, to refer to the number of subordinates a supervisor can effectively manage.

Staging Area: A location at or near an incident scene where tactical response resources are stored while they await assignment.

Unified Command: This is a command structure where each individual with a stake in the outcome share the role of command.

UNIT 4 | **SAR RESOURCES**

4.1 Human Resource

4.2 Animal Resource, K9

4.3 The Scent

4.4 Animal Resource, Equine

4.5 Informational Resources

4.6 Technological Resources

4.7 Search Team Member Roles

Upon completion of this chapter and the related course activities, the student will be able to meet the following objectives:

- Define the three types of human resources (individual, strike team and task force)
- Describe the difference between a "Rapid Search Team" and a "Grid Search Team"
- Explain "Skin Rafts" and the types of K9 Searchers
- Who is Professor John Bownds?
- Describe the importance of a "Missing Person Questionnaire"

4.1 Human Resources

SAR resources consist of three basic resource divisions:

- Group #1, Human and animal
- Group #2, Informational
- Group #3, Equipment, and technology

There are several types of human resources. Practically any task done by a human can fall within this category, however we want to address a few "skilled" tasks performed by humans or "**ground pounder**" (slang term for a SAR team member who searches without a K9 or other animal on land). [1]

The key to success is proper utilization of the resources at hand. When resources arrive on the scene of a disaster, they arrive in one of three ways. They are either an individual or a single piece of equipment or in groups of individuals or equipment.

There are three types of personnel classifications. The first type is the single resource **(Fig. 4-1)**. This is any individual piece of equipment and its personnel complement, or an individual with an identified work supervisor that can be used on an incident.

When we allocate a single resource, we can further classify that single resource based on the type of function it provides. Human SAR Resources can be grouped based on overall skill of the personnel within the group. These groups may contain specialized and highly trained individuals or on-the-spot citizen volunteers from the community.

When you gather a group of similar single resources together that have the same skill set, you have a strike team **(Fig. 4-2)**. A group of different strike teams and support personnel gathered is a task force.

They utilize fast, non-thorough search tactics in areas most likely to produce clues or the subject. These teams should include individuals who are track aware, clue and subject oriented, and familiar with local terrain and dangers.

(Fig. 4-1) BSAR searcher at Mount Dom Dom. Photo courtesy of Pete Cambell.

(Fig. 4-2) International strike team of rescuers participating in ASEAN exercise ARDEX 07 at Mandai Training Village Singapore. Photo courtesy of Koshy.

These teams also operate under standard operating procedures and carry equipment to remain self-sufficient for 24 hours. The term for this type of team is a "Hasty Team."

A Hasty Search Team (Fig. 4-3) is a group of single resources, which could qualify it as a strike team, are small (usually 3 to 5 members) in size but are very well-trained and highly mobile. The group is self-sufficient and clue conscious.

Human (Grid Team)

Another human resource is the grid team. This group of single resources, forms a strike team using vision to search a well-defined, usually small, segment of land. This is done with several individuals standing in a line and then walking together through the area. The grids can be loose or tight in nature. This type of search can be very "thorough" and require many resources that are spaced quite close to each other or can be an "efficient" type search, where fewer resources are used and the speed and spacing is greater.

(Fig. 4-3) A Hasty Team preparing to go out on mission. Photo courtesy of Joseph Bobot.

4.2 Animal Resources - Canine

There are a number of animals used by searchers, from the use of horses for transportation and searching to K9s. An animal resource, probably the most widely recognized resource in search and rescue, is the search dog (Fig. 4-4) or K9.

The use of dogs in SAR is a valuable component in responding to law enforcement requests for missing people. Dedicated handlers and hardworking, well-trained dogs are required in search efforts to be effective in their task. Search and rescue dogs detect human scent.

Although the exact process is still being researched, it may include the detection of molecular level, evaporated perspiration, respiratory gases, or decomposition gases released by bacterial action on human skin or tissues. [2]

(Fig. 4-4) New Orleans, LA, September 19, 2005 A FEMA Urban Search and Rescue dog takes a break by his handlers muddy shoe after searching in neighborhoods impacted by Hurricane Katrina. Image courtesy of Jocelyn Augustino/FEMA.

Types of K9 Searchers

From their training and experience, search and rescue dogs can be classified broadly as either air-scenting dogs or trailing (and tracking) dogs. They also can be classified according to whether they scent discriminate, and under what conditions they can work. Search and rescue dogs are typically worked by a small team on foot but can be worked from horseback. K9 searchers come in two types, scent discriminating and non-scent discriminating.

Scent discriminating dogs have proven their ability to alert only on the scent of an individual person, after being given a sample of that person's scent. Trailing dogs are scent discriminating and require a scent article from the subject, working on-lead or off lead to follow the subject's path.

Non-scent discriminating dogs alert on or follow any scent of a given type, such as any human scent or any cadaver scent. SAR dogs can be trained specifically for rubble searches, for water searches, and for avalanche searches. Air-scenting dogs typically work off-lead, are non-scent discriminating (locate scent from any human as opposed to a specific person) and cover large areas of terrain. These dogs are trained to follow diffused or wind-borne scent flowing back to its source, return to the handler and indicate contact with the subject, and then lead the handler back to the subject. The typical search area may be 40-160 acres and scent sources can be detected from 1/4 mile or more.

Human Remains Detection (HRD) or **cadaver** dogs are used to locate the remains of deceased subjects. Depending on the nature of the search, these dogs may work off-lead (eg, to search a large area for buried remains) or on-lead (to recover clues from a crime scene). [3]

K9 Application

Specific applications for SAR dogs include wilderness, disaster, cadaver **(Fig. 4-5)**, avalanche, and drowning search and rescue or recovery. In wilderness SAR applications, air-scenting dogs can be deployed to high-probability areas (places where the subject may be or where the subject's scent may collect, such as in drainages in the early morning). Whereas tracking/trailing dogs can be deployed from the subject's last known point or the site of a clue.

Handlers must be capable of bush navigation, wilderness survival techniques, and be self-sufficient. The dogs must be capable of working for four to eight hours without distraction (eg, by wildlife). Disaster dogs are used to locate victims of catastrophic or mass-casualty events (e.g., earthquakes, landslides, building collapses, aviation incidents). Many disaster dogs in the US are trained to meet the Federal Emergency Management Agency K9 standards for domestic or international deployment; advanced agility and off-lead training are prerequisites reflecting the nature of these dogs' application. Disaster dogs rely primarily on air-scent and may be limited in mass-casualty events by their inability to differentiate between survivors and recently deceased subjects.

Air-scenting and tracking/trailing dogs are often cross-trained as cadaver dogs, although the scent the dog detects is clearly of a different nature than that detected for live or recently deceased subjects. Cadaver dogs can locate entire bodies (including those buried or submerged), decomposed bodies, body fragments (including blood, tissues, hair, and bones), or skeletal remains; the capability of the dog is dependent upon its training.

How a K9 searches on land

The search dog first finds the scent and begins tracking within the "scent cone" left by the missing person until the scent is no longer detected, then it turns, picks up the scent again and continues along this "zigzag" pattern **(Fig. 4-6)** until the missing person is found. Avalanche dogs work similarly to air-scenting, disaster, or cadaver dogs, and must be able to rapidly transition from a wilderness SAR air-scenting scenario to a disaster scenario focused on pinpointing the subject's location.

How a K9 searches in water

It is also worth mentioning just how a K9 can smell a human under water. We have all seen the K9 on a boat but what is it doing? As a human body decomposes, it releases gases that float to the surface in bubbles **(Fig. 4-7)**. When the bubbles break the surface, they "pop" and release a scent the cadaver dog is trained to alert to. Based on the current and wind, the K9 handler can narrow the search to a given area for divers to enter the body of water and search for the subject.

4.3 The Scent

Residual scent is that persisting in an area after the original source is no longer present. Scent persists in an area to the degree that environmental influences do not degrade whatever it is that forms the scent to the point that it either cannot be sensed or cannot be differentiated.

In a tracking situation, a dog follows residual scent left by someone who has traveled through an area. In an outdoor search for decomposed remains, scent may drift and pool in low areas or may bank up against physical barriers such as trees or bushes. An experienced dog will usually work out this problem and eventually find the scent source.

(Fig. 4-5) Greenland (Aug. 7, 2004) - Master at Arms 1st Class Rudy Hutchinson and Susan Frank, one of the volunteers from Bucks County Search and Rescue are led by cadaver dog, Tucker during the recovery of a Navy P-2V Neptune aircraft that crashed in Greenland in 1962. U.S. Navy photo by Photographer's Mate 2nd Class Jeffrey Lehrberg

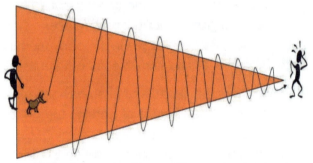

(Fig. 4-6) Illustration of how a K9 searches on land. Image courtesy of J. Bobot.

(Fig. 4-7) Illustration of how a K9 searches on water. Image courtesy of J. Bobot.

Scent in Motion

The effectiveness of search dogs is highly dependent upon the terrain (some surfaces, such as grass, retain scent better than others, like pavement), the age of the trail (fresher is easier to follow), the path (the dog is most likely to lose the trail if there are sharp turns or changes in direction), and the number of contaminating paths that cross the subject's path.

The scent specific Trailing Dog can follow a trail that may be very aged, from hours to days old, because of various factors the least of which is that the scent can be anywhere in the environment and not necessarily on the ground. The bloodhound is the prototypical Trailing dog, although herding and sporting breeds are often successfully trained for either trailing or tracking with trailing being the optimum.

The following will improve the success of a search:

- **Vegetation** —High undergrowth restricts the dissemination of scent **(Fig. 4-8)**.
- **Time & Time of Day** — This is of prime importance. A fresh scent is easier for a dog to track. Night and early morning is best as evaporation is less rapid.
- **Personal Hygiene** —A person, because of circumstances or carelessness, who is unclean gives off a greater amount of body odor.
- **Running** —A person running gives off more scent than a person walking.
- **Weather** —A mild overcast day favors tracking as it limits evaporation of scent.

(Fig. 4-8) By the use of a smoke bomb representing the scent of a person, we can see how the scent travels up an embankment through brush. Image by Dale Thompson.

The following will decrease the success of a search:

- **Temperature** —High (dry) temperature will quickly reduce the scent due to evaporation.
- **Wind** —A strong wind rapidly disperses the scent.
- **Ground Surface** —Dry, bare ground, adversely affects tracking **(Fig 4-9)**.
- **Manure** —Heavily fertilized land may disguise the scent.

(Fig. 4-9) By the use of a smoke bomb representing the scent of a person, we can see how the scent travels down along a road. Image by Dale Thompson.

- **Water** —Substantial running water courses can be an obstacle for tracking dogs.
- **Scene Contamination** —Searchers and vehicles will contaminate the area by leaving a fresh scent or lifting the scent with the tires.

4.4 Animal Resource - Equine

Some consider the horse or mule in Mounted SAR (Search and Rescue) to simply be a method of a non-motorized transportation for a mounted searcher, but that mount has strong potential to be an active search partner.

Management should be aware of the existing potential and encourage stronger partnering, and riders can enhance their search capabilities with better awareness or additional training. One key area where the mount contributes very advantageously is in natural clue detection. The equine is a prey animal, with all the related survival instincts that usually trigger flight before fight response.

The horse (or mule) also is a herd animal and commonly prefers being with known and trusted companions. In general, this combination translates to the equine being very aware of his surroundings and continually monitoring for possible threats, known companions, and noting likely sources for food or water. Sight, hearing, and scent are natural equine detection tools that can provide valuable input to the rider on every search. However, the rider needs to be actively aware of that equine input and perform follow-up as needed

Horses have a well-developed sense of hearing that is notably better than the human's, and their range includes higher frequencies. Ears turn on the horse's head up to 180 degrees to focus directionally for better hearing and can swivel independently. As a prey animal, the equine ears are constantly monitoring for possible threats from all directions. The mount has good potential to hear something the rider doesn't, such as a voice calling in the distance or movement rustling the bushes.

SAR responders **(Fig. 4-10)** on horseback are primarily a search resource, but also can provide off-road logistics support and transportation. Horses are faster, can carry more supplies to stay out longer, offer a higher viewing platform for searching, and provide a more rested rescue worker when a subject is found. Horseback units are also used to transport needed equipment such as medical equipment, block and tackle, litters, and radio equipment.

Mounted SAR responders typically have longer initial response times than SAR resources, due to the time required to pick up trailer, horse(s), and perhaps also water, feed, and equipment.

(Fig. 4-10) Members of Buffalo Trace Mounted Patrol SAR with air ambulance helicopter during a training session in 2008. Photo courtesy of Robert Milward.

Scent-Detecting Mounted SAR

Jorene Downs, Chairwoman of the NASAR Mounted SAR SIG, is a noted authority on Mounted SAR. She said "An additional capability that some riders are already pursuing may well be the most exciting 'next-generation' option as a specialty for Mounted SAR: equine scent detection. The horse (or mule) as a prey animal routinely performs air scenting, complete with scent discrimination ability, and riders should be able to 'read' basic input from the mount. But the equine can also be trained to intentionally use that nose and provide an alert, creating a 'SAR dog' you can ride. Equine olfactory capabilities are similar to a SAR dog, but with a nose that can be raised notably higher off the ground to detect the airborne scent. This has obvious advantages." Veteran MSAR rider and experienced horse trainer Terry Nowacki has successfully demonstrated riding an air-scenting horse during SAR. [4]

4.5 Informational Resources

Personnel in this group can obtain vital search data about the subject or other vital search data. Information about the environment and the weather are very important. Obtaining projected weather forecasts is vital to a successful and safe search operation. Consideration must be given to designating a trained person to conduct a thorough investigation or interviews. The effectiveness of a search operation can be diminished because of a lack of adequate and/or accurate information.

The Search Urgency Calculation will help determine the relative urgency of the SAR situation. Additional information can be obtained by conducting a door-to-door survey to interview neighbors about sightings or additional information that can help the planner. The following places/ persons should be contacted as they are identified and then re-contacted periodically:

- Subjects destination: did they arrive after the search began?
- Friends, co-workers, relatives, companions.
- Local hospital, emergency medical centers, doctor's office.
- Adjacent law enforcement jurisdictions (Have subject placed into LINK system if situation warrants).

Other considerations should be developed, including the possibility of criminal act. A thorough check of the subject's vehicle, home, etc., should be made for clues. It is vital to preserve these clues as physical evidence in the event this incident changes from a missing person incident to a criminal incident.

One of the most important pieces of documentation that can be obtained during the first hours of the search mission is the information on the **Missing Person Questionnaire (MPQ)**. **(See SAMPLE DOCUMENTS at the Appendix E)**

The MPQ provides a format to collect information in an efficient and coherent manner and is used to support a missing person investigation. It may also be used as a guide for conducting an interview. Information used to complete the form may come from multiple sources and from multiple interviews. The MPQ is used to establish the subject profile and determine urgency of the incident. Establishing the urgency of the search incident is very important.

4.6 Technological Resources

A wide range of technical equipment-aided resources provide additional problem-solving capabilities. Some examples of these would be a vertical high-angle rope rescue team, where a mechanical advantage would be required to reach the missing subject or to extricate them to safety. Access is vital and the use of all-terrain vehicles (ATV), boats, snowmobiles and even mountain bikes can make a difference. In a collapsed structure environment, technology has played a vital part in the locating of trapped persons.

Electronic viewing devices, including search cameras, infrared devices, and fiberoptic, are used in conjunction with breaching devices for access beyond obstacles into void spaces. Miniature search cameras specifically designed for USAR are small diameter, pole-mounted devices, but they are limited in depth of penetration into void spaces.

Infrared (IR) imaging systems such as the "FLIR" or forward-looking Infrared are used to see through smoke and dust and identify hot spots or body heat **(Fig. 4-11)** of a missing person. The disadvantage of IR is that all sources of heat are detected, not just subjects, and it cannot see through obstructions. The use of a handheld FLIR device off the fire truck can be taken into the woods at night to aid in the search by displaying heat signatures of objects in the dark.

(Fig. 4-11) Infra-red (FLIR) in action on R100. Image courtesy of Fremantle Sea Rescue, Western Australia.

Flexible **fiberscopes** are another electronic viewing tool that is used to search extremely tight spaces; however, snaking the fiberscope into holes is very difficult. An alternative to the flexible fiberscope is a rigid **borescope**. A borescope is an optical device consisting of a rigid tube used to search in tight spaces. Both scopes have eyepiece on one end, an objective lens on the other linked together by a relay optical system in between.

Acoustic/seismic devices (Fig. 4-12) are used for listening to detect survivors, and their application involves the deployment of an array of pick-up probes around the perimeter of the search area. If sounds are detected, the probes are assessed individually to determine which gives the strongest indication and should be closest to the source of the sound. The array of probes can be redistributed around the original probe giving the strongest indication to more precisely identify the subject's location. Some disadvantages of this method are the presence of interfering signals, limited range, ineffective in concrete, and inability to detect unconscious subjects.

(Fig. 4-12) The above image shows various acoustic and seismic devices. Image courtesy of the U.S. Department of Homeland Security, "Urban Search and Rescue (US&R)" website.

Remotely Operated Vehicles (ROVs) and Search Robotics are the latest in urban search and rescue technology. They are either tethered with power and video cables or wireless and can be sent into hazardous atmospheres to search for subjects. The design of these devices includes some with treads, like a small tank to six and eight-legged walking, mechanical insects.

(Fig. 4-13) Shows the SAR Robots, developed by Houxiang Zhang and colleagues at the University of Hamburg, in Germany. (Image courtesy of the International Journal of Advanced Robotic Systems).

When the conditions are not safe, there becomes a need to use something other than canines or subjects. Humans and canines have limitations: they tire, can make mistakes, cannot function in low hazardous atmospheres and, most importantly, are not expendable. Devices need to be developed that can perform similar functions, perhaps even more effectively. These devices may include:

- ROVs **(Fig 4-13)** for going over rubble with a camera or other sensors, such as IR or sonar to perform subject search or structural assessment, including data transmission capability.

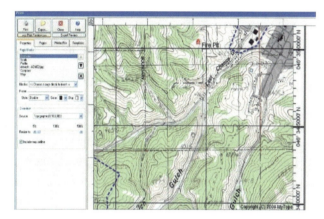

(Fig. 4-14) Screen grab from Maptech® Terrain Pro. Photo courtesy of J. Bobot.

- Flexible, durable "snake" robot to go through the smallest hole to search for subjects.

- Unmanned aerial vehicle, such as helicopters and balloons, to view the site.

- ROV for use in flooded areas, such as basements (with GPS)

Computer Software applications are being developed to assist with the planning and response to search and rescue incidents. **MapTech®** is a topographical mapping software **(Fig. 4-14)**. A Search Manager can easily create any number of accurate maps and quickly determine containment strategies and high probability areas where a missing person is likely to be found. Advanced search and rescue procedures include using Maptech's Terrain Navigator CD-ROMs showing the latest USGS topographic maps with GPS integration, 3-D views, and more.

C.A.S.I.E. (Computer Aided Search Information Exchange) is the brainchild of David Lovelock, M.J. Ebersole and the late John Bownds. Dr. Lovelock, of the University of Arizona, was the principal programmer of the software in the C-language. The program was designed to simplify most of the calculations related to managing a search emergency using modern search theory. CASIE also introduced innovative applications, like Resource Optimization and quantification of the Influence of Clues, as part of a comprehensive package of SAR analysis tools. [5] CASIE is also provided free of charge, less any costs for reproduction or shipping, to the general SAR community to help save lives.

4.7 Search Team Member Roles

A Wilderness Hasty Search team typically has three to five members and four roles other than "searcher." Although the number of team members can be variable dependent upon circumstances, the number of roles remains static. An individual can undertake more than one role and more than one person may be undertaking a role. The roles are:

TEAM LEADER: The role of the team leader is varied, and includes initially acting as an intermediary between search management (or police) and the team in order to ensure an adequate briefing has been received and passed onto the team, ensuring all pertinent information is known, and equally that all irrelevant detail is omitted. This is the first step in ensuring the team is focused on the task. The next, and probably the most important role, is to translate the search managers' strategic aim for the search into a tactical approach that is viable for the sector allocated to the team. While it is expected that search team members will know what is required of them, the team leader before deployment will check that:

- Team members are suitably equipped
- Team members are suitably motivated
- Ensure health and safety briefings have occurred

NAVIGATOR: The navigator is responsible for directing the team to their area, then maintaining knowledge of their position throughout the search. Location information becomes vital in the reporting of significant finds or coordination of a rescue response once the subject is located. Once a search is complete, organizing the movement of a team to the next task or their return to the incident command point are additional responsibilities.

The navigation role can be surprisingly difficult; for example when a segment is an area of woods and does not have boundaries that are well defined on the ground. Often, subtleties of land contours are the only clue, and traditional map reading skills are supplemented with things such as use of natural navigation. Searches may depend on certain major navigation clues from the sun, prevailing weather and sounds from major air and road routes.

MEDIC: The person acting as nominated team medic is responsible for all aspects related to team medical duties. This involves carrying adequate medical equipment. Statistically, the most likely outcome on a search is that no medical intervention is needed.

The most likely scenario in which medical assistance is provided, is to an injured team member and this is a key role of the medic. In the event of a subject being located, and with time to implement an ideal plan, the medic would be the person to approach. However, this can be compromised in scenarios such as a same sex person being required or a subject suddenly materializing in front of another team member. The medic in these circumstances takes over as and when required. A range of qualifications may currently be found in use such as first aid at work and wilderness first aid. Many teams will have members who have advanced medical training by virtue of their employment such as paramedics, nurses, and doctors.

RADIO OPERATOR AND COMMUNICATIONS: The radio operator may not be the only person in the team with access to a radio, but they will be the person formally designated to maintain contact with search control and coordinate all communication activities. They will be responsible for updating other team members of major developments as they become apparent through monitoring of radio traffic. At times of either necessity (eg loss of VHF contact), or at times of a confidential nature (eg finding a missing person deceased), communication may be via mobile phone. Radio training is generally delivered within a team and is based on general principles such as use of plain language phrases and NATO phonetics.

SEARCH TEAM MEMBER: All team members are deployed primarily with searching for the subject in mind. Some, such as the team leader may be periodically utilized to concentrate on other matters. However, for those acting as basic searcher, their role is always focused on this task. While taking overall strategic guidance from their team leader, they are expected to act autonomously and will utilize key skills such as the searchers cube and purposeful wandering. As and when required, other aspects of training such as crime scene management will be required.

FOOTNOTES

(1) Bannerman, Foster, Hill, Hood, Thrasher & Wolf, (1999). Introduction to Search & Rescue. National Association for Search & Rescue.

(2) ww.vsrda.org/how-scent-and-airflow-works article by Jennifer Pennington

(3) Thomas Bauman. (2007). Maximizing Cadaver Training. Police K9 Magazineww.vsrda.org/how-scent-and-airflow-works article by Jennifer Pennington.

(4) "Mounted SAR: Equine Clue Detection" a whitepaper by Jorene Downs, 2006

(5) David Lovelock, M.J. Ebersole and John Bownds (2010) University of Arizona, Department of Mathematics, CASIE Program.

VITAL VOCABULARY

Air-scenting K9: Dogs that primarily use airborne human scent to find subjects, whereas trailing dogs rely on scent of the specific subject.

Borescope: An electronic device consisting of a rigid tube used to search extremely tight spaces.

Cadaver: The remains of a deceased human being.

Clue Consciousness: A general concept that searchers must search for clues and not only the subject and consists of a combination of the three characteristics of the sensor, the object and the environment.

Fiberscope: An electronic viewing tool consisting of a flexible tube that is used to search extremely tight spaces.

Grid Team: A group of single resources, like a hasty team, used to search well-defined, usually small, segment of land.

Hasty Search Team: This is a group of single resources, which could qualify as a strike team, are small (usually 3 to 5 members) but are very well-trained and highly mobile.

MapTech®: A topographical mapping software package that can easily create any number of accurate maps and quickly determine containment strategies and high probability areas where a missing person is likely to be found.

Missing Person Questionnaire (MPQ): This document provides a format to collect information in an efficient and coherent manner and is used to support a missing person investigation.

Remotely Operated Vehicles (ROVs): Mechanical searchers are either tethered with power and video cables or wireless and can be sent into hazardous atmospheres to search for subjects.

Single Resource: An individual piece of equipment and its personnel complement used on an incident.

Skin Rafts: Scent-carrying skin cells that drop off living humans at a rate of about 40,000 cells per minute.

Strike Team: A group of people with the same skills needed to perform a given task as a cohesive group.

Task Force: A group of people with varying skills needed to complete a given task.

Tracking/Trailing K9: Dogs that are scent discriminating and require a scent article from the subject, work on lead or off lead to follow the subject's path.

UNIT 5 | SAR COMMUNICATIONS

5.1 Communication Types

5.2 Amateur & MARCS Radio Systems

5.3 Verbal & Visual Emergency Signals

5.4 Using the Radio

5.5 COSPAS-SARSAT System

5.6 Electronic Distress Signals

5.7 Incident Communications

5.8 After Action Reports (AARs)

> Upon completion of this chapter and the related course activities, the student will be able to meet the following objectives:
> - Explain the use of MARCS
> - Describe the two verbal distress signals
> - Explain the three types of electronic distress beacons
> - Identify the ICAO ground signals
> - Be able to use the phonetic alphabet
> - Describe the COSPAS-SARSAT system
> - What is an AAR and when is it used?

5.1 Communication Types

A SAR incident, or any emergency incident for that matter, involves many people communicating during all aspects of the incident. There may be several groups of people using multiple communications methods.

Essentials of Communications

- A message
- A message source
- A transmission medium
- A message destination
- Communication objective
- An interpretation

There are five types of communication methods that are deployed during a SAR incident:

#1: Face to face communications - this can be in the form of staff meetings, team briefings or all-hands briefings.

#2: Investigative/Search data collection - where personnel interview people, gather weather reports, conditions, history of the area and other information that is vital to the planning of the search.

#3: Information only communications - where a representative, such as the Public Information Officer (PIO) will provide the press with information only and not include questions from the press.

(Fig. 5-1) Castle Rock, Colorado June 18, 2002 -- Chris Krengel is a member of ARES, (Amateur Radio Emergency Service) which is helping to provide communication around the Hayman fire just south of Denver, Colorado. Photo courtesy of Michael Rieger/FEMA News Photo

#4: Press conference - where a representative, such as the PIO will give an open interview with both status updates, information and allow for questions from the press.

#5: Electronic communications - communication via radio systems; Amateur (HAM) Radio, MARCS/UHF/VFH radios, cellular communications and satellite communications.

5.2 Amateur & MARCS Radio Systems

Amateur (HAM) Radio operation is licensed by an appropriate government entity, for example, by the Federal Communications Commission (FCC) as coordinated through the International Telecommunication Union. An estimated two million people **(Fig. 5-1)** throughout the world are regularly involved with amateur radio. [1] The term "amateur" does not imply a lack of skill or quality, but rather that amateur radio and its operators work outside of an official, governmental or commercial capacity.

The **MARCS (Multi-Agency Radio Communication System)** is an 800 MHz radio and data network that utilizes state-of-the-art trunked technology to provide statewide interoperability in digital clarity to its subscribers. [2] The MARCS system provides statewide, secure, reliable public service wireless communication for public safety and first responders. In all cases, it is essential that the information exchange be as clear, concise, and accurate as possible. Additionally, there can be occasions when one must be selective about the kind of information to exchange, or of its recipients, such as if a search for clues becomes a criminal investigation.

5.3 Verbal & Visual Emergency Signals

Verbal Emergency Signals

The use of verbal emergency signals is usually one's best case scenario. Verbal signals are usually transmitted over various radio frequencies to those who are monitoring them. Aircraft and ships have two very distinct verbal signals when they are in need of assistance or wish to convey a message to those around them, also known as distress signals.

Audible Distress & Urgency Signals:

- Distress signal – **MAYDAY** is used to indicate that a craft is in distress and requires immediate assistance and has priority over all other communications.

- Urgency signal – **PAN-PAN** (pronounced PAHN-PAHN) is used when the safety of a craft is in jeopardy or an unsafe situation exists that may eventually involve a need of assistance, and has priority over all but distress traffic.

Ships and aircraft are not the only ones able to use the term "mayday." The "mayday" radio message can be used by ground personnel as well. The radio message "mayday" should be used by fire fighters, rescue technicians, searchers and other personnel on the scene of a search or disaster incident. This radio call is used to report their status as being in distress and needing rescue. Any report of "mayday" will receive priority radio traffic. The term "mayday" will be reserved ONLY to report a person in distress, other than the subject(s). The radio message "Emergency Traffic" should be used to inform units there is an ongoing emergency and not to interrupt unless with another emergency. [3]

Visual Emergency Signals

Commonly used visual distress signals include flares, signal mirrors, dye markers, smoke, and flags. In addition to these signals, daylight visual signals may include fluorescent material and night devices may include strobes, incandescent or chemical lights, pyrotechnics or reflective materials.

Some examples of visual distress signals include:

- A square flag having above or below it a ball or anything resembling a ball.

- Flames, (flames are very effective at night, and have been sighted as far away as 50 miles).

- Red flares, which can be seen up to 35 miles at night with an average of 10 miles at night, and about 1 to 2 miles during daylight.

- Orange smoke, effective up to 12 miles during the day if winds are less than 10 knots, with an average 8-mile range.

- Slowly and repeatedly raising and lowering arms outstretched to each side.

- Flashes from a signal mirror, with an average detection range of five miles, but sometimes detectable up to 45 miles.

- Dye-stained water, normally green or red, has been sighted up to ten miles away, with an average detect ability of three miles.

The International Civil Aviation Organization (ICAO) is an agency of the United Nations that codifies the principles and techniques of international air navigation and fosters the planning and development of international air transport to ensure safety. The ICAO has adopted a standard set of ground-to-air signals **(Fig. 5-2)** that can be made from debris from the wreckage of a plane, logs, rocks or sections of a parachute.

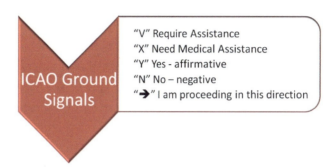

(Fig. 5-2) The International Civil Aviation Organization recommends the above ground signals. Image by J. Bobot.

It is recommended that the letters be at least 10 feet in length and one foot in diameter. The objects used to form the signal should be of a contrasting color to the surface they are on. [4]

5.4 Using the Radio

The radio is one of the most important tools that a SAR technician can have. Being able to communicate your location and needs is vital for the safety of the search crew and the subject. Always to remember to keep your messages concise as it takes less power to listen to your radio than it does to transmit. One should also be vigilant that if you can hear radio traffic, the entire world can hear it too. Do not transmit personal information about the patient unless directed to do so by medical control.

TABLE 5-1	
Radio Communication Procedural Words	
Affirmative	Means "yes
Break	Used to separate portions of a message or one message from another
Negative	Means "no"
Out	Indicates the end of a transmission when no reply is expected or required
Over	Indicated the end of a transmission when an immediate reply is expected
Roger	Means "I have received your transmission satisfactorily"
Standby	Means to wait

It is important to use common speech, as opposed to codes and signals. A "10-80" can mean a different thing for each department/agency participating. However, there is a time in SAR communications that a radio code should be used, when the missing subject is located.

Radio Communication Procedural Words

When using the radio, there is are some procedural rules to follow **(Table 5-1)**.

When marking another unit on the radio, it is proper to first identify the person you are calling, then give your identifier. The following are situations and the proper radio syntax.

It is vital that we comply with local operating rules (e.g., **Federal Communications Commission or FCC)**. The Federal Communications Commission (FCC) is an independent agency of the United States government, created, directed and empowered by Congressional statute (see 47 U.S.C. § 151 and 47 U.S.C. § 154), and with many of its commissioners appointed by the current President.

When talking on any communication device, we need to be concise (short and to the point). It is also vital that during an incident, we do not use codes or signals - no unapproved jargon, even if your department requires it. It is vital that we remember "we have two ears and one mouth, thus listen twice as much as you speak."

We also need to use the standard **phonetics** when spelling. Many letters sound the same when pronounced over the air: B, D, T, P and V may all wind up sounding like "Ee" after the radio has had its fun with them. If you need to pronounce a letter over the air, use the NATO standard phonetics. The ICAO spelling alphabet, also called the NATO phonetic alphabet or the international radiotelephony spelling alphabet, is the most widely used spelling alphabet **(Table 5-2)**.

The International Civil Aviation Organization (ICAO) alphabet assigns code words to the letters of the English alphabet acrophonically (Alfa for A, Bravo for B, etc.) so that critical combinations of letters (and numbers) can be pronounced and understood by those who transmit and receive voice messages by radio or telephone regardless of their native language, especially when the safety of navigation or persons is essential.

TABLE 5-2
NATO Phonetic Alphabet

A	Alpha	(AL-fah)
B	Bravo	(BRA-voh)
C	Charlie	(CHAR-lee)
D	Delta	(DEL-tah)
E	Echo	(ECK-oh)
F	Foxtrot	(FOKS-trot)
G	Golf	(GOLF)
H	Hotel	(HOH-tell)
I	India	(IN-dee-ya)
J	Juliet	(JU-lee-ett)
K	Kilo	(KEE-loh)
L	Lima	(LEE-mah)
M	Mike	(MIKE)
N	November	(no-VEM-ber)
O	Oscar	(OSS-kah)
P	Papa	(PAH-PAH)
Q	Quebec	(KAY-bek)
R	Romeo	(ROW-me-oh)
S	Sierra	(SEE-air-ah)
T	Tango	(TANG-go)
U	Uniform	(YOU-ni-form)
V	Victor	(VIK-tah)
W	Whiskey	(WISS-kee)
X	X-ray	(ECKS-ray)
Y	Yankee	(YANG-kee)
Z	Zulu	(ZOO-loo)

Please learn them and don't make up new ones on the spot. If you are calling command on the radio and need to be picked up after you mission and tell them you are at trail head on Williams Road. You may be asked to spell it… whiskey-india-lima-lima-india-alpha-mike-sierra.

The paramount reason is to ensure intelligibility of voice signals over radio links. The standard phonetics were chosen so that no two of them can be confused under poor conditions.

When we need to read off a series of numbers, one digit at a time. The number "345" would not be pronounced as three-hundred, forty-five but rather "three-four-five". The number "100" is not pronounced as one hundred, but rather "one-zero-zero". We need to pay particular attention to the number nine (9). It is pronounced as "niner" to distinguish it more from five (5).

5.5 COSPAS-SARSAT System

COSPAS-SARSAT program is an international satellite-based search and rescue (SAR) distress alert detection and information distribution system **(Fig. 5-3)**, established by Canada, France, the United States, and the former Soviet Union in 1979.

(Fig. 5-3) How the COSPAS-SARSAT System works. Image courtesy of the from the U.S. National Oceanic and Atmospheric Administration, Satellite, and Information Service. Image courtesy of the U.S. National Oceanic and Atmospheric Administration.

The COSPAS-SARSAT System consists of both a ground segment and a space segment and is responsible for monitoring distress radio beacons, SAR signal processors aboard satellites, satellite downlink receiving and signal processing stations called LUTs (local user terminals), operation of the Mission Control Center (the AFRCC) that distribute distress alert data generated by the LUTs. [5]

- **COSPAS** = Cosmicheskaya Systyema Poiska Aariynyich Sudov. Which loosely translates into: "The Space System for the Search of Vessels in Distress".
- **SARSAT** = Search And Rescue Satellite Aided Tracking.

COSPAS-SARSAT Rescues as of July 30, 2010

Number of People Rescued (to date) in the US: 169

Rescues at sea: 91 people rescued in 34 events Aviation rescues: 36 people rescued in 9 events

Terrestrial rescues: 42 people rescued in 22 events

Worldwide – Over 28,000+ People Rescued. United States – 6,403 People Rescued (since 1982)

The space segment of the Cospas-Sarsat system currently consists of SAR processors aboard 4 geosynchronous satellites called GEOSARs and 5 low-earth polar orbit satellites called LEOSARs.
In short, Cospas-Sarsat takes the "search" out of Search & Rescue.

COSPAS-SARSAT began tracking the two original types of distress radio-beacons in 1982 (EPIRB's & ELT's). More recently, a new type of distress radio beacon (PLB's) became available (in 2003 in the USA) **(Fig. 5-4)**.

(Fig. 5-4) Commercial Personal Locator Beacons. From left to right you have the SPOT®, ResQFix ® 406 GPS/PLB end the McMurdo FastFind ® Plus.

5.6 Electronic Distress Signals

An electronic distress signal is an internationally recognized means for obtaining help. Distress signals are commonly made by using radio signals, displaying a visually detected item or illumination, or making an audible sound from a distance.

The activation of an electronic distress signal indicates that a person or group of people, ship, aircraft, or other vehicle is threatened by grave and imminent danger and requests immediate assistance. Use of distress signals in other circumstances may be against local or international law.

In order for distress signaling to be most effective, two functions must be communicated:

- Alert or notification of a distress in progress.
- Position or location (or localization or pinpointing) of the party in distress.
- Types of electronic signaling devices:
- **EPIRBs** (Emergency Position-Indicating Radio Beacons), which signal maritime distress.
- **ELTs** (Emergency Locator Transmitters), which signal aircraft distress.
- **PLBs** (Personal Locator Beacons), are for personal use and are intended to indicate a person in distress who is away from normal emergency services.

Aeronautical, maritime, and land mobile facilities operate on different radio frequencies and normally are not authorized to communicate on the other's frequency. Aircraft typically have at least one radio, so it may be easiest for the air facility and land facility to use an aeronautical frequency. If the land facility does not have a portable aircraft radio, then equipping an aircraft with a radio operating on ground frequencies may provide communications.

Aircraft normally communicate on voice channels only, and usually use at least one channel. Both military and civilian aircraft use HF (AM/SSB) for long-range. Civil aircraft use VHF (AM) for short-range, and military aircraft use UHF (AM) or VHF for short-range. If the ground aeronautical radio station that is working the aircraft is known, contact may be established through it.

Civil commercial aircraft on both long-range and short-range flights normally maintain communications with Aeronautical Radio Incorporated (ARINC) radio stations.

Merchant vessels have the capability to communicate on Marine Frequency (MF) or HF voice frequencies. INMARSAT provides a full range of communications, including voice, data, Telex and facsimile depending on the type of terminal installed on board. The NAVTEX system can also be used to contact vessels equipped with NAVTEX receivers. When attempting to establish contact with a merchant vessel, a call should be made on the DSC distress frequencies for GMDSS-equipped vessels, or 2182 kHz voice or 156.8 MHz voice.

5.7 Incident Communications

The Communications Plan (ICS 205), Radio Log (SAR 133), and Clue Log (SAR 134) provide information on all radio frequency or trunked radio system talk group assignments for each operational period, radio traffic and any clues found. The communications plan is a summary of information obtained about available radio frequencies or talk groups and the assignments of those resources by the Communications Unit Leader for use by incident responders.
(See SAMPLE DOCUMENT at the end of the unit)

5.8 After Action Reports (AARs)

An After Action Report (AAR) is a great tool to use for assessing team missions after they're completed. This type of report can be very short or quite lengthy, depending on the scope and timeframe of the mission being analyzed, but no matter the length, the report always serves the same purpose: evaluation and improvement.

What Is An AAR?

An AAR is a way of reflecting on a mission after its completion. Sharing the results of your mission, both positive and negative, can help future teams fulfill their own missions and avoid the pitfalls you encountered along the way. The aim is to maximize the learning, so you don't make the same mistakes twice. Every team member should be included and contribute to the AAR, because every voice counts.

What to Include in an AAR?

Ideally, a group will work on an AAR as a team. After a mission has been completed, the team should gather as soon as possible to go over what went right, what went wrong and what could be improved upon. Here are some of the questions that should be asked and answered for an AAR:

What was supposed to be achieved by this mission?

- What was actually achieved?

- Why are there differences?
- What aspects of the mission work?
- What didn't work and why?
- What would you change if given a chance?

The first three questions establish what happened during the mission's execution and ensure all team members are in agreement. The last three questions give the team the opportunity to reflect on the value of the mission and decide what needs improvement.

FOOTNOTES

(1) U.S. Federal Communications Commission. (2010). "Amateur Radio Service"

(2) State of Ohio, Department of Administrative Services, Information technologies. (2010) "MARCS FACTS", www.das.ohio.gov.

(3) "Aeronautical Informational Manual", Official Guide to Basic Flight Information and ATC Procedures published by The U.S. Department of Transportation, Federal Aviation Administration, August 15, 2019

(4) U.S. Army Field Operations Guide (FM 3-05.70) Chapter 19: Signaling Techniques, May 2002

(5) http://www.sarsat.noaa.gov/sarsat.html. (2010) The SARSAT Overview. The NOAA National Satellite and Information Service.

VITAL VOCABULARY

All-Hands Briefing: This form of communications usually occurs once during any given operational meeting where all of the staff at the incident meet for a generalized briefing.

Amateur (HAM) Radio: Usually a volunteer group of civilian radio hobbyist who use various types of radio communications equipment to communicate with other radio amateurs for public services, recreation and self-training.

COSPAS-SARSAT System: This system consists of both a ground segment and a space segment and is responsible for monitoring distress radio-beacons.

Federal Communications Commission (FCC): Is an independent United States government agency that was established by the Communications Act of 1934 and is charged with regulating interstate and international communications by radio, television, wire, satellite and cable. The FCC's jurisdiction covers the 50 states, the District of Columbia, and U.S. possessions.

MARCS (Multi-Agency Radio Communication System): Is a statewide 800 MHz radio and data network that utilizes secure, reliable public service wireless communication for public safety and first responders.

MAYDAY: Is a verbal distress signal used to indicate that a craft is in distress and requires immediate assistance and has priority over all other communications.

PAN-PAN: Is a verbal urgency signal used when the safety of a craft is in jeopardy or an unsafe situation exists that may eventually involve a need of assistance and has priority over all but distress traffic.

Phonetics: Is a branch of linguistics that comprises the study of the sounds of human speech.

UNIT 6 | PERSONAL CARE AND SAFETY

6.1   Prevention

6.2   Physical Fitness & Physiology

6.3   Clothing

6.4   Hygiene

6.5   Mental Health and Support

6.6   Cold Weather Conditions

6.7   Hot Weather Conditions

6.8   Survival Skills

6.9   Expanding Your Comfort Zone

> Upon completion of this chapter and the related course activities, the student will be able to meet the following objectives:
> - Understand the importance of a good pre-plan
> - Know how and when to use PPE
> - Describe the various "heat loss" methods
> - Know signs of hypothermia
> - Know what a CISD is used for
> - Define the seven necessities of life
> - Explain the four steps to manage fear

6.1 Importance of Pre-Planning
Precautions Prior to Departure

There are several precautions you can take to avoid the need for an extensive search and rescue operation. Obtaining maps and knowing how to use them in conjunction with a compass is a basic outdoor skill. Too often discounted, it is the surest way to avoid becoming lost. The wilderness **(Fig. 6-1)** is remote, dangerous and unforgiving for those not prepared.

(Fig. 6-1) The true picture of "wilderness", Forrester Island Wilderness in the U.S. state of Alaska. Image courtesy of the US Fish & Wildlife Service.

Pre-planning such as taking time to write out your trip schedule and plans, and leaving them with someone, is routinely ignored. Pre-planning greatly aids in the efficiency and timely response of a search effort. Also, should you become lost, you need to know whether to stay put or find your own way out. Either way, you must not wander around aimlessly, making it more difficult for an SAR team to locate you.

Here are the steps outdoor enthusiasts should always follow when heading into the backcountry away from civilization:

- Let someone know the route and when you expect to return. Notify them when you do return or if your plans change.
- Bring several layers of synthetic or wool clothes. You can get very hot hiking but can cool down quickly after stopping. Make sure that you have a windproof and waterproof layer.
- Bring a hat and sunglasses. Always wear sunscreen to protect your skin.
- Wear good footwear with ankle support and a firm sole with a secure grip.
- Carry a compass and map of the area. Learn how to use them!
- Carry emergency equipment such as matches, solar blanket, a first aid kit, whistle, signal mirror, and a flashlight.
- Take ample food and water, even if it's a short hike near home. DON'T DRINK FROM STREAMS! YOU CAN GET SICK DOING THIS!
- Keep your party together. DON'T SEPARATE!

A backcountry area in general terms is a geographical region that is isolated and remote. It is usually undeveloped with difficult or no general access. The term usually applies to various regions that are reasonably close to urban areas but are not immediately accessible by street. The term wilderness or woodland is a natural environment that has not been significantly modified by human activity. While the term "backcountry" is roughly comparable to the term "wilderness," they are not necessarily equivalent. "Wilderness" implies more the condition, whereas "backcountry" implies more the location.

SAR Safety

Safety during all aspects of a search and rescue operation is vital. We cannot help those in need if we become a victim. Pay attention to the hazards called out in IAP if you are at an incident. Regardless of the environment, remember:

- Trained technical personnel should be used for technical environments such as caves, cliffs, water, etc.
- Communication is key - keep everyone informed.
- Use accepted procedures to care for and protect the subject.
- Even though there may be an "Official" Safety Officer on the scene – we ALL need to take the roll of safety officer and remember that safety is the number one priority of everyone!

Wilderness Defined

The wilderness or a remote geographical location is defined as one that is more than one hour from definitive medical care. The distance may not be geographical but situational such as an urban area after a major disaster. There are some key hazards to being in the wilderness or working on a SAR team in these environments.

Wilderness Hazards

- Both subjects and rescuers are at risk for injury and illness.
- Definitive medical care can be delayed hours or days.
- Some injuries/illnesses are more common in remote locations.
- Supplies may be limited.
- Difficult decisions must be made.

Personal Protective Equipment (PPE)

Personal protective equipment (PPE) refers to the respiratory equipment, garments, and barrier materials used to protect rescuers and medical personnel from exposure to biological, chemical, and radioactive hazards. The goal of personal protective equipment is to prevent the transfer of hazardous material from subjects or the environment to rescue or health care workers. It also pertains to clothing, like pants, uniforms, etc. gloves, boots, vest, etc. It's use decreases the spread of bloodborne pathogens.

- Why? Trauma is messy!
- Risk of exposure to diseases.
- Most serious diseases are bloodborne.
- Use gloves and eye, face, and mouth protection.

- Use Universal Precautions
- Use Personal Protective Equipment
- Use Disposable Equipment
- Use Proper Disinfection and Decontamination Techniques!

PPE Types

Different types and levels of PPE may be used depending on the specific hazard or hazards present. PPE also may be needed to protect searchers from other hazards, such as electric shock hazards or hazards associated with exposures to hazardous substances that may be encountered during emergency response and recovery operations.

- The following are some of the important steps employers with emergency response and recovery workers need to take with respect to PPE:
- Conduct a hazard assessment to determine what safety and health hazards searchers may encounter;
- Determine what PPE searchers need (uniforms, helmets, gloves, eye protection, etc.);
- Provide the proper PPE to the crews or require them to operate;
- Train personnel in the proper use of PPE, including how to put it on and take it off correctly, and how to clean, maintain and dispose of it after or between uses;
- Ensure that PPE is used properly and whenever necessary;
- Regularly review and update the PPE program as hazards change.

6.2 Physical Fitness & Physiology

We all need to get the proper rest, food and water intake and exercise in our lives. We need to find that balance between work, play and rest. We need to be ready for that call to assist someone, no matter when it comes in.[1] Physical and mental fitness is integral to the primary search and rescue objective of "working for the subject." SAR personnel must have a working knowledge of human biological survival.

How your body works and what it needs is a vital aspect of being a healthy and safe searcher. When it comes to the physical aspect of SAR, there are four areas that we need to keep up-to-par: strength, agility, flexibility and endurance (SAFE).

Search and rescue personnel should go through a work capacity test, or physical fitness test, on a periodic basis. These tests are used to ensure that persons assigned to activities are physically capable of performing the duties required of them. Before training for the test or the duties of the job, an individual must first complete a health screening questionnaire (or medical history) designated by the hiring agency or authority of jurisdiction. That agency may require a medical examination as part of the qualification process. Once individuals have received medical clearance, they may begin training for the work capacity test. Those who have been regularly active may begin training as soon as they receive medical clearance.

Light Duty testing: "Duties mainly involve office-type work with occasional field activity characterized by light physical exertion requiring basic good health. Activities may include climbing stairs, standing, operating a vehicle, and long hours of work, as well as some bending, stooping, or light lifting. Individuals almost always can govern the extent and pace of their physical activity." —NWCG 310–1

The walk test for light duty is designed to determine the ability to carry out required duties. It consists of a one-mile test with no load (pack). A time of 16 minutes, the passing score for the test, ensures the ability to meet emergencies and evacuate to a safety zone. Other testing can be that of a hearing and vision test as well as basic vital signs such as a resting blood pressure of better than 140/90.

Moderate: "Duties involve field work requiring complete control of all physical faculties and may include considerable walking over irregular ground, standing for long periods, lifting 25 to 50 pounds, climbing, bending, stooping, squatting, twisting, and reaching. Occasional demands may be required for moderately strenuous activities in emergencies over long periods. Individuals usually set their own work pace." —NWCG 310–1

The field test for those with moderately strenuous duties consists of a two-mile hike with a 25-pound pack in under 30 minutes.

Admitting Limitations

Make a realistic assessment of your physical abilities. Being unable to admit to others that you have a limitation is worse than being in poor physical condition during a mission. The time to realize that you are unfit is not when you are on the trail searching for a missing child. Everyone is different - set your own limits and communicate them to your team. We are only as strong as the weakest member of our team.

Blister Care

- Attend to "hot spots," or irritation, immediately. This is the best way to prevent blisters.
- A blister is a burn of the skin caused by friction forming a blister.
- Cut a hole the size of the blister in moleskin and layer to protect it.
- If rupture is needed, pierce corner with sterile needle and clean ASAP.

Blister Care Procedure

- Do not "pop" blister if possible.
- Use of moleskin is best care.
- Cut center out of a section of moleskin the size of the blister.
- Center moleskin and apply.

- Cover with a bandage.
- The hold in the moleskin will prevent contact with bandage.

Hydration

Hydration is vital for any physical activity. Searching for a lost person is no different – it is a physical activity. Heavy activity significantly increases caloric requirements. We must understand that we are made up mostly of water, about two-thirds. There are two conditions that can affect body hydration. Water intoxication (also known as **hyperhydration** or water poisoning) is a potentially fatal disturbance in brain functions that results when the normal balance of electrolytes in the body is pushed outside of safe limits by overconsumption of water. Normal, healthy (physically, nutritionally and mentally) individuals have little reason to worry about accidentally consuming too much water.

TABLE 6-1 Dehydration Affects

%	Effect
1%	Leads to thirst.
2%	Causes feelings of anxiety, reduced appetite and a decrease in work capacity by 20%.
6%	Leads to loss of coordination and coherent speech.
10%	Causes thermoregulation failure. Cells begin to die.
11%	Inability to correct by water consumption – urgent medical attention is required.
20%	Leads to death.

An inactive person requires a minimum of one to two liters of water per day while an active searcher may need as much as eight to 10 liters of water per day.

Mild Dehydration Signs & Symptoms	Moderate Dehydration Signs & Symptoms	Severe Dehydration Signs & Symptoms
- Thirst, dry mouth and lips - Decreased urine volume, abnormally dark urine - Unexplained tiredness, irritability - Lack of tears when crying - Headache and sometimes blurred vision - Dizziness when standing due to orthostatic hypotension	- There may be no urine output at all. - Lethargy or extreme sleepiness. - Seizures. - Dry, pale skin. - Sunken fontanel (soft spot) in infants. - Fainting or near syncopal episode. - Sunken eyes and poor skin turgor.	- Muscle cramps. - A sudden episodes of visual disturbances. - Decreased blood pressure (hypotension). - Delirium, and unconsciousness. - Swelling of the tongue - Death!
Treatment		
- BSI / PPE - Monitor vitals - The best treatment for minor dehydration is drinking water, adding electrolytes and stopping fluid loss - In more severe cases, rehydration, through oral rehydration therapy or intravenous therapy is needed. - In the case of serious lack of fresh water, drinking seawater, alcohol or urine does not help		

Decreases in normal water levels is called **dehydration**. Dehydration (hypohydration) is defined as an excessive loss of body fluid. It is literally the removal of water from the cellular tissue. Physiologically, dehydration, despite the name, does not simply mean loss of water, as water and solutes (mainly sodium) are usually lost in roughly equal quantities. Our body is very sensitive to changes in body water levels.[2]

The human body requires a fresh supply of water every day **(Table 6-1)**. Not only is water one of the most abundant nutrients available, but it's also the most important. Water helps regulate and maintain your body temperature, transports nutrients and oxygen, removes waste products, and moistens your mouth, eyes, nose, hair, skin, joints, and digestive tract. Limiting your water intake can result in dehydration, elevated body temperature, fatigue, decreased performance, and increased risk of heat-related illness. Water is more essential than food. This is why searchers carry water purification in the 24-hour pack. You will likely run out of water in the backcountry. Being prepared to filter is critical.

Nutrition

What you eat today is what you will work on tomorrow. The U.S. Department of Agriculture has adopted a 2,000-calorie diet as the basis for calculating a daily reference. Eating a proper diet and incorporating a fitness regiment is very important. As our bodies require about 2,000 calories per day during normal life, the environment may require that you increase that caloric intake an additional 870 - 1,000 calories for strenuous work and even up to 2,000 additional calories in cold environments. The body uses energy (calories) to simply keep the body warm.

Trail Snack Suggestions

- Nuts: A mix of nuts is fine, whatever ones you enjoy the most. They're light, easy to carry and provide a good punch on the energy and nutrition fronts.

- Fresh Fruit: Apples and bananas are easy to carry and tasty to eat. What's great about fruit is there is high water content which helps as you sweat and lose water.

- Dried Fruit/Trail Mix: Dried Fruit is less bulky than fresh and has a longer shelf life. Take a mix of dried fruit and nuts, a handful here and there is a tasty little power pack while out on the trail!

- Chocolate: Chocolate is a great energy booster. It works very fast. If you're approaching the end of your hike and you come up against a final steep peak but you're not feeling 100% up to it, a bite or two of chocolate can do the trick to give you that little boost to push on.

- Hard Candy: They're functional and they score highly on the psychological side too.

- Granola/Cereal Bars: There are lots of organic varieties of these which are usually made with more of a focus on nutrition. However, some are just bars of refined sugar when you look at them in detail so it's worth taking a good look at the ingredients. Again, packable, lightweight and not bulky.

- Seeds: Similar to nuts, you can just take a handful when you fancy and eat them. Again, very nutritious, and tasty. Many varieties pack a really good energy punch too.

6.3 Clothing

Dressing in Layers

When you step outdoors, the ancient art of layering becomes your smart-technology thermostat. This tried-and-true strategy lets you regulate comfort by slipping layers on and off as your activity level or the weather changes.

Even if you don't wear all three layers at the outset, it's a good idea to take all layers on every outing: You can peel off layers if things heat up, but you can't put on layers that you didn't bring along.

Cold-weather layers:

Midweight polyester long underwear top and bottom; a jacket with synthetic insulation; midweight fleece pants; waterproof/breathable rain jacket and pants.

Rainy-weather layers (cool temps):

Lightweight polyester long underwear top and bottom; lightweight fleece jacket; synthetic hiking pants; lightweight waterproof/breathable rain jacket and pants (with plenty of vents).

Hot-weather layers:

Polyester briefs and a short-sleeve synthetic top; convertible nylon hiking pants; lightweight wind jacket. You have literally dozens of alternatives and options for each of these layers. The trick is to go with options that make the most sense for where you're headed, what you're doing and what you're able to spend. It's also key that you take the time to adjust layers as conditions change. If the rain and wind let up, remove your shell. If hiking alone isn't warming you up, add a middle layer. And many people add a middle layer (on top) and/or outer layer at every rest stop, just to avoid getting chilled.

Base Layer: Moisture Management

As the next-to-skin layer, a base layer's job is moving perspiration away from your skin, aka "wicking." In cool or cold conditions, wicking long-underwear-style base layers are needed to keep your skin dry. That's essential because it helps to keep you from becoming chilled or worse—hypothermic. This is very important when considering the types of socks and footwear. Both need to breath and be able to pull heat and moisture away from the feet to prevent conditions such as "trench foot."

Middle Layer: Insulation

The insulating layer helps you retain the heat that's radiated by your body. The more efficiently this layer traps that heat, the warmer you'll be.

Outer Layer: Rain and Wind Protection

The outer layer (or shell layer) protects you from wind, rain and snow. Shells range from pricey mountaineering jackets to simple wind-resistant jackets. Most allow at least some perspiration to escape; virtually all are treated with a durable water repellent (DWR) finish to make water bead up and roll off the fabric. Your outer shell is an important piece in stormy weather, because if wind and water are allowed to penetrate to inner layers, you can get seriously chilled.

High Visibility Safety Apparel (HVSA)

High visibility safety apparel (HVSA) **(Fig 6-2) is** clothing that workers wear in order to improve their visibility. HVSA includes reflective vests, hard hats, coveralls, and bibs.

(Fig. 6-2) Example of a Hi-VIS vest to improve the searcher of being seen in all conditions. Image courtesy of J. Bobot

Unlike working in an office where hazards are minimal, on SAR missions there are moving vehicles and other hazards that have the potential to cause significant injuries. In these workplaces, proper precautions need to be taken in order to ensure that workers are as safe as possible.

Because hi-vis clothing is made of brightly colored fabrics and reflective materials, those who wear them are more visible. Not only does this clothing make it easier for motorists to see SAR searchers walking along a roadway at night, but it also makes them more visible to motorists during the daytime, particularly in inclement weather when inclement weather is an issue. In addition to the SAR workers safety, it allows for the missing subject to see the searchers from a distance and allow them to signal them for rescue.

Heat Loss Methods

Thermoregulation (temperature control) is an important aspect of human life. Most body heat is generated in the deep organs, especially the liver, brain, and heart, and in contraction of skeletal muscles. Our bodies can lose heat several ways (Fig. 6-3):

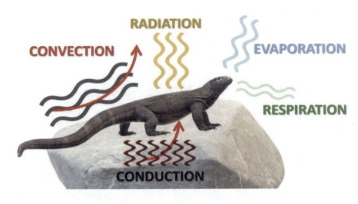

(Fig. 6-3) Types of heat Loss Methods. Image courtesy of J. Bobot.

- **Radiation:** In cold environments, our body is warmer than the air temperature and heat will leave the body and radiate into the air, even if standing in one place. To reduce heat loss through radiation, our body must be properly covered and protected.

- **Conduction:** When we come into contact with a cold surface, such as a rock or the ground, the body is robbed of heat as it transfers to the colder surface.

- **Convection:** Air currents pass over exposed skin surfaces cooling the skin and making the body work harder to maintain normal temperature.

- **Evaporation:** Our bodies lose heat through sweating. The most dangerous thing a person can do in cold environments is to begin to sweat. Once you stop moving, the once warm wetness will change into cold, icy water on the body and cool the body under the protection of your clothing.

- **Respiration:** When we breathe, the warm, moist air that has been warmed in our lungs is replaced with cold air from the outside. This reduces the core body temperature.

Humans have been able to adapt to a great diversity of climates, including hot humid and hot arid. High temperatures pose serious stresses for the human body, placing it in great danger of injury or even death. For humans, adaptation to varying climatic conditions includes both physiological mechanisms as a byproduct of evolution, and the conscious development of cultural adaptations

The skin assists in homeostasis (keeping different aspects of the body constant e.g. temperature). It does this by reacting differently to hot and cold conditions so that the inner body temperature remains constant. Vasodilation (opening of the blood vessels) and sweating are the primary modes by which humans attempt to lose excess body heat.

The brain creates much heat through the countless reactions which occur. The head has a complex system of blood vessels, which keeps the brain from overheating by bringing blood to the thin skin on the head, allowing heat to escape. The effectiveness of these methods is influenced by the character of the climate and the degree to which the individual is acclimatized.[3]

6.4 Hygiene

Personal hygiene is very important while out in the wilderness. It is vital that you keep this in mind when you are out on missions and while at extended incidents. Poor hygiene can lead to a number of health issues from infections, rashes, intestinal illnesses and other preventable diseases.

Using the bathroom in the wilderness, though it may be uncomfortable, it is often a necessity. Holding your stool or urine can cause issues and can lead to abdominal pain, cramps and urinary tract infections. To decrease the risk of spreading pathogens, do the following:

- Deposit human waste at least 200 feet away from water sources and campsites
- To protect vegetation, urinate on bare ground or rocks
- Bury your stool and use biodegradable bath tissue
- Pack out any paper or waste including feminine items.
- Pack a hygiene kit with alcohol-based hand sanitizer, extra bags, baby wipes and any other items you need.

6.5 Mental Health and Support

Search and rescue is difficult work that requires emotional resilience and good mental health care and support. Taking care of yourself is critical to remaining able to respond. This includes tending to your mental well being. Repeated exposure to traumas or difficult situations can bring up issues for a searcher. If you notice yourself not enjoying your usual activities, changing your social habits, drinking more, withdrawing from friends or teammates, or a change in sleep patterns, consider that you might be experiencing a reaction to the work we do.

Peer support teams are a great resource for SAR teams. If your team has one, consider contacting them. If your team doesn't, reach out to any trusted friend or teammate to talk through what you are experiencing. It is known that talking through problems with friends or colleagues can be beneficial. Ask your team about the availability of professional outside counselors as well. Mental health issues can come at any time and for any reason, so be vigilant in caring both for yourself, and for your teammates.

Critical Incident Stress Debriefing

After dealing with death or a disturbing scene such as finding a decomposing body or the recovery of a child, the searcher or team may require **Critical Incident Stress Debriefing**. A "critical incident" is any event that causes an unusually intense stress reaction. It can be a body recovery, the death of a child, an unresolved search, or an accident on the incident. The distress people experience after a critical incident limits their ability to cope, impairs their ability to adjust, and negatively impacts the work environment.[4]

Debriefing is a specific technique designed to assist others in dealing with the physical or psychological symptoms that are generally associated with trauma exposure. Debriefing allows those involved with the incident to process the event and reflect on its impact.

Critical Incident Stress Debriefing is a process that prevents or limits the development of post-traumatic stress in people exposed to critical incidents. Professionally conducted debriefings help people cope with and recover from an incident's aftereffects. CISD enables participants to understand that they are not alone in their reactions to a distressing event and provides them with an opportunity to discuss their thoughts and feelings in a controlled, safe environment. Optimally, CISD occurs within 24 to 72 hours of an incident.

Critical incidents produce characteristic sets of psychological and physiological reactions or symptoms (thus the term syndrome) in all people, including emergency service personnel. Typical symptoms of Critical Incident Stress include:[5]

- Restlessness & Irritability
- Excessive Fatigue or other Sleep Disturbances
- Anxiety or Startle Reactions
- Depression & Moodiness
- Muscle Tremors
- Difficulties Concentrating
- Nightmares
- Vomiting
- Diarrhea
- Suspiciousness

The physical and emotional symptoms that develop as part of a stress response are normal but have the potential to become dangerous to the responder if symptoms become prolonged. Researchers have also concluded that future incidents (even those that are more "normal") can be enough to trigger a stress response. Prolonged stress saps energy and leaves the person vulnerable to illness. Under certain conditions, there is potential for life-long aftereffects. Symptoms are especially destructive when a person denies their presence or misinterprets the stress responses as something wrong with them.

6.6 Cold Weather Conditions

We can only survive for a few hours in extreme cold or hot weather conditions without mitigation. The initial phase of cold-related conditions is called frost nip. This condition will progress into frostbite. Frostbite is most likely to happen in body parts farthest from the heart and those with large exposed areas. If the body is exposed to low temperatures, the body can begin to suffer from hypothermia. Any condition which decreases heat production, increases heat loss, or impairs thermoregulation, however, may contribute to these conditions. Thus, hypothermia risk factors include: any condition that affects judgment, the extremes of age, poor clothing, chronic medical conditions, substance abuse, homelessness, and living in a cold environment.

Hypothermia also occurs frequently in major trauma. Body temperature is usually maintained near a constant level of 36.5–37.5 °C (98–100 °F) through biologic homeostasis or thermoregulation. If exposed to cold and the internal mechanisms are unable to replenish the heat that is being lost, a drop in core temperature occurs. As body temperature decreases, characteristic symptoms occur such as shivering and mental confusion.

Hypothermia – Stage 1 Signs & Symptoms	Hypothermia – Stage 2 Signs & Symptoms	Hypothermia – Stage 3 Signs & Symptoms
- Body temperature drops by 1-2°C (1.8-3.6°F) below normal temperature (35-37°C or 95-98.6°F). - Temperature (35-37°C or 95-98.6°F). - Mild to strong shivering occurs. - Unable to perform complex tasks with the hands; the hands become numb. - Blood vessels in the outer extremities constrict, lessening heat loss to the outside air. - Breathing becomes quick and shallow. - Goose bumps form, raising body hair on end in an attempt to create an insulating layer of air around the body. - May feel sick to their stomach, and very tired. - May experience a warm sensation, as if they have recovered, but they are in fact heading into state 2.	- Body temperature drops by 2-4°C (3.8-7.6°F) below normal temperature (33-35°C or 91-94.8°F). - Shivering becomes more violent. - Muscle mis-coordination becomes apparent. - Movements are slow and labored, accompanied by a stumbling pace. - Mild confusion, although the victim may appear alert. - Surface blood vessels contract further as the body focuses its remaining resources on keeping the vital organs warm. - The victim becomes pale. - Lips, ears, fingers and toes may become blue.	- Body temperature drops below approximately 32 °C (89.6 °F). **Shivering usually stops.** - Difficulty speaking, sluggish thinking, and amnesia start to appear. - Inability to use hands and stumbling is also usually present. - Exposed skin becomes blue and puffy. - Unable to walk. - Incoherent/irrational behavior including terminal burrowing or even a stupor. - Pulse and respiration rates decrease significantly, but fast heart rates (ventricular tachycardia, atrial fibrillation) can occur. - Major organs fail. - Clinical death occurs. Because of decreased cellular activity in stage 3 hypothermia, the body will actually take longer to undergo brain death.
Hypothermia – Stage 1 Treatment	**Hypothermia – Stage 2 Treatment**	**Hypothermia – Stage 3 Treatment**
- BSI / PPE - Drying & sheltering - Gradual warming - Supplemental oxygen - Monitor vitals - It is vital that you warm the core of the body first or the cold blood will be forced towards the heart and may cause death! - In the field, a mildly hypothermic person can be effectively rewarmed through close body contact from a companion and by drinking warm, sweet liquids if well conscious.	- BSI / PPE - Avoid rough drying and handling. - Remove to a warm environment. - Require immediate evacuation and treatment in a hospital. - Supplemental oxygen. - Monitor vitals. - These patients are at high risk for arrhythmias (V-Fib), and care must be taken to minimize jostling and other disturbances until they have been sufficiently warmed.	- BSI / PPE - Avoid rough drying and handling. - Remove to a warm environment. - Require immediate evacuation and treatment in a hospital. - Supplemental oxygen. - Monitor vitals. - These patients are a high risk for arrhythmias (V-Fib), and care must be taken to minimize jostling and other disturbances until they have been sufficiently warmed.

Other Cold-related Conditions

- Can either be present alone or in combination with hypothermia include:
- Chilblains are superficial ulcers of the skin that occur when a predisposed individual is repeatedly exposed to cold.
- Frostnip is a superficial cooling of tissues without cellular destruction.
- Frostbite involves the freezing and destruction of tissue with large bullae present.
- Bullae: A blister more than 5 mm (about 3/16 inch) in diameter with thin walls that is full of fluid.
- Trench foot or immersion foot is due to repetitive exposure to wet, non-freezing temperatures.
- Raynaud's Disease is a disorder causing discoloration of the fingers, toes, and occasionally other areas. This condition may also cause nails to become brittle with longitudinal ridges.

Frostbite Care Considerations

Feet - Remove the victim's boots and socks if he does not need to walk any further to receive additional treatment.

Thawing the feet and forcing to walk on them will cause additional pain/ injury.

Place the affected feet under clothing and against the body of another person – keep dry.

6.7 Hot Weather Conditions

Hot-weather emergencies occur when the body produces or absorbs more heat than it can dissipate. When the elevated body temperature is sufficiently high, hyperthermia is a medical emergency and requires immediate treatment to prevent disability and death.

The human body normally cools itself by perspiration, or sweating, which evaporates and carries heat away from the body. However, when the relative humidity is high, the evaporation rate is reduced, so heat is removed from the body at a lower rate causing it to retain more heat than it would in dry air. The heat-regulating mechanisms of the body eventually become overwhelmed and unable to effectively deal with the heat, causing the body temperature to climb uncontrollably. Hyperthermia is a relatively rare side effect of many drugs, particularly those that affect the central nervous system.

If the problem isn't addressed, heat cramps (caused by loss of salt from heavy sweating) can lead to heat exhaustion (caused by dehydration), which can progress to heatstroke. Heatstroke, the most serious of the three, can cause shock, brain damage, organ failure, and even death.

Heat Cramps Signs & Symptoms	Heat Exhaustion Signs & Symptoms	Heat Stroke Signs & Symptoms
- Irritability, loss of appetite. - Prickly heat rash. - Nausea and vomiting. - Muscle spasm/twitching. - Moist cool skin. - Painful muscle cramps (limbs and abdomen)	- Heat cramps may remain. - Profuse perspiration. - Cold, clammy, pale skin. - Headache with nausea and vomiting. - Weak, thready and fast pulse. - Poor coordination. - Pupils dilate. - Syncope. - Rule out hyponatremia.	- Skin is flushed, red, hot and dry. - Dry swollen tongue. - High body temperature. - Pupils constrict. - Confusion and disorientation. - Lethargy may progress to unconsciousness.

Sunburn

Your skin can burn if it gets too much sun without proper protection from sunscreen and clothes. To help heal and soothe stinging skin, it is important to begin treating sunburn as soon as you notice it. The first thing you should do is get out of the sun—and preferably indoors.

6.8 Survival Skills

These are techniques a person may use in a dangerous situation (e.g. natural disasters) to save themselves or to save others. Generally speaking, these techniques are meant to provide the basic necessities for human life: water, food, shelter, habitat, and the need to think straight, to signal for help, to navigate safely, to avoid unpleasant interactions with animals and plants, and for first aid. Many of these skills are the ways to enjoy extended periods of time in remote places, or a way to thrive in nature. Some people use these skills to better appreciate nature and for recreation, not just survival.

When faced with a survival situation, the slightest discomfort can be multiplied. Tend to minor cuts and scrapes immediately, as they can become infected and add stress to your situation. It is important that you check and see what equipment you may have and what condition it is in. A knife (or cutting tool) is one of the most important pieces of equipment you will need.

Seven Necessities of Life

SAR survival means continuing to exist by whatever means possible. In a survival situation, actions and needs must be prioritized. Those who operate on the outskirts of their comfort zones react better in emergencies. To function safely, one needs to understand the seven Necessities of Life:[6]

- **Positive Mental Attitude (PMA)** - It only takes three seconds to lose your PMA! Often overlooked but a vital priority in survival situations. Simply stated, it is the "will to live" – an overwhelming urge to survive. It is also a whole person concept where it must be both a mental and physical body processes.

- **Air** - We can only last three minutes without air! Breathing is essential to maintain life. A person can only survive a few minutes without oxygen.

- **Shelter** - In extreme conditions, a person can only survive about three hours without proper clothing or shelter. A shelter can be anything that protects the body. Our clothing can function as a shelter, but efforts must be taken to improve our survival by improving our shelter.

- **Rest** - You can keep running on adrenalin for about 30 hours before you collapse! Energy levels significantly impact our ability to cope. When we rest, we conserve energy for future use and rid the body's tissues of waste. It also allows time for reflection, planning, prevents acting in haste or desperation, and provides an opportunity for mental rest.

- **Signals** - Your ultimate objective is being rescued, so you should plan on gathering the proper materials needed to signal help. You should have about three hours of signal materials on hand or permanently placed. If you are lost or immobilized, you must find some way to attract attention to yourself.

- **Water** - You can only last about three days without water! As we know, we are made mostly of water and we have discussed the problems that can result from dehydration. In a survival situation you should ration your sweat and activity, not your water. In extreme conditions, the absence of water can cut survival time to only days.

- **Food** - Most of us can live up to three weeks without food. If you do not have water, do not eat. The body uses large quantities of water in the digestive process, water you may not be able to spare. Eating may make you emotionally feel better, but without water, you will simply be dehydrating your body through digestion. Food is not a necessity for "short-term-survival, however it does help morale." In cold environments, additional calories are needed to maintain body temperature.

6.9 Expanding Your Comfort Zone

Your comfort zone is a state of being where you base your decision to do or not to do something based on fear or comfort. Your comfort zone limits vary based on experience and knowledge. Anxiety and stress are created when people are forced outside their zone.

Look for opportunities to expand your comfort zone. There are many things that you can do to increase your comfort zone. Search and rescue is a very demanding occupation, both emotionally and physically. Perhaps start a fitness program or forming a hiking group with other team members. This will improve your physical fitness level, thus expanding your ability to search longer and stronger. One can expand your emotional comfort zone through education and training. When we are competent and skilled, we tend to focus less on the possibility of failure. If you have never started a fire using two sticks, the time to try it is NOT when you are faced with a survival situation. Survival situations brings its own level of fear and fear of failure will simply add to the already mounting stress.

Four Steps to Handle Fear:

Fear is something that we all face and in order to conquer or harness that fear, we need to first be able to recognize it. We must realize it can happen to you. Again, by being informed we can expand our comfort zone. This can also be done by having procedures mapped out and setting realistic goals.

The use of affirmative self-talk is a great way to help "keep your cool" and focus. If you have others with you in a survival situation, remember teamwork.

There is a psychology to survival. It takes much more than the knowledge and skills to build shelters, get food, make fires, and travel without the aid of standard navigational devices to live successfully through a survival situation. Some people with little or no survival training have managed to survive life-threatening circumstances. Some people with survival training have not used their skills and died.

A key ingredient in any survival situation is the mental attitude of those involved. Having survival skills is important; having the will to survive is essential. Without a desire to survive, acquired skills serve little purpose and invaluable knowledge goes to waste.

FOOTNOTES

(1) US Department of Health and Human Services / US Department of Agriculture. (2005). "Dietary Guidelines for Americans"

(2) Dehydrationsymptoms.org. (2009). "The Effects of Dehydration".

(3) Guyton, A.C., & Hall, J.E. (2006) Textbook of Medical Physiology.

(4) Raphael, Beverly; Wilson, John (2003). Psychological Debriefing: Theory, Practice and Evidence. Cambridge: Cambridge University Press.

(5) "Psychological Debriefing for Post-Traumatic Stress Disorder". www.div12.org. Society of Clinical Psychology: Division 12 of The American Psychological Association.

(6) Bannerman, Foster, Hill, Hood, Thrasher & Wolf, (1999). Introduction to Search & Rescue. National Association for Search & Rescue.

VITAL VOCABULARY

Critical Incident Stress Debriefing (CISD): This concept embraces the tenets of a crisis theory which believe that after exposure to a traumatic event: 1) people may need additional coping skills to deal with the event and 2) people are usually open to acquiring new skills after being exposed to critical incidents.

Dehydration (hypohydration): This is defined as an excessive loss of body fluid.

Frost Nip: This is the initial stages of frostbite.

Frostbite: This is the medical condition where localized damage is caused to skin and other tissues due to extreme cold.

Heat cramps: These are muscle spasms that result from loss of large amount of salt and water through exercise.

Heat Exhaustion: This can be a precursor of heatstroke resulting in weakness, nausea and dehydration.

Heat stroke: This is defined by a body temperature of greater than >40.6 °C (105.1 °F) due to environmental heat exposure with lack of thermoregulation causing loss of consciousness and even death.

Homeostasis: The ability or tendency of an organism or cell to maintain internal equilibrium by adjusting its physiological processes.

Hyperhydration: (water poisoning) is a potentially fatal disturbance in brain functions that results when the normal balance of electrolytes in the body is pushed outside of safe limits by over-consumption of water.

Hypothermia: This condition usually occurs from exposure to low temperatures and is frequently complicated by alcohol.

Raynaud's Disease: This is a medical condition that causes some areas of your body (fingers, toes, tip of your nose and ears) to feel numb and cool in response to cold temperatures or stress.

Thermoregulation: Thermoregulation is the ability of an organism (the body) to keep its body temperature within certain boundaries, even when the surrounding temperature is very different.

UNIT 7 | 24 – HOUR SAR PACK

7.1 The Tools of the Trade

7.2 The Three-Level Approach

7.3 The SAR Pack

7.4 Fitting a Backpack

7.5 Pack Weight

7.6 Ten SAR Pack Essentials

7.7 Packing a Backpack

7.8 Other Equipment

7.9 NASAR Approved 24-Hour Pack List

Upon completion of this chapter and the related course activities, the student will be able to meet the following objectives:

- Explain the need for a "SAR 24-Hour Pack"
- Identify the various SAR Equipment and their characteristics

7.1 The Tools of the Trade

The SAR 24-hour pack is a key tool of the searcher trade. This is the house on your back and allows you to be self-reliant and comfortable. A "24-hour pack" is the absolute minimum that should be carried during a mission **(Fig. 7-1)** and is dictated by the National Association for Search and Rescue (NASAR). The name means that the contents of the pack should be able to support you for 24 hours if needed.

When it comes time to purchase a pack, everyone should be "fitted" for a pack (any reputable sporting goods store can do this). We all tend to have that cool piece of equipment or some extra comfort gear; however, those items should not be kept in your 24-hour pack.

(Fig. 7-1) Example of a SAR Pack (left) and a wilderness medical pack (right). Image courtesy of J. T. Bobot.

Your 24-hour pack must allow you to conduct search operations and safely spend up to 24 hours in the field. Careful thought should be given to the equipment needed for search effectiveness, balanced with how much weight you are comfortably able to operate with. The inventory of your 24-hour pack should be dynamic, not static; changing as circumstances (i.e. seasons) change.

A process of ongoing evaluation is also important; as your experience grows, the items in your 24-hour pack should be adjusted accordingly. Keep in mind that the 24-hour pack is just one (very important) element of your over-all "search package." Your training, skills, and, probably most important, your physical and mental readiness, are critical for mission success in whatever your team encounters!

7.2 The Three-Level Approach

Virtually all backpacks have large openings at the top and are known as top-loading packs. A seldom-seen alternative is a panel-loading pack which uses a zippered sidewall flap. Some packs have a zippered opening at the bottom of the pack, known as the sleeping bag compartment. Lots of people love the convenience of this compartment. Since a sleeping bag is not one of the items you will carry in your pack all the time, this is a great place for medium weight gear that you may want quick access to. The following is an approach to looking at gear and where it should go: [1]

- **Level 1:** The clothing you wear, and basic survival items (i.e. what's in your pockets, and on your belt - like a sheath knife).

- **Level 2:** Basic operational equipment and other survival items. This level would include your radio, map & compass, flashlight (s), snacks, grid ribbon, etc. - things you need and use as you conduct field operations. These items may be carried in a radio harness and a butt pack, a multi-pocketed vest, or a load bearing harness.

- **Level 3:** Your backpack. Here is where your extra clothing, water, food, and other bulky items go. A mid-sized, internal frame pack is probably a good bet for this function.

7.3 The SAR Pack

You need a pack that both fits your figure perfectly and suits your gear-stowing needs. For the best fit, go by the length of your torso, not your height. As you browse packs, keep in mind that each manufacturer is different -- so read the sizing instructions on each backpack. After you narrow down the size, zero in on backpack features. A panel-loading backpack, which zips open at the top and down each side, will allow you easy access to your things. With a top-loading pack, you may have to unload half your pack to reach what you need. The internal-framed backpack is more popular than the external-framed pack. It holds the backpack close to your body, which makes it easier to balance, and you carry 80 percent of the pack's weight on your hips. The external-framed backpack is less expensive, and because the frame holds the pack away from your body, it's cooler on hot days.

A quality backpack **(Fig. 7-2)** should have padded straps that go over the shoulders, across the chest and around the hips. Women's packs are made with narrower straps and shorter torso lengths. If you plan to carry water bottles, make sure the pack has external pockets correctly sized for this. If you plan on using a pack bladder or hydration system, confirm that it's compatible with your backpack. Some backpacks come with a hydration system.

(Fig. 7-2) The Terra 35 by The North Face, even at full capacity handles the weight with ease. Image courtesy of Dan Human.

Once you've narrowed down your choices, try each one on with added weight. The backpacking store should have weighted bags to put in the backpack. These bags typically contain lead or other dense packing, so they won't exactly replicate the feel of a loaded pack, but they'll give you some idea. Walk around the store, look up, squat down, and, if possible, walk up and down a flight of stairs. The backpack shouldn't hit the back of your knees when you squat, hit your neck or head when you look up or shift around when you move.

7.4 Fitting a Backpack

As with boots, proper fit is the key with a backpack. The weight of a pack is secondary, since a well-designed, heavier backpack may give you a more comfortable ride than a much lighter pack carrying the same load.

The key for any pack is to try it out with plenty of weight in it. All outdoor shops should have weights and stuffing for testing packs. Fill up the pack with weight approximate to that you would be carrying on the trail. Try to distribute the weight in the pack as best you can (This can be hard because the stores usually have 10 to 20-pound sacks of lead shot or BB's and wads of paper but try your best). Your torso length—not your height—is the key measurement. [2]

After you have achieved a good fit (and, hopefully, the salesperson concurs) take the pack for a test drive, as follows:

- Bend over and touch your toes. Sway, dramatically, from side to side. Jump up and down. Throughout these maneuvers, the pack should stick to you like glue. It should not feel sloppy, nor, if it's properly packed, should it throw you off balance.

- Walk around the store many times. Walk up and down stairs. Walk out in the parking lot, thru the nearby park, or wherever--assuming it's okay with the salesperson.

7.5 Pack Weight

When you are choosing your gear and packing your pack, make sure you put your water in FIRST and then your gear. We have a tendency of including all the really "cool" gear and every piece of "cool" gear adds to the weight! A backpacker needs anywhere from a half to two gallons (two to eight liters), or more, per day. [3]

You should never carry heavy equipment on the very bottom of your pack, those items need to be in the center. Your heaviest items should be placed 1) on top of your sleeping bag compartment and 2) close to your spine. Rope is one such item. It is heavy and people make the mistake of putting it in the sleeping bag compartment. This should be just above, close to the center of your pack for the best weight distribution.

You will not use the rope as much as you think, nor will you be needing "quick" access to it. Taking a few items out to gain access to your rope is better than hiking with weight in the bottom. Loading your pack and preparing for a trip or mission can be a daunting task. There are several things that you can do to make your preparations easier.

Analyze your current equipment kit. A computer spreadsheet and a postal scale provide one cornerstone to the foundation for lightening your load. The ability to visualize every item in your kit - and their weights - allows you to see the impact of gear selection on the big picture.

Select the lightest equipment that fully meets your need. Next (financial resources permitting), begin to replace your heavier gear with lighter items. But don't go too light with your pack until reducing the weight of the rest of your load - or your musculature will pay the price for an overloaded "ultra-light" pack.

You also need to plan for different seasons and weather. Carefully look at your clothing, shelter, and outerwear to make sure that it's appropriate for the season. Choose jackets with down fill insulation. Down insulation will always be (at least in the foreseeable near future) lighter than synthetic alternatives for the same amount of insulating value. However, carrying down assumes that you possess the necessary skills and attentiveness to care for it in inclement weather - down provides precious little insulating value if it gets very wet.

Only take what you need. I advocate leaving luxuries behind. Look for lighter alternatives, go without, or carefully select one or two key items for any particular mission. Look for items that have multiple uses. Start treating your gear as a system of components that work together. The ability to recognize synergistic relationships between your gear, or to select gear that performs multiple uses, is a key skill in reducing your pack weight and increasing the level of simplicity in your approach to lightweight backpacking. The classic example of ultra-light multi-use gear: the tarp can replace a poncho, which serves as both shelter and raingear.

Each SAR team member should provide their own pack and is responsible for its development and maintenance -- and ensuring that it is present and ready for every mission. Many SAR teams consider the 24-hour pack so important that they bring them to meetings and all trainings.

7.6 Ten SAR Pack Essentials

1) **Map** - Topographical maps are strongly recommended.

2) **Compass** - know-how and an understanding of declination (the difference between a 'magnetic' and 'true' bearing) is important.

3) **Flashlight** - Ensure you have an extra bulb & batteries. A head lamp is very useful. If possible, choose equipment that all uses the same size batteries.

4) **Extra food, water and filtration** - Carry food which requires little or no preparation (i.e. food bars). Sadly, there is no longer any uncontaminated surface water in the lower 48 states. Bring it with you and be prepared to treat all other water.

5) **Extra clothing** - Include a hat and gloves with your extra clothing. Rain protection is a must, wool is always a good choice for layering. A space blanket is an ideal addition to any kit.

6) **Fire starter** - Must be waterproof. It is a good idea to have three options for fire starting (i.e. a lighter, waterproof matches & magnesium/flint). Practice makes all the difference.

7) **Candle/fuel tablets** - These are remarkably effective as hand warmers, a quick hot beverage, or for making a fire much easier to start.

8) **Knife** - The Swiss Army knife is an excellent, basic choice. The addition of a larger camping type knife is also quite useful (i.e. gathering firewood).

9) **First Aid kit** - Basic First Aid & CPR training should be considered a critical part of your First Aid kit. Latex gloves and a CPR shield are important parts of your kit.

10) **Signaling device** - At a minimum carry a whistle. Signal mirrors are very effective, as are smoke signals & flares (potential fire hazard).

7.7 Packing a Backpack

There's no one way to pack a backpack. Everyone will pack their backpacks differently. But some general guidelines will make it easier for you to access the things you need when you need them. They'll also make your pack easier to carry during a long day.

When you're packing a backpack for a mission where you'll cover moderate terrain and remain on the trail, it's best to pack the lighter items in the bottom of the pack and heavier items toward the top.

This keeps your center of gravity relatively high, which many people find makes the weight easier to manage. The heavier items should be packed closest to your back.

However, if you plan to search in rough terrain or off-trail, try arranging some of your heavier items in the bottom of your backpack. This lowers your center of gravity, which will improve your balance. Because women naturally have a lower center of gravity, they often prefer to pack their backpacks this way for all trips.

Some of the things you pack for your trip you won't use. But a first aid kit, bear spray and other emergency items shouldn't be left behind, and they shouldn't be relegated to the bottom of your backpack. Although you may never use these items, if you need them, you don't want to dump out your entire backpack to find them. Designate outside pockets for things you'd need in a hurry, like a flashlight, map or whistle. And always return those items to the same place after you use them. Once you have purchased your pack and all of your required SAR equipment - **Mark your gear!!!!**

(Fig. 7-3) A carabineer with colored tape around it to identify it's owner. Image courtesy of J. Bobot.

Use multi-colored electrical tape **(Fig. 7-3)** and come up with an unique color code for your gear! Why? When there is a pile of equipment on the ground after a rescue from five or six people… you will want to quickly and easily locate your stuff.

7.8 Other Equipment

There are several items in the pack list that need to be looked at closer. They are either very important or are items that are not widely known.

Moleskin (Blister Care)

Moleskin is a product used by hikers, runners and walkers all over the world. It is soft and cloth-like on one side and adhesive on the other. It is useful for blisters that have not formed, are already formed or have popped open. Originally referring to the short, silky fur of a mole, moleskin is heavy cotton fabric, woven and then sheared to create a short soft pile on one side. The word is also used for clothing made from this fabric. It is also used in adhesive pads stuck to the feet to prevent blisters.

(Fig. 7-4) A package of Moleskin. Photo courtesy of J. Bobot.

To use moleskin **(Fig. 7-4)**, cut a piece of moleskin roughly the size of the area. Then fold the moleskin in half. Cut a hole in the moleskin that is about the size of the blister. Unfold the moleskin, and place it over the blister, with the blister through the hole. This cushions the blister but does not cover it.

Carabiners

A carabiner or karabiner **(Fig. 7-5)** is a metal loop with a sprung or screwed gate. The loop part opposite the gate is referred to as the spine. It can quickly and reversibly connect components in safety-critical systems.

(Fig. 7-5) Assorted carabiners, clockwise from top left - D shape wire gate, straight gate, oval shape straight gate, auto lock, twist lock. Pictured center is a standard carabiner rating. Photo courtesy of Wikimedia Commons.

Locking carabiners have the same general shape as non-locking carabineers but have an additional sleeve around the gate. The sleeve can be released along the gate and, when it is at one end of the gate, cannot be opened (except by releasing the sleeve and moving it to the other end of the gate). This provides security against the carabineer opening accidentally, for example, if struck against a rock or if caught in a loop of rope. The sleeve can be either auto-locking or a twist-lock. A **locking carabiner** MUST be used anytime a rescue is being conducted.

Some carabiners have an auto-locking gate. These gates allow for quick locking and prevent the user from forgetting to lock the carabiner. The disadvantages are that the spring can wear out or break, preventing it from locking, and it is harder to use with one hand because you must hold the gate lock to keep it from locking again. Another popular style of carabiners have a twist/screw type of gate. These gates are like a nut on a bolt. They are sleeves that twist up and down and must be engaged and disengaged manually.

Non-locking carabiners have a sprung swinging gate that can be opened to insert or remove a rope, webbing sling, or other climbing hardware. The gate snaps shut under the spring's pressure. The gate used depends on the use and preference of the user.

Cordage (Prusik)

A Prusik cord is a small (6- 8 mm in dia. and 6 ft in length) cord that is used as a friction hitch or knot. The cord is used in conjunction with a larger diameter rope **(Fig 7-6)** to be allowed move up and down the rope until pressure is exerted on it, causing it to "bite" into the larger rope, stopping its movement.

The prusik is applied in climbing, canyoneering, mountaineering, caving, rope rescue, and by arborists. The term Prusik is a name for both the loops of cord and the hitch, and the verb is "to prusik." More casually, the term is used for any friction hitch or device that can grab a rope.

(Fig. 7-6) A loop of smaller diameter cord is wrapped around a rope forming the Prusik knot. Photo courtesy of Wikimedia Commons.

Webbing

Climbing-specific nylon webbing **(Fig. 7-7)** is generally tubular webbing, that is, it is a tube of nylon pressed flat. It is very strong, generally rated at 17.7 kilonewtons. This is converted to well over 3,000 pounds of force. [4]

Generally, webbing is made into loops for use as climbing equipment. Such loops, called runners, slings, or quickdraws, have many uses in climbing, including racking gear, building anchors, extending a piece of protection, or even attaching directly to a rock or a tree for an anchor. These loops are made one of two ways-- sewn or tied.

(Fig. 7-7) Various colors of tubular webbing. Photo courtesy of RescueDirect.com

Water Treatment Options

As noted earlier in the chapter, most water is not potable and must be treated before consumption. The lightest and easiest method is with iodine tablets. These are inexpensive, easy to use and need no maintenance. They can leave a taste in the water, and they don't remove particles. They also need time to work, usually 30 minutes or so.

Portable water purification devices, also known as point-of-use (POU) water treatment systems and field water disinfection techniques – are self-contained units that can be used by recreational enthusiasts, military personnel, survivalists, and others who must obtain drinking water from untreated sources (e.g., rivers, lakes, etc.). The objective of these personal devices is to render un-chlorinated water potable (that is, safe for drinking purposes).

Many commercial portable water purification systems **(Fig. 7-8)** are available for hiking, camping, and other travel in remote areas. These devices are not only used for remote or rural areas. They can also be used to treat safe municipal water for aesthetic purposes by removing chlorine, bad taste, heavy metals like lead and mercury, and odors.

Large rivers may be polluted with sewage effluent, surface runoff, or industrial pollutants from sources far upstream. However, even small streams, springs and wells may becontaminated by animal waste and pathogens. The presence of dead animals upstream is not uncommon. In most parts of

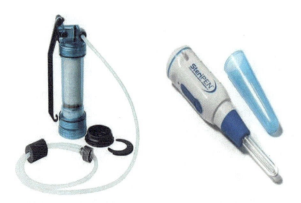

(Fig. 7-8) Portable Water Filter (left) and the SteriPen (right). Photo courtesy of J.Bobot

the world, water may be contaminated by bacteria, protozoa or parasitic worms from human and animal waste or pathogens which use other organisms as an intermediate host.

There are several methods of obtaining potable water while in the wilderness. One such way is the use of a water filter system, which pull water through a carbon filter to remove the impurities from the water. There are many different types of filters and the best way to find the one that will be best for you is to ask around, read reviews and use different systems to test them. Some need gravity or time to work, some require pumping water through a filter, some can store lots of filtered water, and others filter as you drink.

Leg Protection (Gaiters)

Gaiters are a type of protective clothing **(Fig. 7-9)** for a person's ankles and legs below the knee. Gaiters are worn when walking, hiking or running outdoors amongst dense underbrush or in snow, with or without snowshoes. Heavy gaiters are often worn when using crampons to protect the leg and ankle from the spikes of the opposite foot. Gaiters strap over the hiking boot and around the person's leg to provide protection from branches and thorns and to prevent mud, snow, etc. from entering the top of the boot.

(Fig. 7-9) Gaiters worn by the tourist. Photo courtesy of Carivaldi

Trekking Poles

Trekking poles have become standard equipment for many searchers. The reasons why are simple: They enhance stability and support on all types of terrain, they are an extension of your sight when tracking and even can be used as a splint or tent pole. When shopping for trekking poles, your key considerations should be weight, price, shock absorption, shaft construction and the type of grip. Trekking poles **(Fig. 7-10)** offer several practical advantages:

- They provide better balance and footing.
- On downhill hikes especially, they decrease the amount of stress on your legs and joints.
- On uphill climbs, poles transfer some of your weight to your shoulders, arms and back, which can reduce leg fatigue and add thrust to your ascents.
- They make crossing streams, loose rocks and slippery surfaces such as ice and snow patches easier and safer.
- They help you establish a walking rhythm.
- They can push back overhanging vegetation from the trail and probe soggy terrain for holes and boggy spots.

Trekking poles are most helpful to those with weak or damaged knees or ankles, particularly when going downhill, because the poles absorb some of the impact that your body would normally sustain. It should be noted that using trekking poles will not decrease your overall energy expenditure since you'll be using your arms more than you would when walking without poles. They do; however, help distribute your energy usage in a way that can help your hiking endurance.

(Fig. 7-10) Pair of trekking poles. Photo courtesy of Daniel Case.

Extra Gear

We all have a few, some of us even more, pieces of gear that we just can't live without, but not always needed out in the field on a mission. We also need to have support equipment for when the mission lasts longer than a few hours, like a tent, sleeping bag, etc., or different gear for summer and winter weather conditions. It is good to have this equipment readily available to load in your vehicle when you respond to an incident. Keeping an extra box or duffel of gear to swap in and out of your pack is good practice and can make it easier to get out the door quickly.

(Fig. 7-11) A place to keep all of your SAR gear where you can pick and choose what you need for a mission. Photo courtesy of J. Bobot

7.9 NASAR Approved 24-Hour Pack List

Such a pack holds those items that will assist the holder in functioning safely, effectively, and efficiently during a SAR incident. Some items may be carried on a belt, in pockets, or strapped to the person. This is the minimum equipment is recommended to be carried on all missions in non-urban or wilderness areas. Your local equipment requirements may vary. Consult a physician for recommendations about analgesics and other drugs that you may carry in the SAR pack.

FOOTNOTES

(1) https://www.switchbacktravel.com/how-to-pack-backpack

(2) https://www.rei.com/learn/expert-advice/backpacks-adjusting-fit.html

(3) "Comparisons and Conversions". pp. 2nd paragraph. Retrieved 2009-05-08.

(4) https://www.convertworld.com/en/mass/kilonewton/kn-to-kg.html

(5) https://www.cdc.gov/parasites/crypto/index.html

(6) *Henry, Mark (2003), The US Army of World War I, Oxford: Osprey.*

VITAL VOCABULARY

Carabiner: This is a metal loop with a sprung gate used to quickly and reversibly connect components in safety-critical systems.

Moleskin: This is a soft cotton flannel padding can be cut to any size for relief of painful corns, calluses, and tender spots.

Pathogen: Is an infectious agent, or more commonly germ, is a biological agent that causes disease to its host.

Potable: A term used to describe safe drinking water.

Prusik: Is a friction hitch or knot used to put a loop of cord around a rope.

Tubular Webbing: Is a tube of nylon pressed flat. It is very strong, generally rated in excess of 9kN, or about 2,020 pounds of force.

UNIT 8 | INCIDENT & SCENE SAFETY

8.1 General Scene Safety

8.2 Driving

8.3 Snakes, Plants and Animals

8.4 Altitude

8.5 Lightning

8.6 Water Hazards

8.7 Helo Ops

8.8 Aircraft Crash Sites

8.9 Marijuana Grows and Drug Labs

> Upon completion of this chapter and the related course activities, the student will be able to meet the following objectives:
>
> - Identify dangerous spiders, snakes, and plants
> - Understand the dangers of rivers (strainers, sweepers, and hydraulics)
> - Identify various altitude issues
> - Understand helicopter safety
> - Be aware of the dangers of meth labs and marijuana grows
> - Explain how to use a signal mirror

8.1 General Scene Safety

Safety is a primary concern in any search and rescue incident. Making sure that all searchers remain safe is vital to the mission. If searchers are injured, resources will have to be pivoted away from the search. Safety is a consideration even before searchers are called out. Training is done to make sure skills remain sharp, individuals do physical activities to maintain their readiness for a callout, equipment is checked and maintained for mission readiness. Once a callout happens, driving is the first risk of many searchers face. Being aware of risks, training with your team and maintaining vigilance about safety is critical to success in search and rescue.

Safety is part of the IAP and searchers should be sure to review the safety plan, medical plan and hazards portion of the IAP upon arrival at a scene. If at any point, you or your team is not comfortable that appropriate plans are in place, or that an assignment is safe, you should bring that to the attention of the appropriate person in the command post.

8.2 Safe Driving

Standard Operating Guidelines: Responding In Your Private, Non-Emergency Vehicle

When responding to the station or scene of an emergency in a private vehicle, all applicable motor vehicle laws must be strictly adhered to. Privately owned non-emergency vehicles are not granted any exemptions to the vehicle traffic laws that apply to authorization emergency vehicles.

PRIVATE VEHICLES ARE NOT EMERGENCY VEHICLES AND THEREFORE ARE NOT AFFORDED ANY EXEMPTIONS OR SPECIAL PRIVILEGES UNDER STATE LAW.

Due to the stress that a timely response generates, you need to make an extra conscious effort to operate your vehicle in a safe manner. You should pay close attention to:

- Speed limits and road, weather, and light conditions.
- Intersections with and without control devices.
- Passing and turning.

When parking at the scene, keep your vehicle as far away as reasonably possible and in a safe position; try to keep the vehicles on one side of the street and, if possible, out of the street.

Did you know that more than 270 firefighters and emergency responders have died in the last two decades from accidents involving their vehicles? In 1995, 18 firefighters died in the line of duty; nine of those firefighters died in their own personal cars. Twenty-five percent of the annual firefighter fatalities occurred while responding to and returning from alarms. These figures do not include the many emergency services personnel or the people they are sworn to protect who are injured annually from vehicle-related accidents.

8.3 Snakes, Plants and Animals

Snake Dangers

Prevention is key to avoiding a snakebite. People should take the following steps to prevent a snake bite:

- Do not try to handle any snake, even to attempt to determine if it was poisonous.

- Stay away from tall grass and piles of leaves when possible.

- Avoid climbing on rocks or piles of wood where a snake may be hiding.

- Be aware that snakes tend to be active at night and in warm weather.

- Wear boots, long pants and gaiters when working outdoors.

- Wear leather gloves when handling brush and debris.

- Always step "ON" any log or rock that you could step over. This gives the snake a chance to flee.

(Fig. 8-1) Know the area you are working. Watch for signs and warnings. Image courtesy of Alan Levine from Strawberry, United States.

Venomous snakes found in the United States include rattlesnakes, copperheads, cottonmouths/water moccasins, and coral snakes. They can be dangerous to outdoor workers including farmers, foresters, landscapers, groundskeepers, etc. and any other people who spend time outside.

Although rare, some people with a severe allergy to snake venom may be at risk of death if bitten. It has been estimated that 7,000–8,000 people per year receive venomous bites in the United States, and "about five of those people die according to the Center for Disease Control (CDC).

The number of deaths would be much higher if people did not seek medical care. It is important that you understand snakebite prevention, what snakes are in your area (Fig. 8-1) and what they should do if they are bitten.

A venomous snake (Fig. 8-2) is a snake that uses modified saliva, snake venom, usually delivered through highly specialized teeth such as hollow fangs, for the purpose of prey immobilization and self-defense. In contrast, non-venomous species either constrict their prey, or simply overpower it with their jaws.[1]"

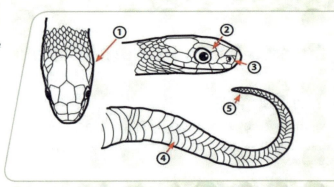

Nonvenomous Snakes

1. Head usually oval when viewed from above, but may be somewhat triangular.
2. Pupils round.
3. No pits – only nostrils present.
4. Divided scales on underside of tail.
5. Although many snakes vibrate their tail when upset, nonvenomous snakes never have rattles.

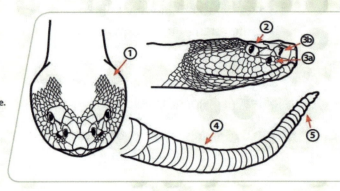

Venomous Snakes

1. Head distinctly triangular, when viewed from above.
2. Pupils elliptical.
3. Pits(a) as well as nostrils(b) present.
4. Undivided scales on underside of tail.
5. Except for the Northern copperhead, tail ends in a rattle.

(Fig. 8-2) Poisonous vs. Non-poisonous snake characteristics. Image courtesy of WildOhio.gov

Poisonous Plants

Many native and exotic plants are poisonous to humans when ingested or if there is skin contact with plant chemicals. However, the most common problems with poisonous plants arise from contact with the sap oil of several ever-present native plants that cause an allergic skin reaction—poison ivy, poison oak, and poison sumac.

Poison ivy, poison oak, and poison sumac release an oil, urushiol, when the leaf or other plant parts are bruised, damaged, or burned. When the oil gets on the skin an allergic reaction, referred to as contact dermatitis, occurs in most exposed people as an itchy red rash with bumps or blisters. The rash, depending upon where it occurs and how broadly it is spread, may significantly impede or prevent a person from working.

Urushiol binds to the skin on contact, where it causes severe itching that develops into reddish colored inflammation or non-colored bumps, and then blistering. These lesions may be treated with Calamine lotion, Burow's solution compresses or baths to relieve discomfort, though recent studies have shown some traditional medicines to be ineffective. Over-the-counter products to ease itching—or simply oatmeal baths and baking soda—are now recommended by dermatologists for the treatment of poison ivy.

The oozing fluids released by scratching blisters do not spread the poison. The fluid in the blisters is produced by the body and it is not urushiol itself. The appearance of a spreading rash indicates that some areas received more of the poison and reacted sooner than other areas or that contamination is still occurring from contact with objects to which the original poison was spread.[2]

Although over-the-counter topical medications may relieve symptoms for most people, immediate medical attention may be required for severe reactions, particularly when exposed to the smoke from burning these poisonous plants.

Hazardous Plant Dermatitis Signs and Symptoms	Hazardous Plant Dermatitis Treatment
<ul><li>Itchy skin.</li><li>Redness or red streaks.</li><li>Hives.</li><li>Swelling.</li><li>An outbreak of small or large blisters, often forming streaks or lines.</li><li>Crusting skin (after blisters burst).</li><li>Anaphylaxis.</li></ul>	<ul><li>BSI / PPE</li><li>Remove contaminated clothing.</li><li>If within 10 minutes of exposure, wash area with soap and water, dry and apply lightly, rubbing alcohol. A rash from poison ivy, oak, or sumac usually lasts 1 to 3 weeks. Most rashes go away without treatment. While your skin heals, it often itches. (After 10 minutes, only 50% of the resin is removable, and by 30 minutes only 10%.)</li><li>Cortisone creams, whether over the counter or by prescription, are only helpful if applied right away, before blisters appear, or much later, when the blisters have dried up.</li><li>Compress with Burow's solution (available without prescription) can help dry the ooze faster.</li><li>Oral antihistamines, such as diphenhydramine (Benadryl), may help the itch somewhat.</li><li>Evacuate immediately.</li></ul>

U.S. Geographic Distribution

One or more of the most common poisonous plant species are found throughout the United States (except Alaska and Hawaii). These plants can be found in forests, fields, wetlands and along streams, roadsides, and even in urban environments, such as parks and backyards.

Toxicodendron radicans (Poison ivy) is a poisonous North American plant that is well known for its production of urushiol. Poison ivy **(Fig. 8-3)** can be found growing as a trailing vine, as a shrub or as a climbing vine that grows on trees or some other support.

Toxicodendron vernix (Poison Sumac) are shrubs and small trees that can reach a height of one to 10 meters (3.3–33 ft). The leaves of poison sumac **(Fig. 8-4)** are spirally arranged. The flowers are in dense panicles or spikes, each flower very small, greenish, creamy white or red, with five petals.

(Fig. 8-3) Poison Ivy (Toxicodendron radicans). Image courtesy of Gordon E. Robertson.

(Fig. 8-4) Winged Sumac leaves and flowers (Toxicodendron vernix). Image courtesy of Matthew C. Perry

Toxicodendron pubescens (Atlantic Poison-oak) is an upright shrub with three leaflets on each leaf. The leaflets of poison oak are usually hairy, and are variable in size and shape, but most often resembling white oak leaves; they usually turn yellow or orange in autumn.[3]

Large Mammal Precautions

- Properly secure food stores away from camp.
- Make noise when traveling.
- Keep cooking area away from sleeping area.
- Use proper containers.
- No food in tents.
- Know what animals are indigenous to the area you are in.
- Don't treat any wild animal as a pet.

8.4 Altitude Precautions and Safety

We all enjoy that tremendous view from a high summit, but there are risks (**Fig. 8-5**) in going to high altitude, and it's important to understand these risks. **Atmospheric pressure** is the force per unit area exerted against a surface by the weight of air above that surface in the Earth's atmosphere.

The Travel Scenario

Here is a classic scenario for developing high-altitude illness or **acute mountain sickness (AMS)**. You fly from New York City (sea level) to a Denver at 5,000 feet (1,525 meters). That afternoon you rent a car and drive up to the trailhead at 8,000 feet (2,438 meters). You hike up to your first camp at 9,000 feet (2,745 meters). The next day you hike up to 10,500 feet (3,048 meters). You begin to have a severe headache and feel nauseous and weak. If your condition worsens, you may begin to have difficulty hiking. Scenarios like this are not uncommon, so it's essential that you understand the physiological effects of high altitude, both for yourself and people you may search for.

The percentage of oxygen in the air remains essentially constant with altitude at 20.94%. However, the air pressure (and therefore the number of oxygen molecules) drops with altitude. At 18,000 feet, air and oxygen pressure is one-half what they are at sea-level and one-third at 29,000 feet. Thus, as you increase the altitude you decrease the air pressure. If you decreased the air pressure, you decrease the amount of oxygen. This is where we run into trouble as we climb.

How high is high? A minority of people, about 20 percent, have some symptoms of altitude sickness if they ascend to about 8,000 feet (2,500 meters) above sea level and sleep there. However, most people will **acclimatize** to 10,000 feet (3,000 meters) with relative ease, perhaps having symptoms after the first night. Acclimatizing to heights of 10,000–16,000 feet (3,000–5,000 meters) is much more difficult, and it is here that it is absolutely necessary to ascend slowly and return to a lower altitude to sleep if you have been traveling around at a higher altitude during the day. More than 50 percent of people will become ill if they ascend rapidly from sea-level to 11,000 feet (3,500 meters) without acclimatization, and everyone will if they ascend rapidly to 16,000 feet (5,000 meters). It is thought to be impossible to permanently acclimatize to heights above 18,000 feet (5,500 meters). It is possible to spend several weeks sleeping as high as 20,000 feet (6,000 meters) once acclimatized, but gradual deterioration of physical well-being will still occur.

(Fig. 8-7) The field of activities carried out by the Engadin base; Switzerland is characterized by the seasonal fluctuations in the tourism sector. Winter sport enthusiasts, as well as mountain climbers on the famous peaks of the Bernina Massif and the steep rock faces of the Bregaglia mountain range, are among its most frequent patients. Image courtesy of the Rega 9 base in the Engadine, Switzerland.

Specialized rescue teams **(Fig. 8-7)** are usually stationed in close proximity to mountains due to the high probability that someone will suffer injury or illness when climbing.

High Altitude 5,000 to 11,500 feet (1,500 to 3,500 meters) - The onset of physiologic effects of diminished inspiratory oxygen pressure (Pio_2) includes decreased exercise performance and increased ventilation (lower arterial Pco_2). Minor impairment exists in arterial oxygen transport (arterial oxygen saturation [Sao_2] at least 90%), but arterial Po_2 is significantly diminished. Because of the large number of people who ascend rapidly to 8,000 to 11,500 ft., high-altitude illness is common in this range.

Very High Altitude 11,500 to 18,000 feet (3,500 to 5,500 meters) - Maximum Sao_2 falls below 90% as the arterial Po_2 falls below 60mmHg. Extreme hypoxemia may occur during exercise, during sleep, and in the presence of high-altitude pulmonary edema or other acute lung conditions. Severe altitude illness occurs most commonly in this range.

Extreme Altitude above 18,000 feet (5,500 meters) - Marked **hypoxemia, hypocapnia,** and **respiratory alkalosis** are characteristic of extreme altitudes. Progressive deterioration of physiologic function eventually outstrips acclimatization. As a result, no permanent human habitation occurs above 18,000 ft. A period of acclimatization is necessary when ascending to extreme altitude; abrupt ascent without supplemental oxygen for other than brief exposures invites severe altitude illness.

Regions above 25,000 feet (7,500 meters) are referred to as the "death zone." You will deteriorate noticeably while you remain at such high altitudes, some of your body's major systems will shut down and climbers will only remain there for two or three days.

Death rates from altitude sickness above 23,000 feet (7,000 meters) are estimated at four percent of all people who venture that high. The following are some tips to help you adjust to high altitude conditions:

- Give the body time by gaining altitude slowly.

- Sleep at the high trailhead before starting the ascent.

- Drink plenty of water in small but frequent amounts.
- Eat a high-carb diet several days before the ascent.
- Keep muscles warm.
- Avoid alcohol and sleeping pills.
- Don't ascend with respiratory infections/problems.
- Get old! Susceptibility to altitude illness seems to decrease with age.

Altitude-Related Medical Conditions

Acute Mountain Sickness (AMS) is a medical condition that is caused by acute exposure to low air pressure (usually outdoors at high altitudes). It commonly occurs above 2,400 meters (approximately 8,000 feet).

Primary symptoms of AMS related conditions Headaches are the primary symptom used to diagnose altitude sickness, although a headache is also a symptom of dehydration. A headache occurring at an altitude above 2,400 meters (8,000 feet), combined with any one or more of the following symptoms, may indicate altitude sickness.[4]

Minor Symptoms:

- Lack of appetite, nausea, or vomiting
- Fatigue or weakness
- Dizziness or lightheadedness
- Insomnia
- Pins and needles
- Shortness of breath upon exertion
- Nosebleed
- Persistent rapid pulse
- Drowsiness & General malaise
- Peripheral edema (swelling of hands & feet)

Severe symptoms (life-threatening altitude sickness):

- Pulmonary edema (fluid in the lungs)
- Symptoms similar to bronchitis
- Persistent dry cough
- Fever

- Shortness of breath even when resting
- Cerebral edema (swelling of the brain)
- Headache not responding to analgesics
- Unsteady gait
- Gradual loss of consciousness
- Increased nausea
- Retinal hemorrhage

High Altitude Cerebral Edema (HACE) is a severe (frequently fatal) form of altitude sickness. HACE is the result of swelling of brain tissue from fluid leakage and almost always begins as acute mountain sickness. AMS and HACE are syndromes that probably occur along a continuum of severity from mild, benign AMS to severe, life-threatening HACE. They strike people who travel too fast beyond altitudes to which they are adjusted.[5]

Common symptoms of HACE appear in order as followed:

- Confusion
- Changes in behavior
- Fatigue
- Difficulty speaking
- Vomiting
- Hallucinations
- Blindness
- Paralysis of a limb
- Seizure
- Unconsciousness
- Total paralysis
- Coma

High Altitude Pulmonary Edema (HAPE) results from fluid build-up in the lungs. The fluid in the lungs prevents effective oxygen exchange. As the condition becomes more severe, the level of oxygen in the bloodstream decreases, and this can lead to impaired cerebral function and even death. Physiological and symptomatic changes often vary according to the altitude involved. The Lake Louise Consensus Definition for High Altitude Pulmonary Edema has set widely used criteria for defining HAPE symptoms.

Symptoms: at least two of:

- Difficulty in breathing (dyspnea) at rest

- Cough
- Weakness or decreased exercise performance
- Chest tightness or congestion

Signs: at least two of:

- Crackles or wheezing (while breathing)
- Central cyanosis (blue skin color)
- Tachypnea (rapid shallow breathing)
- Tachycardia (rapid heartrate)
- Bluing of fingers, toes, lips

(Fig. 8-8 Dead cows lined up along a metallic fence. Lightning struck the fence, and the current traveled along the fence killing the cows. Image Courtesy Ruth Lyon-Bateman.

8.5 Lightning Safety

In the United States, there are an estimated 25 million lightning flashes each year. During the past 30 years, lightning killed an average of 58 people per year. This is higher than 57 deaths per year caused by tornadoes and average 48 deaths to hurricanes. Be aware of changing weather conditions, monitor weather service announcements and be in contact with a meteorologist if possible. Get accurate weather predictions and timelines to help planning search missions.

When Thunder Roars, Go Indoors! Remember, there is NO safe place outside in a thunderstorm. Your first and only truly safe choice is to get to a safe building or vehicle. If you absolutely can't get to safety, this section may help you slightly lessen the threat of being struck by lightning while outside. Don't kid yourself - you are NOT safe outside.

Know the weather patterns of the area. Listen to the weather forecast for the outdoor area you plan to visit. The forecast may be very different from the one near your home. If there is a high chance of storms, use extreme caution on search missions.

These actions may slightly reduce your risk of being struck by lightning:

- If camping, hiking, etc., far from a safe vehicle or building, avoid open fields, the top of a hill or a ridge top.

- Stay away from tall, isolated trees or other tall objects. If you are in a forest, stay near a lower stand of trees.

- If you are camping in an open area, set up camp in a valley, ravine or other low area.

- Stay away from water and metal, which are excellent conductors of electricity. The current from a lightning flash will easily travel for long distances. (**Fig. 8-8**)

8.6 River Crossing and Water Hazards

River crossings can be dangerous. If you are in any doubt as to the safety of a river, you should not attempt a crossing. If the river is too dangerous to cross at this point, look for a safer crossing point. Alternatively, be prepared to out-wait the waters or find another route. Every river is different, but some of the dangers to look out for include:

- Deep or fast-flowing water **(Fig. 8-9)**.
- Strainers, dead trees in the river which can catch things underwater (including you).
- Submerged, sharp, or slippery rocks.
- An uneven or unstable bottom.

Not all of these dangers will be visible upon a casual inspection. **Strainers** are formed when an object blocks the passage of larger objects but allows the flow of water to continue - like a big food strainer or colander. These objects can be very dangerous, because the force of the water will pin an object or body against the strainer and then pile up, pushing it down under water.

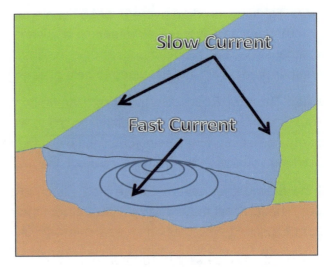

(Fig. 8-9) Location of Currents. Image courtesy of J. T. Bobot.

For a person caught in this position, it will be difficult or impossible to get to safety, often leading to a fatal outcome. If you are in a river **(Fig. 8-10)**, swimming aggressively away from the strainer and into the main channel is your best bet. If you cannot avoid the strainer, you should swim hard towards it and try to get as much of your body up and over it as possible.

(Fig. 8-10) A fallen tree creates both a strainer (at trunk to left) and a sweeper hazard (branches to right). Image courtesy of the Commonwealth of Pennsylvania, Fish and Boat Commission.

Sweepers are trees fallen in or heavily leaning over the river, still rooted on the shore and not fully submerged. Its trunk and branches may form an obstruction in the river like strainers. In fast water, sweepers can pose a serious hazard.

Holes, or "**hydraulics**", (also known as "stoppers" or "souse-holes"), are formed when water pours over the top of a submerged object, causing the surface water to flow back upstream toward the object. Holes can be particularly dangerous.

In the Water

If you are carried away over rapids, obviously you should try to stay afloat. Attempt to maneuver yourself so that your feet point downstream and you are sitting up slightly. This presents your legs and bottom to oncoming obstacles. It also should be stated that if a person is found after submersion in cold water, that emergency resuscitation be started even if the duration of submersion is unknown. The rule:

> "No patient should be pronounced dead until they are warm and dead."

Children in particular have a good chance of survival in water up to three minutes, or 10 minutes in cold water (10 to 15 °C or 50 to 60 °F). Submersion in cold water can slow the metabolism drastically. [6] There are rare but documented cases of survivable submersion for extreme lengths of time. It is reported that in one case a child named Michelle Funk survived drowning after being submerged in cold water for 70 minutes. In another case, an 18-year-old man survived 38 minutes under water. This is known as cold water drowning. Cold is one of the greatest threats to the lives of everyone on the water. Certain techniques can improve your chance of surviving long enough to be rescued.

- Wear a lifejacket. A full lifejacket helps to keep the head and airway clear of the water, even when strength and mental capacity is waning. It will also make adopting heat-loss reducing postures much more stable.

- The more clothes you have on, the better. Do not get undressed to enter the water. A person wearing two layers of woolen clothing will lose less than a quarter of the heat a person wearing only a swimsuit will lose.

- Wear as many layers of wool as possible, covered with a waterproof layer. The wool will trap warmer layers of water closer to the body.

- Try not to panic. Panic can impair breathing and hasten the drowning process. Hyperventilation can occur when a person is unexpectedly immersed in the water.

- Where possible, get out of the water. In water the body loses heat 20 to 30 times faster than it does in air. Even if you feel colder out of the water, try to clamber on top of an overturned boat or any floating wreckage.

8.7 Helicopter Safety

Helicopter operations during an emergency are unique due to the emergency nature of the flight. The FAA, operators and the medical community play a vital role in promoting a positive safety culture that ensures the safety of passengers, flight crews, and medical professionals on these flights. There are approximately 840 emergency medical service helicopters operating today **(Fig. 8-11)**, most of which operate under FAA Part 135 rules. Aviation safety decisions are separate from medical decisions. The decision to conduct a flight with a patient on board does not mean that flight safety can be compromised in any way.

Once the medical need for air transportation is determined, it is up to the operator to make the air transportation decision based on pre-flight factors such as weather, maintenance, and crew readiness. If you are requesting helicopter assistance—at a minimum, pilots want to know the following:

- Whether or not it will be a long line pickup, and if so, how long of a line will be required. Otherwise, is there a suitable landing zone in the area.

- Approximate wind speed and direction of the wind at the rescue site.

- Air temperature in the summertime (heat affects thickness of the air and therefore affects lift capacity).

- Obstacles in the area of the landing zone (type, height, location, etc.)

- Type of terrain in the landing zone (sand, snow, rocks, trees, swampy, bushy, etc.).

- Slope of the landing zone (more than ten degrees can be cause for concern).

- The size of the standard landing zone should be 100 feet x 100 feet but can be as small as 75 feet x 75 feet if need be.

(Fig. 8-11) MedFlight Helicopter, a not-for-profit, air and ground critical care transportation company based in Columbus, Ohio. Photo courtesy of MedFlight Public Relations.

Landing Zones (LZ)

Select a touchdown area that is as flat as possible. The slope should not be more than 10 degrees. You should always ensure the touchdown surface is firm. Parking lots, roads, sport fields, and other locations are most desirable. Always remember that the pilot has the final say on the selection of the LZ. For the safety of the ground personnel and the aircraft, ensure the touchdown area is free of debris and obstructions. If able, wet the LZ if it is dusty or has loose gravel and keep spectators and vehicles away from the landing zone. **(Fig. 8-12)**.

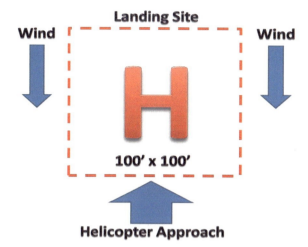

(Fig. 8-12) Helicopter Landing Zone Guidelines. Image courtesy of J. Bobot.

When Helicopter is on Approach

Designate a landing officer (Ground Contact) to communicate with the helicopter crew as soon as they are dispatched. Notify the emergency dispatch center of the frequency you intend to communicate on. Watch the helicopter glide slope rules **(Fig. 8-13)**.

Be ready to provide the helicopter crew with a description of:

- The landing zone. Include the size of the landing zone, how it is marked, a list of any nearby obstructions.

- Notify the helicopter crew when you have them in sight. Immediately notify the crew if any last-minute hazards are detected or if an unsafe condition develops.

- Any other conditions such as weather and any patient information for the flight crew.

Helicopter safety should be taken very seriously!

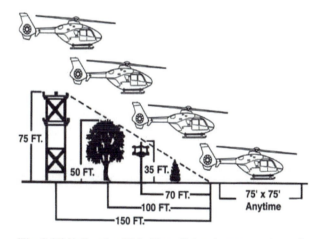

(Fig. 8-13) Helicopter Glide Slope Rules. Image courtesy of the Dartmouth-Hitchcock Advanced Response Team.

Helicopters are exciting and dangerous. When being transported by a helicopter, remember - You are cargo! It is vital that you do what you are told.

Here are a few other safety tips that should be followed around helicopters: [7]

- If you have a helmet, secure the chin strap. No other hats should be worn, and nothing loose on your body.
- Cover up, head to toe. Wear full-coverage goggles and gloves as well as ear protection.
- Always walk, never run, around a helicopter. If the landing zone is uneven, never approach or depart from the uphill side.
- Always use the downhill side where you are in the pilot's view.
- Don't touch anything on the helicopter unless directed to do so by a crew member and remain clear of the tail rotor and main rotor at all times.
- At night, don't flash any bright lights at the aircraft and keep headlights on low beam, away from the LZ.
- Don't approach the helicopter until motioned to do so by a crewmember and use only the preferred or accepted entry points **(Fig. 8-14)**.

When helicopter is Departing

The Ground Contact will notify the pilot when the landing zone is clear of all ground personnel. Maintain all protective devices against flying debris. Notify your dispatch that the helicopter has lifted off and if possible, their destination. If possible, try to maintain a secure landing zone with all personnel and emergency equipment for five minutes after the helicopter departs. If an in-flight emergency develops, this will allow the pilot to return safely to a secure landing zone.

(Fig. 8-14) Helicopter approach points.
Image courtesy of J. Bobot.

8.8 Aircraft Crash Sites

Movement in the vicinity of crash sites can be extremely hazardous for ground parties on account of toxic fumes, dangerous substances and explosives. There have been aviation mishaps where search and rescue personnel became ill or died as a result of exposure to gases and hazardous materials that were present at aircraft accident sites. Modern aircraft use composite materials for some of their structure, skin, and access panels. Significant health hazards exist at crash sites from the effects of crash damage and fire on composite materials. When burnt, these materials release fibers and resins that may be toxic through inhalation and/or skin and eye contact.

Damaged composites may also produce needle-like edges that render handling hazardous **(Fig. 8-15)**.

Carbon fibers are electrically conductive and may short-circuit nearby electrical equipment. Certain exotic metals (radioactive substances) can also be found in aircraft types, and they are also poisonous.

The inhalation, ingestion or absorption of radioactive substances is hazardous, as low-level radiation will continue to be emitted inside the body, possibly resulting in damage to surrounding tissues and organs.

(Fig. 8-15) Air India Express Flight 812 was a scheduled passenger service from Dubai to Mangalore which at around 01:00 UTC on 22 May 2010, overshot the runway on landing, fell over a cliff and caught fire, spreading wreckage across the surrounding hillside in Bajpe, India. Image is of rescue workers at the crash site. Image courtesy of Neil Pinto.

The following precautions should be observed at all aircraft accident sites:

- Attendance at crash sites should be limited to essential personnel.
- Personnel should wear Personnel Protective Equipment (PPE).
- All work at the crash site should be conducted upwind of the wreckage wherever possible.
- The location of helicopter landing zones in close proximity to crash sites should be avoided to prevent the possible spread of contamination.
- Eating, drinking, and smoking in or around the crash site should be prohibited.
- Aircraft technical personnel familiar with the aircraft type should be utilized in the location, identification, and salvage of hazardous materials and remnants.
- Environmental health personnel should also be notified when suspected dangerous substances are present at the accident site.
- SAR personnel who were working at the accident site should shower as soon as possible after leaving the area.

8.9 Marijuana Grows & Drug Labs

The hazards we face in Search and Rescue are not always natural, sometimes they're manmade. One of the ways our fellow human beings make our lives more exciting is by growing dope or mixing drugs in the backcountry. The best defenses against clandestine activity such as pot farms and meth labs is alertness and trained clue awareness — qualities that searchers bring with them automatically.

Marijuana Farms - Unless you stumble right into a pot farm, there aren't very many clues that identify this activity. Marijuana growers are especially active in April, when growers are planting their crop, and in September and October, **(Fig. 8-16)** when they harvest it. During these times, growers are likely to be living in their farms. Thanks to forfeiture laws, outdoor farms are moving onto Federal lands, including national forests.

(Fig. 8-16) DEA Marijuana growing between a farmer's corn crop. Photo courtesy of METRICH Enforcement

Meth Labs - The marijuana farm's ugly brother is the methamphetamine lab. Methamphetamine **(Fig. 8-17)** is most structurally similar to amphetamine. Synthesis is relatively simple, but entails risk with flammable and corrosive chemicals, particularly the solvents used in extraction and purification.

From time to time, one hears of an ordinary suburban house exploding because someone was mixing up meth inside. Make no mistake, meth labs are dangerous. It is true whether they're active or abandoned. It is true for the drugs, the chemicals, the waste products and the people. Making meth requires some highly potent chemicals. Merely touching some of them can poison a person.

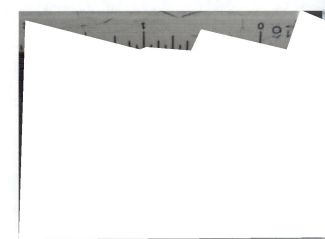
(Fig. 8-17) Methamphetamine crystals. Photo courtesy of the United States Department of Justice.

The leftover waste from a meth lab is a full-blown Hazmat site **(Table 8-1)**, and cleanup requires specially trained people with head-to-toe protective suits and respirators. When on a wilderness or urban search, always keep an eye out for the listed materials. Any of these items alone can easily be explained as simply discarded or trash. However, where you start seeing these items grouped together, an immediate use of caution is recommended.

Tip-offs to a drug lab's presence start with the chemicals. The smell of ether is a genuine warning sign. Other signs are gray five-gallon chemical cans scattered about, lots of propane, and/or a gas-powered generator. The house (or trailer, or bus — some labs are mobile) may have blacked out windows, often with aluminum foil.

Other Items to watch for

Signs of a methamphetamine lab include large quantities of common household products. Used as designed, these household products are generally safe. Mixed, they can become explosive and/or give off toxic fumes.

Equipment is needed to make methamphetamine. This equipment can be left in an igloo-type cooler and left in the woods for several days. You want to look for piles of trash containing items used to manufacture the drug.

The Bottom Line - Chances are you will never discover a marijuana farm or a meth lab during your entire SAR career. But knowing what the signs are, and how to react, will give you the edge in case you do.

TABLE 6-3	
Signs of a Methamphetamine Lab	
Chemicals	Trichloroethane
Acetone	Toluene
Alcohol (isopropyl)	Aluminum foil
Common cold pills	Blender
Drain cleaner	Bottles
Ether	Cheesecloth
Iodine	Coffee filters
Heet (gas additive)	Funnels
Lithium batteries	Gas can
Matches	Hot plate
Muriatic acid	Jugs / coolers
Anhydrous ammonia	Paper towels
Red Devil lye	Propane tank
Salt (table or rock)	

- If you suspect a meth lab, leave at once and report it.
- Do not open any coolers.
- Do not touch any items.
- Handling methamphetamine waste residue can burn your skin and eyes and breathing in the gases can send you to the hospital.
- Handling these chemicals with unprotected skin or getting the dust in your eyes can cause serious damage.

8.10 Basic Principles of Signaling

There are some basic principles of signaling that one should understand. It is vital that you have signals ready for immediate use and know how to use them. Searchers also need to be vigilant in looking for signals. There are two main ways to get attention or to communicate — visual and audio. The means used will depend on the situation and the materials available.

Types of signals

There are several types of signal that can be used to draw attention to your position. They are broken down into the following categories: electronic, fire or smoke, mirror, noise, visual (ground signals), and color. While subjects may use fire or smoke, searchers are more likely to use electronic or mirror signals.

Electronic & Signal Mirrors

There are several types of electronic signaling devices. The most used is the Personal Locator Beacon or PLB. A PLB is probably the single most important piece of survival gear a pilot or backwoods adventurer can carry.

A PLB is activated by the push of a single button and it sends out a distress signal via satellite to a special receiver. By the means of a GPS function within the PLB, rescue crews can locate you. There have been many rescues contributed to a PLB and more PLBs are finding their way on the market.

(Fig. 8-18) An emergency signal mirror. The aim indicator is in the center. Image courtesy of J. Bobot.

The signal mirror **(Fig. 8-18)** is probably one of the safest and widely practiced signaling methods. The US military has trusted signal mirrors for many years and have included them in most all survival kits. On a sunny day, a mirror is your best signaling device. If you don't have a mirror, polish your canteen cup, your belt buckle, or a similar object that will reflect the sun's rays. Direct the flashes toward searching aircraft. Haze, ground fog, and mirages may make it hard for a pilot to spot signals from a flashing object. So, if possible, get to the highest point when signaling.

How to use a signal mirror:

- Reflect sunlight from the mirror onto your hand.

- Slowly bring up the mirror to eye level and look through the sighting hole (if one is present). You will see a bright spot or light. This is the aim indicator.

- Sweep the mirror across the horizon even if you cannot see the aircraft or boat but may only hear it. Mirror flashes can be seen for many miles, even in hazy weather conditions **(Fig. 8-29)**.

(Fig. 8-29) Signal mirror technique. Image courtesy of the US Army Field Manual, No. 21-76, Survival.

If you can't determine the aircraft's location, flash your signal in the direction of the aircraft noise.

> **Note:**
> Pilots have reported seeing mirror flashes up to 160 kilometers away under ideal conditions.

FOOTNOTES

(1) Dr. Johnson, Steven A. Department of Wildlife Ecology & Conservation, University of Florida (2010). "Frequently Asked Questions about Venomous Snakes"

(2) Barceloux, D. (2008). "Medical Toxicology of Natural Substances: Foods, Fungi, Medicinal Herbs, Plants, and Venomous Animals"

(3) Keeler, Harriet L. (1900). "Our Native Trees and How to Identify Them".

(4) Roach, Robert; Stepanek, Jan; and Hackett, Peter. (2002). "Medical Aspects of Harsh Environments"

(5) www.mountaindays.net. (2010), "Climbing Dictionary & Glossary"

(6) Clare Murphy. (2009) BBC News Health report. "Toddler survives pool drowning"

(7) Duquette, Alison and Dorr, Les. (2009). "Fact Sheet – Helicopter Emergency Medical Service Safety"

VITAL VOCABULARY

Acclimatize: This is the process of an individual organism adjusting to a gradual change in its environment, (such as a change in temperature, humidity or altitude) allowing it to maintain performance across a range of environmental conditions.

Acute Mountain Sickness (AMS): Is a medical condition that is caused by acute exposure to low air pressure (usually outdoors at high altitudes).

Atmospheric Pressure: This is the force per unit area exerted against a surface by the weight of air above that surface in the Earth's atmosphere.

Clandestine: Marked by, held in, or conducted with secrecy.

High Altitude Cerebral Edema (HACE): This is a severe (frequently fatal) form of altitude sickness from swelling of brain tissue from fluid leakage and almost always begins as acute mountain sickness.

High Altitude Pulmonary Edema (HAPE): This condition results from fluid build-up in the lungs that prevents effective oxygen exchange.

Hydraulics: (also known as "holes", "stoppers" or "souse-holes"), are formed when water pours over the top of a submerged object, causing the surface water to flow back upstream toward the object.

Hypoxemia: This is the abnormally low percent of oxygen saturation of arterial hemoglobin (red blood cells).

Hypocapnia: This is a state of reduced carbon dioxide in the blood.

Latrodectism: Is the clinical syndrome caused by the neurotoxic venom, that can be injected by the bite of any spider that is a member of the spider genus Latrodectus, in the family Theridiidae.

Necrosis: This condition is caused by factors external to the cell or tissue, such as infection, toxins, or trauma that causes premature death of the cells in living tissue.

Neurotoxin: A chemical (venom) that alters the normal activity of the nervous system in such a way as to cause damage to nervous tissue.

Respiratory Alkalosis: This condition generally occurs when some stimulus (like altitude) makes a person hyperventilate - expelling CO2 from the circulation where it alters the dynamic chemical equilibrium of carbon dioxide in the circulatory system.

Strainers: These are objects that have formed in rivers that block the passage of larger objects but allows the flow of water to continue.

Sweepers: These are trees fallen in or heavily leaning over the river, still rooted on the shore and not fully submerged.

Urushiol: Is an oily organic allergen found in plants of poison oak, poison ivy, poison sumac.

UNIT 9 | LAND NAVIGATION

9.1	Cardinal Points	9.8	The US National Grid Standard
9.2	The Compass	9.9	Use of Geospatial Addresses
9.3	Foot Travel & Orienteering	9.10	Universal Transverse Mercator (UTM)
9.4	The Map	9.11	Elevation, Revisions & Benchmarks
9.5	The USGS, 7.5 Minute, 1:24,000 Topo Map		
9.6	Map & Compass Together		
9.7	Introduction to the USNG		

Upon completion of this chapter and the related course activities, the student will be able to meet the following objectives:

- Define the "Cardinal Points"
- Identify the parts of a compass
- Explain the various types of "north"
- Define the term "Declination"
- Identify the types of maps
- Identify the parts of a Topo Map and the characteristics of contour lines
- Explain how to determine your "pace"
- Know how to plot USNG/UTM coordinates and headings

Land navigation is one of the most important skills to have in the backcountry and while recreating outdoors. Reading a map and translating the map to the physical surroundings is crucial to understanding not only where you are, but how to best travel and what hazards may exist. Search personnel use maps for planning, plotting search segments and assignments to be completed, and SAR members in the field must know how to find those assignments, travel within them, and read terrain to find things like a landing zone for a helicopter or best route for rescue personnel to access a patient.

Relying on technology, especially phones, is often what gets people into situations where they need search and rescue to come help them, so understanding how to navigate without technology is an important skill. Certainly technology is helpful to the searcher, who will likely use a phone-based app to see search assignments on the app and use it to track their work so that the IC can see where searchers have been. But phone batteries can die, service can be spotty and apps can crash, so the map and compass method is critical to be proficient in.

9.1 Cardinal Points

The four cardinal directions or **cardinal points** are the directions of north, south, east, and west, commonly denoted by their initials: N, S, E, W. East and west are at right angles to north and south, with east being in the direction of rotation and west being directly opposite. The four cardinal directions **(Fig. 9-1)** correspond to the following degrees of a compass:

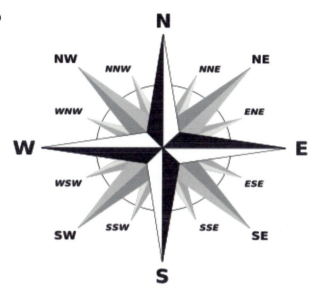

North (N): 0° = 360° East (E): 90°
South (S): 180° West (W): 270°

(Fig. 9-1) A compass rose showing the four cardinal directions, the four ordinal directions, plus eight further divisions. Image courtesy of Wikimedia Commons.

Intermediate points between the four cardinal directions form the points of the compass. The intermediate (intercardinal, or ordinal) directions are north-east (NE), north-west (NW), south-west (SW), and south-east (SE). An ordinal, or intercardinal, or intermediate, directions:

- Northeast (NE), 45°, halfway between north and east, is the opposite of southwest.
- Southeast (SE), 135°, halfway between south and east, is the opposite of northwest.
- Southwest (SW), 225°, halfway between south and west, is the opposite of northeast.
- Northwest (NW), 315°, halfway between north and west, is the opposite of southeast.

The directional names are also routinely and very conveniently associated with the degrees of rotation in the unit circle, a necessary step for navigational calculations (derived from trigonometry) and/or for use with Global Positioning Satellite (GPS) Receivers.

9.2 The Compass

The compass is the first part of orienteering. The second part is the map. A compass is a navigational instrument for determining direction relative to the Earth's magnetic poles. It consists of a magnetized pointer (usually marked on the North end) free to align itself with **Earth's magnetic field**. Magnetic North Pole is different from the geographic **North Pole**.

The geographic North Pole is defined as the point in the northern hemisphere where the Earth's axis of rotation meets the Earth's surface. The magnetic north and south poles are the ends of the magnetic field around the earth. The magnetic field is created by magnetic elements in the earth's fluid outer core and this molten rock does not align perfectly with the axis around which the earth spins.

There are actually many different sources of magnetic activity around and in the world. All those influencing factors combine to create the north and south attractions at each spot on the globe. The actual strength and direction of 'north' is slightly different everywhere, but it is generally towards the 'top' of the planet.

A simple tool based on the earth's magnetic field that has been around for centuries, the compass will, if used correctly, find the right direction.

Compass Styles

There are two standard compass styles **(Fig. 9-1)** that are widely used. The Lensatic compass and the Orienteering compass.

In wilderness search and rescue, it is recommended that the "orienteering" style compass be the one of choice although both have the same basic features. Modern compasses usually use a magnetized needle or dial inside a capsule completely filled with fluid (oil, kerosene, or alcohol is common to prevent freezing).

(Fig. 9-1) Example the Lensatic (left) and Orienteering (right) compass. Image courtesy of J. Bobot.

While older designs commonly incorporated a flexible diaphragm or airspace inside the capsule to allow for volume changes caused by temperature or altitude, modern liquid compasses utilize smaller housings and/or flexible materials for the capsule itself to accomplish the same result. The fluid dampens the movement of the needle and causes the needle to stabilize quickly rather than oscillate back and forth around magnetic north. The parts of the compass can be seen below **(Table 9-2)**.

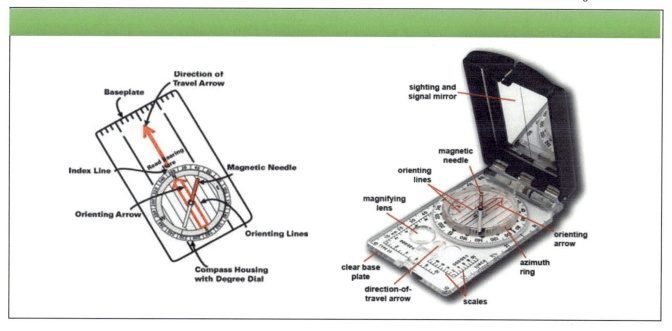

Limitations of the compass are few and are more trustworthy than any electronic device. The compass is very stable in areas close to the equator, which is far from "magnetic north".

As the compass is moved closer and closer to one of the magnetic poles of the Earth, the compass becomes more sensitive to crossing its magnetic field lines.

Good Compass Posture

Good compass posture is vital to accuracy in navigation. There are several key points to remember when using a compass

- Stand still with feet supporting your body with elbows bent so that both hands can hold the compass directly in front of body.

- Hold compass at either chest-level or eye-level.

- Use the compass mirror to view the dial **(Fig. 9-3)**.

Using a Compass: Putting "The Red in the Shed"

(Fig. 9-3) Proper compass sight picture. Image courtesy of J. Bobot

Think of the rhyme "Red in the Shed" to remember how to face north. As you perform the steps below, remember the following.

Dialing in a **heading or bearing**...

- Dial in your heading, or direction of travel, and find the "red" magnetic needle.

- Think of the orienteering arrow in the bezel as the "shed."**(Fig.9-4)**. The arrow usually looks like a garden shed.

- Moving your entire body, not turning at your waist and stop when the magnetic needle is over the top of the orienteering arrow (or "shed").

- You are now facing the direction that you dialed in.

(Fig. 9-4) Example of the "Shed" also known as the orienting arrow. (It looks like a shed). Image courtesy of J. Bobot.

Determining a heading...

- Point the compass to a distant point you wish to travel too.

- Using the folding mirror, look down on to the face of the compass and locate the bezel.

- Twist the bezel until the "red shed" lines up below the magnetic needle.

- Lower the compass and read the heading that lies above the index line. That will be the heading you will travel on.

Compass headings are read in degrees (ex. 120°). There are several things one needs to remember when reading a compass to ensure accuracy. These are:

- Ensure that direction of travel arrow is pointing in the same direction as your toes.

- When you move the compass to a specific heading, move your entire body as a solid extension.

- Hold the compass level so that the needle may move freely to settle on a direction.

Following a Compass Heading (Azimuth)

- Point your toes in direction you wish to travel and sight a prominent object in the distance.

- Close your eyes for several seconds, open them, and confirm you can find the object.

- Reconfirm your heading to object, lower the compass, and start walking.

9.3 Foot Travel & Orienteering

Foot Travel

A **Pace** is the measured distance of a full stride from the position of the heel when it is raised from the ground to the point the same heel is set down again at the end of the step **(Fig.9-5)**.

Everyone has different length legs and our strides very. Certain conditions affect your pace count in the field, and you must allow for them by adjusting.

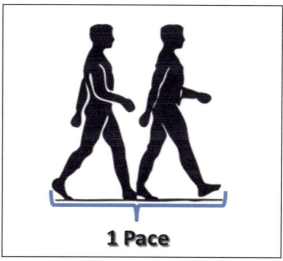

(Fig. 9-5) Example of one pace. Image courtesy of J. Bobot.

- Your pace lengthens on a down slope and shortens on an upgrade.

- A head wind shortens the pace and a tail wind increases it.

- Sand, gravel, mud, snow, and similar surface materials tend to shorten the pace.

- Excess clothing and boots with poor traction affect the pace length.

- Poor visibility, such as in fog, rain, or darkness, will shorten your pace.

Determine Your Pace Variance (PV)

For a searcher to measure distance in the field, the searcher needs to know how long their individual pace is based on various terrain styles. This is achieved by conducting a Pace Variance experiment in a variety of terrain styles. This is also required if you were to conduct an AMDR experiment where you are required to measure the distance from an object without the use of a tape wheel or other measuring device.

Experiment Set Up:

Step 1: Measure a Sample Distance (SD), such as 50 meters, within the terrain you could be searching in, i.e. flat & level terrain, down-hill, up-hill and mixed. You can also add others, such as snow, swamp/marsh, rocky, etc. In order to be as precise as possible, the searcher should have all of these different pace variances for various terrain style stored in their SAR LOG.

Step 2: Once the distance is laid out in the terrain you are experimenting in, walk that distance three times, tracking your Pace Count (PC) for each leg and calculate the average Pace Count (APC).

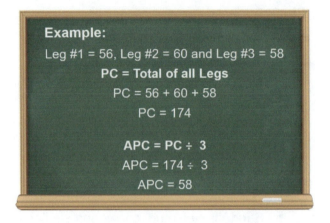

Example:
Leg #1 = 56, Leg #2 = 60 and Leg #3 = 58
PC = Total of all Legs
PC = 56 + 60 + 58
PC = 174

APC = PC ÷ 3
APC = 174 ÷ 3
APC = 58

Step 3: Once you have your Average Pace Count (APC), you must divide it by the Sample Distance (SD) to calculate your Pace Variance (PV).

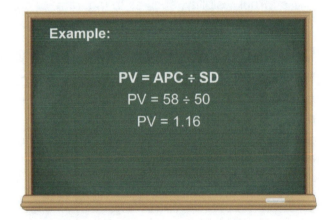

Example:

PV = APC ÷ SD
PV = 58 ÷ 50
PV = 1.16

How to Use Your Pace Variance (PV)

You can use your Pave Variance (PV) to determine the Distance (D) you have travelled based on you Pace Count (PC) or what your Pace Count (PC) would be for a given Distance (D) in meters. Based on your personal PV, solve the following problems:

$$PC = D \div PV$$
$$PC = 185 \div 1.16$$
$$PC = 159 \text{ paces}$$

You are told to travel along a stream that is 185 meters long. How many paces is that?

$$D = PC \times PV$$
$$D = 164 \times 1.16$$
$$D = 190 \text{ meters}$$

You travel 164 paces down a trail to the victim. How many meters is that?

There are many methods to keep track of the distance traveled (pace) when walking. Some of these methods are put a pebble in your pocket every time you have walked 100 meters, tie knots in a string; or put marks in a notebook. Another method is the use of **Ranger Beads (Fig. 9-6)**. Do not try to remember the count; always use one of these methods or design your own method.

Navigation in the wilderness means knowing your starting point, your destination, and your route to get there. Check your position regularly. Make it a habit of keeping your map and compass handy and refer to them every hour or so to locate your position (more often in low visibility). Keep track of your starting time, rest breaks and lunch stop, and general hiking pace.

(Fig. 9-6) Example of Ranger Beads.
Image courtesy of J. Bobot.

To orient the Map to You - take the topographical map and locate where your position is on the map. Is there a building you are near or identify the ridgeline or some other terrain feature? Once you have done that you have oriented the map to you.

9.4 The Map

A map is a visual representation of an area - a symbolic depiction highlighting relationships between elements of that space such as objects, regions, and themes. Many maps are static two-dimensional, geometrically accurate (or approximately accurate) representations of three-dimensional space, while others are dynamic or interactive, even three-dimensional. Although most commonly used to depict geography, maps may represent any space, real or imagined, without regard to context or scale, e.g. brain mapping, DNA mapping, and extraterrestrial mapping.

Types of Maps

There are many types of maps in existence. SAR personnel should be able to take the principles of land navigation and orienteering and apply them to whatever maps are made available during a search. However, SAR does have its standard and often available map of choice. It is the USGS, 7.5 minute quadrangle map. The following is a short list of various maps that searchers may be faced with.

- **Planimetric Maps:** Show both natural and man-made features such as roads, streets or other points of interest (a state road map). They are usually to scale.

- **Site Specific Maps:** These maps are not usually to scale and simply show points of interest such as a metro or state park and identifies park attractions and facilities.

- **Fire Service Maps:** These maps give more terrain details than most Planimetric maps, but charted to a scale that is not good for foot travel.

- **Relief Maps:** this map (or terrain model) is a three-dimensional representation, usually of terrain. When representing terrain, the elevation dimension is usually exaggerated by a factor between five and ten; this facilitates the visual recognition of terrain features.

- **Surveyors' Maps:** These maps are generally available for most areas, but should be used only when no other maps are available. These maps show virtually no terrain features and a very limited amount of road information.

- **Topographical Maps:** These are the most used maps in search and rescue. They are produced by the United States Geological Survey (USGS) and are scaled in a suitable fashion for foot travel (7.5 & 15 minute maps). These maps depict in detail ground relief (landforms and terrain), drainage (lakes and rivers), forest cover, administrative areas, populated areas, transportation routes and facilities (including roads and railways), and other man-made features.
[1]

- **Orthophoto Qaud Maps:** These maps are a new cross between an aerial photographs with a topographical map overlay on top of it so that it depicts the images of buildings, roads, etc. and elevation.

Longitude & Latitude

Longitude is the angular distance of a point's meridian (or line of longitude). This is an imaginary arc on the Earth's surface from the North Pole to the South Pole that connects all locations running along it with a given longitude. It is usually expressed in degrees, minutes, and seconds. Lines of longitude are often referred to as meridians and is the geographic coordinate most used incartography and global navigation for east-west measurement.

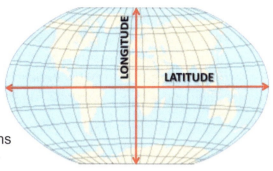

(Fig. 9-8) Longitude lines run north-south and Latitude lines from east-west. Image courtesy of J. Bobot.

Latitude gives the location of a place on Earth north or south of the equator. Lines of Latitude are the imaginary horizontal lines shown running east-to-west (or west to east) on maps that run either north or south of the equator **(Fig. 9-8)**. Technically, latitude is an angular measurement in degrees ranging from 0° at the equator (low latitude) to 90° at the poles. [2]

9.5 The USGS, 7-5 minute, 1:24,000 Topo Map

The key objective of this map **(Fig. 9-9)** is to depict a three-dimensional feature like elevation on a flat surface. This is done by placing lines on the map that form contours of the terrain. The **scale ratio 1:24,000 represents that 1" on the map equals** 24,000" on the earth. It also means that one of "anything" on the map (km, meters, feet, etc.) equals 24,000 of those on the earth. [3]

(Fig. 9-9) Sample topographical map showing the various colors and features. Image courtesy of MapTech Software.

"Quadrangle" is a specific surveying term for the basic subdivision of the United States Public Land Survey System. In this system, a quadrangle is an area that can be subdivided into 16 townships, and has limits generally measuring 24 miles (39 km) on each side, although this distance is not exact due to the effects of surveying and mapping the curved surface of Earth. [4]

Things to Know on a Topographical Map

A topographical map usually contains three directional references **(Fig. 9-10)**. They are true north, grid north and magnetic north. These references can usually be found in the lower portion of the map in symbolic form.

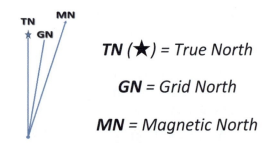

TN (★) = True North

GN = Grid North

MN = Magnetic North

(Fig. 9-10) Longitude lines run north-south and Latitude lines from east-west. Image courtesy of J. Bobot.

- True North is the direction to the geographical north pole or at the Earth's axis points and is represented by a « symbol or "TN".

- Grid North is the direction the grid lines are aligned to the map and is represented by "GN".

- Magnetic North is the direction of the north needle points on a compass and is represented by "MN". [5]

Understanding these references will be very important when we start to navigate using a compass and a map.

Colors on a Topographical Map

Topographical maps are in color and each color represents a key feature of the terrain.

Green - Vegetation
Light Brown - Contour Lines
Dark Brown - Index Lines
White - Clear
Blue - Water
Purple - Map Revisions
Black - Structures and Roads

See the USGS handout on page 159 to see examples of symbols and the use of color.

Types of Slopes

Searchers will need to determine not only the height of a hill, but the degree of the hill's slope as well. The rate of rise or fall is known as its **slope**. [6]

The speed at which equipment or personnel can move is affected by the slope of the ground or terrain feature. This slope can be determined from the map by studying the **contour lines** — lines on a topographical map that denote elevation. The closer the contour lines, the steeper the slope; the farther apart the contour lines, the gentler the slope. The space between the contour lines is always 20 feet. The distance moves from horizontal to vertical as the lines move closer together.

Four types of slopes that concern the land navigators are as follows: Remember, the closer the contour lines, the steeper the slope.

Gentle Slope - Contour lines (lines that denote elevation) showing a uniform, gentle slope will be evenly spaced and wide apart. **Steep Slope** - Contour lines showing a uniform, steep slope on a map will be evenly spaced, but close together **(Fig. 9-11)**.

Concave Slope - Contour lines showing a concave slope on a map will be closely spaced at the top of the terrain feature and widely spaced at the bottom. **Convex Slope** - Contour lines showing a convex slope on a map will be widely spaced at the top and closely spaced at the bottom **(Fig. 9-12)**. [6]

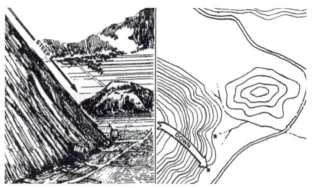
(Fig. 9-11) Gentle Slope (top) and Steep Slope (bottom). Image courtesy of the US Army Field Manual #3-25.26.

(Fig. 9-12) Concave Slope (top) and Convex Slope

(Fig. 9-13) Ridgeline. Image courtesy of J. Bobot.

The Ridgeline Features

A **ridgeline** is a geological feature that features a chain of mountains or hills that are of a continuous elevated crest for some distance **(Fig. 9-13)**. Ridges are usually termed hills or mountains as well, depending on size. All terrain features are derived from a complex landmass known as a mountain or ridgeline.

The term ridgeline is not interchangeable with the term ridge. A ridgeline is a line of high ground or individual ridges, usually with changes in elevation along its top and low ground on all sides from which a total of 10 natural or man-made terrain features are classified **(Fig. 9-14)**. You can use your hand to help remember a few of the different characteristics of a ridgeline **(Fig. 9-15)**.

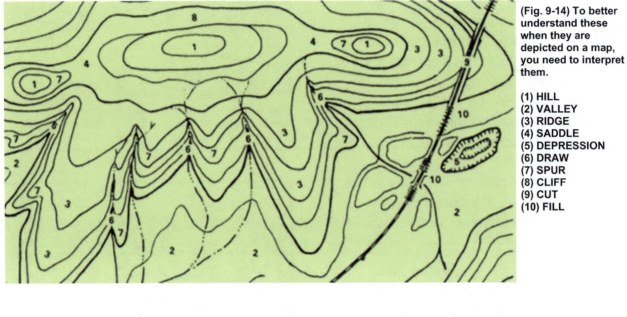

(Fig. 9-14) To better understand these when they are depicted on a map, you need to interpret them.

(1) HILL
(2) VALLEY
(3) RIDGE
(4) SADDLE
(5) DEPRESSION
(6) DRAW
(7) SPUR
(8) CLIFF
(9) CUT
(10) FILL

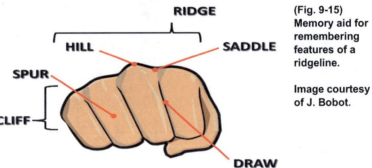

(Fig. 9-15) Memory aid for remembering features of a ridgeline.

Image courtesy of J. Bobot.

The Ten Terrain Features of a Ridgeline

1. Hill - A hill is an area of high ground. From a hilltop, the ground slopes down in all directions. A hill is shown on a map by contour lines forming concentric circles. The inside of the smallest closed circle is the hilltop, or peak.

2. Saddle - A saddle is a dip or low point between two areas of higher ground. A saddle is not necessarily the lower ground between two hilltops; it may be simply a dip or break along a level ridge crest. If you are in a saddle, there is high ground in two opposite directions and lower ground in the other two directions. A saddle is normally represented as an hourglass.

3. Valley - A valley is a stretched-out groove in the land, usually formed by streams or rivers. A valley begins with high ground on three sides, and usually has a course of running water through it. Contour lines forming a valley are either U-shaped or V-shaped. The closed end of the contour line (U or V) always points upstream or toward high ground.

4. Ridge - A ridge is a sloping line of high ground. If you are standing on the centerline of a ridge, you will normally have low ground in three directions and high ground in one direction with varying degrees of slope.
If you cross a ridge at right angles, you will climb steeply to the crest and then descend steeply to the base. Contour lines forming a ridge tend to be U-shaped or V-shaped. The closed end of the contour line points away from high ground.

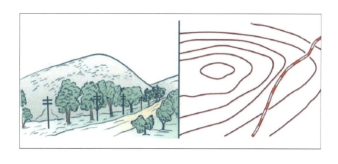

5. Depression - A depression is a low point in the ground or a sinkhole. It could be described as an area of low ground surrounded by higher ground in all directions, or simply a hole in the ground. Usually only depressions that are equal to or greater than the contour interval will be shown. On maps, depressions are represented by closed contour lines that have tick marks pointing toward low ground.

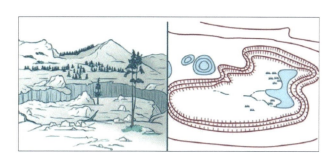

6. Draw - A draw is a less developed stream course than a valley. In a draw, there is essentially no level ground and, therefore, little or no maneuver room within its confines. If you are standing in a draw, the ground slopes upward in three directions and downward in the other direction. A draw could be considered as the initial formation of a valley. The contour lines depicting a draw are U-shaped or V-shaped, pointing toward high ground.

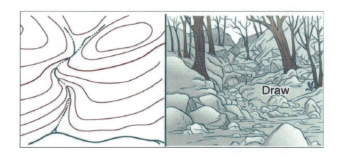

7. Spur - A spur is a short, continuous sloping line of higher ground, normally jutting out from the side of a ridge. A spur is often formed by two rough parallel streams, which cut draws down the side of a ridge. The ground sloped down in three directions and up in one direction. Contour lines on a map depict a spur with the U or V pointing away from high ground.

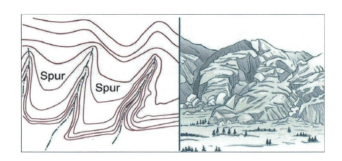

8. Cliff - A cliff is a vertical or near vertical feature; it is an abrupt change of the land with a slope is so steep that the contour lines converge into one. Cliffs are also shown by contour lines very close together and, in some instances, touching each other.

Measuring Distances on a Topo Map

One method is to measure the distance using a piece of paper **(Fig. 9-15)**, marking the ends of the route. If there are grid lines on the map, use the grid line on the border to determine the distance. Each small square on the edge is 100 meters.

If you need to measure something that is not straight, the use of paper can be very difficult. It is recommended that you use a piece of string **(Fig. 9-16),** like the one on your compass. The string can be conformed to follow the route on the map. Once you have the distance, you can mark the string and lay it out along the edge of the map.

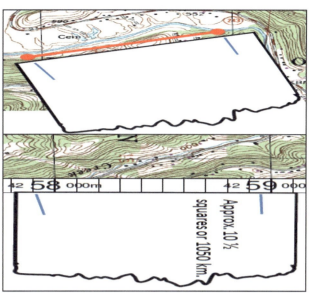

(Fig. 9-15) Using the edge of a piece of paper to measure a distance on a topo map and determining the length by using the 100m marks on the edge. Image courtesy of J. Bobot.

The Map Margins

There is a lot of information along the margin of a topographical map that is used for reference. The scale is in the bottom margin of a topographic map. On a USGS map, the scale is given in feet and sections of a mile and kilometer. The 1:24,000 scale map displays an area of 7.5 minutes of both latitude and longitude, which is marked in the margins. Typically, the margins also contain Universal Transverse Mercator (UTM) coordinates in meters to pinpoint locations.

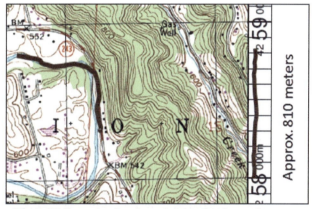

(Fig. 9-16) Example of a piece of string that is used to measure a route and placed on the border to measure. Image courtesy of J. Bobot.

The margin also displays magnetic and grid (true) north. The declination of magnetic north is important information for compass orienteering. In addition, the contour interval, the elevation difference between lines, is also given in the margin. On the 1:24,000 scale map, contour intervals are usually ten or 20 feet. The map name and the USGS notes are also available. [7]

Topographic maps are typically named by the most famous feature within the map. Topographic maps show house locations and other features. This information, along with the publication date printed in the margins, helps track development through time.

Location of Topographical Map Margin Information: (For More Information, see guide at the end of the unit)

- **Upper Right:** The map's Quadrangle name and adjacent quadrangle map name.

- **Lower Right:** Quadrangle Location, Revision Dates, Road Key and USGS Map Identification Number and adjacent Quadrangle Map Name.

- **Corners:** The Universal Transverse Mercator (UTM), State Plane and geographic coordinates (lat/long) at the map margin corners.

- **Bottom:** Road Key, The scale and the Contour Interval. A 1:24,000 USGS topographical map states that 1 inch = 2,000 feet. [8]

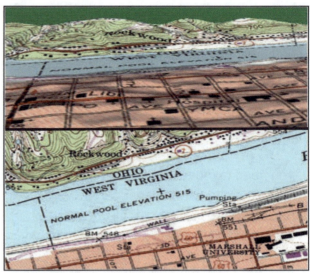

(Fig. 9-17) The two images show the 3D view (top) and the 2D topographical view (bottom). Image courtesy of MapTech Software.

3D Vs. 2D Representation

When you look at a topographical map, you will need to be able to determine the elevation (contour lines) and compare it to the actual world view **(Fig. 9-17)**.

9.6 Map & Compass Together

Headings

Now that we know a bit about the map and the compass, we need to be able to put them together. In order to start using your map and compass together, you need to orientate them to each other and to you. To determine a compass heading (grid heading) you will need a compass, your known or starting location, a ruler & pencil and your ending location.

To Determine a Grid Heading...

- Take your ruler and pencil and draw a straight line from your starting location to your ending location. This is your route line.

(Fig. 9-18) Example of how to position your compass on a map to obtain a grid heading. Image courtesy of J. Bobot.

- Place the compass with the "Direction of Travel" arrow pointing to your destination along the line you have drawn **(Fig 9-18)**.

- Turn the dial until the "N" is toward the top of your map and adjust the compass until one of the orienteering lines are on or parallel to one of the grid lines on the map. Make sure that your compass is still flush up against your route line.

- With your orienting lines on or parallel to the grid lines on the map, your dial will be in the proper position to read your grid heading.

- **THE NEEDLE POSITION DOES NOT MATTER WHEN DOING THIS!**

- Remove your compass from the map and read the heading that is at or over the small little mark called the index line. That is your grid heading.

- **Remember, in order to use this heading in the field, we will need to adjust for declination, discussed later!**

Orient your Map and Compass

To orient a map means to line it up with the terrain, so that North on the map is pointing to North on the terrain. A map so lined up is easier to interpret. To line up with the terrain:

Line up your map with what you see around you. Place your map in such a way that the terrain features line up with your map's features. For instance, line up roads, mountains, water towers—any terrain features that stand out enough to make orienting the map possible.

To line up your map and compass:

1. Determine your position on the map. (GPS, UTM, Landforms, etc.)
2. Place the map flat on the ground.
3. Turn the bezel of the compass so that N or "North" is over the index line.
4. Place the compass on the map and point the compass to the "top" of the map or north and line it up to an orienteering line with the direction of travel arrow all pointing north.
5. Now, turn the map with the compass to the direction you are looking – putting the "red in the shed" and now you have determined your heading and oriented your map.

Using the Grid Overlay to Determine a Heading

A map tool that can be used to determine a heading is the Grid Overlay Tool. This tool has many functions and determining a heading is just one of them.

- Draw a line from your starting point to your ending point on the map.

- Using the darker center cross lines of the grid on the grid overlay, place the center (where the lines cross over) on your starting point. This will usually not fit perfectly in that 1,000-meter box.

- Make sure that at one of the vertical lines on the grid reader is parallel with one of the grid lines on the map.

- Follow the line to the edge of the grid overlay and read the compass degrees that are printed around the edge of the overlay. They are in 5- and 1-meter increments **(Fig. 9-19)**.

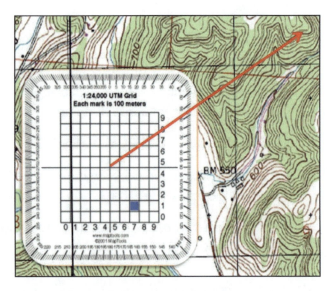

(Fig. 9-19) Example of a grid overlay to determine a heading. The red line above depicts a grid heading or 57 degrees. Image courtesy of J. Bobot.

Declination

You need to compensate for these differences, called declination. This difference is between grid north, true north, and magnetic north. To do this remember this when calculating declination:

When the declination is EAST, subtract the declination from your grid heading… **East is "least" (-)**

When the declination is WEST, add the declination to your grid heading… **West is "best" (+)**

Two problems complicate your easy use of map and compass. First, the surface of the earth is curved, while the surface of your map is flat. This creates problems between what your map shows as north (grid north) and what is really north (true north).

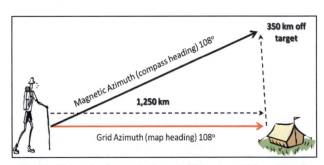

(Fig. 9-20) Illustration as to how "off" you could be without correcting for declination. Image courtesy of J. Bobot.

Second, the earth's magnetic pole is not the same as the earth's axis. This creates a difference between what your compass shows as north (magnetic north) and what is north (true north). **(Fig. 9-20)**

Declinations are constantly changing and that means what is written on a map you buy this year will be incorrect next year. The difference depends on where the north pole moves to and what your current declination is **(Fig. 9-21)**. [9]

In order to use the compass OFF of the map… you must adjust for the declination.

Example:

Take your grid heading that you obtain from the topographical map either by using your compass or with a grid overlay. (160°)

Find the declination in degrees. (4° East) and note if it is on the east side or the west side of the declination symbol. Subtract if east, add if west.

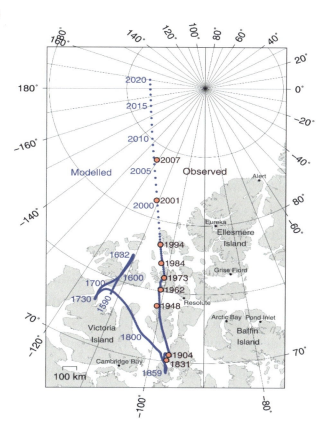

(Fig. 9-21) The movement of Earth's north magnetic pole across the Canadian Arctic in recent centuries, continuing in recent years across the Arctic Ocean towards Siberia. Photo courtesy of Cavit - Own work Observed pole positions taken from Newitt et al., "Location of the North Magnetic Pole in April 2007", Earth Planets Space, 61, 703–710, 2009 Modelled pole positions taken from the National Geophysical Data Center, "Wandering of the Geomagnetic Poles" Map created with GMT. Image courtesy of Cavit.

> **Formula:** Field usable heading = grid heading +/- declination.
>
> 160° - 4° = 156°
>
> The OPPOSITE must occur when taking a heading with your compass and plotting it on the map!
>
> **Compass heading of 160° + 4° = 164°**

Datum

A datum describes the model that was used to match the location of features on the ground to coordinates and locations on the map. Every map that shows a geographic coordinate system such as UTM or Latitude and Longitude with any precision will also list the datum used on the map.

Most USGS topographic maps are based on an earlier datum called the North American Datum of 1927 or NAD 27. You should always set your GPS unit's datum to match the datum of the map you are using.

On a USGS topographic map the datum information is in the fine print at the bottom left of the map. The datum will always be NAD 27. [10]

9.7 Introduction to the USNG

The Federal Geographic Data Committee's **U.S. National Grid (USNG)** standard provides a nationally consistent language of location that has been optimized for local applications. All street maps use a standard set of street names and addresses to locate places. The USNG does not replace this practice; it complements it. Private citizens, public agencies, and commercial enterprises can use USNG. It has obvious applications in navigation, command and control, and public safety response (e.g., police, fire, rescue, National Guard).

The simple linear increments of USNG has shown itself to require less training time to master and produces fewer operator errors than the more complex angular increments of latitude and longitude – such that the USNG be effectively taught at the 5th grade level. [11]

The USNG is an alphanumeric point reference system that has been overlaid on the Universal Transverse Mercator (UTM) numerical grid. Every modest size home in a discrete area (city) can be described using 8-digits (e.g., 1234 5678). By adding a two-letter prefix (e.g., XX 1234 5678) the location is uniquely identified regionally (state-wide).

This alphanumeric designator can be used today with consumer GPS receivers costing less than $100.

The USNG improves interoperability, military support to civil authorities, and reduces operational friction – facilitating crisis and disaster response at all levels – from federal to local government. The Army National Guard is trained to use the USNG format as the USNG and the Military Grid Reference (MGRS) values are identical when referenced to WGS 84 or NAD 83 datum.

The USNG expands the utility of topographic, street, and other large-scale maps by adding several powerful features:

- It provides a grid reference system that is seamless across jurisdictional boundaries
- It provides the foundation for a universal map index; it enables user-friendly position referencing on appropriately gridded paper and digital maps, with Global Positioning System (GPS)receivers; and World Wide Web map portals.

9.8 The US National Grid Standard

The USNG may be the only unambiguous way to describe locations when the end-user is operating either in an area away from the established road network, or in an area impacted by a natural disaster where road signs have been destroyed **(Fig. 9-22)**.

The US National Grid (USNG) standard established a nationally consistent grid reference system, just as all street maps use a common set of street names.

(Fig. 9-22) Joplin, Mo., June 4, 2011 -- Debris fill the streets of Joplin after a EF-5 tornado touched down on May 22, 2011. Where are the street signs, addresses, where are you? Photo courtesy of Steve Zumwalt FEMA

The most important use of the USNG is the fact that during post-disaster situations, there may not be any street signs and rescue resources may be coming from hundreds of miles away to assist a community in need and are not familiar with the area. A tornado can totally obliterate a community and as long as there are USNG maps, rescue personnel will be able to respond to any location.

USNG provides a seamless plane coordinate system across jurisdictional boundaries and map scales; it enables precise position referencing with GPS, web map portals, and hardcopy maps. Unlike latitude and longitude, the USNG is simple enough that it can be taught and effectively used at the 5th grade level. It enables a practical system of geoaddresses or a geospatial address and a universal map index.

The coordinates (16R BU 1028 0976) is a worldwide unique location known as the geospatial address or geoaddress **(Fig. 9-23)**. It is unique in the fact that the "16R" can only be found once on the entire planet, while the "BU" may be repeated, it is also unique to a given state and the states surrounding it.

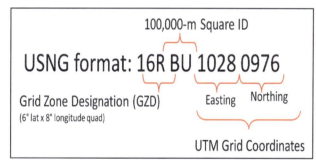

(Fig. 9-23) The geospatial address. Image courtesy www.fgcd.gov/USNG Website.

You will note, the USGS does not portray the latitude letter designation. In the northern hemisphere these start with the letter N at the equator and proceed consecutively northward in 8° increments (with the omission of the letter O). The world is broken down into 8° bands of latitude. Combined with UTM Grid Zones, these 8° latitude by 6° longitude blocks are known as Grid Zone Designation (GZD) **(Fig. 9-24)**.

(Fig. 9-24) The Grid Zone Designators (GZD) on the USNG Index Map for the continental United States. Image courtesy www.fgcd.gov/USNG

The difference between UTM coordinates and the US National grid, is only on a large scale, using the GZD and 100,000-meter grid values. Otherwise, the standard UTM coordinated system is used. The USNG is the topographical map for urban environments. USAR personnel will count on these maps just like a wilderness SAR responder counts on their maps to navigate. [12]

The Grid Zone Designators are further broken down in to **100,000-meter grid** squares and are represented by a two-letter grid value within the Index Map **(Fig. 9-25)**. The Square grid value: "10280976" is a smaller local area and is the same as the **Universal Transverse Mercator (UTM)** coordinate.

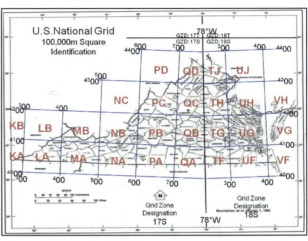

(Fig. 9-25) The Grid Zone Designators (GZD) showing the two-letter position coordinates. Image courtesy www.fgcd.gov/USNG Website.

Given 2 to 10 digits; each additional digit pair improves precision by an order of magnitude squared.

9.9 Use of Geospatial Addresses

These physical locations, also known as geospatial addresses, are becoming more widely used and added to the normal addresses you may find on any business card **(Fig. 9-26)**. Other examples of use include in New Orleans during Hurricane Katrina response, and adoption by the State of Florida, FEMA Urban Search and Rescue (US&R), USGS, Census Bureau, DoD, Garmin & Magellan GPS, and others. [13]

(Fig. 9-26) A business card with a USNG geoaddress on it to identify where the building is located in the event of a disaster. Image courtesy www.fgcd.gov/USNG

9.10 Universal Transverse Mercator (UTM)

The Universal Transverse Mercator (UTM) coordinate system is a grid-based method of specifying locations on the surface of the Earth that is a practical application of a two-dimensional Cartesian coordinate system.

UTM Grids Lines

These lines are shown on all USGS quadrangle maps as little blue tick lines along the margin. Each tick mark is indicated at 1,000-meter intervals. Coordinates are measured north and east in meters. One-meter equals 39.37 inches, or slightly more than one yard. In order to use the lines, you will need to draw them on the map or use mapping software. The lines (horizontal and vertical) form boxes and indicate 1,000 meters square intervals.

How to Plot UTM Coordinates

We will walk through the plotting of a UTM Coordinate. We will say that we are standing at the road junction marked with the star on your topographic map. A GPS unit set to display positions in UTM coordinates, would report the location at: **10S BU 0559731 / 4282182**

The coordinates represent a physical location on the earth's surface. The more digits represented, the more accurate (or closer) you are. We know that the "10S" represents the GZD and the "BU" represents the 100,000-meter grid. The first set of numbers after the USNG identifiers, **0559731**, represent a measurement of East-West position, within the zone, in meters. It's called an **easting**. The second set of numbers, **4282182**, represent a measurement of North-South position, within the zone, in meters. It's called a **northing**.

For example, in the combined coordinates (both easting and northing of 42818 / 21634, the digits would represent the following accuracy:

- 4 digits - <u>42</u> & <u>21</u> - locates a point with a precision of 1,000 meters (a neighborhood size area).

- 6 digits - <u>428</u> & <u>216</u> - locates a point with a precision of 100 meters (a soccer field size area).

- 8 digits - <u>4281</u> & <u>2163</u> - locates a point with a precision of 10 meters (the size of a modest home).

- 10 digits - <u>42818</u> & <u>21634</u> - locates a point with a precision of 1-meter (within a parking spot).

Plotting UTM Coordinates

We read topographical map coordinates by reading to map **left to right then bottom to top**. The most common and "field usable" coordinates would be the following: 5973 / 8218 or as accurate as 10 meters. **(See end of unit for a step-by-step guide)**

9.11 Elevation, Revisions & Benchmarks

There are two different brown lines on a topographical map, one is dark brown (denotes the elevation) and light brown (denotes the interval, usually every 20 feet). The dark contour line will have the elevation (above sea level) written on the line **(Fig. 9-27)**.

As we have discussed before, when talking about slopes and cliffs, the closer the contour lines, the steeper the grade. If you are above or below a dark contour line, simply add or subtract 10 or 20 feet from for each light contour line. The contour interval will be marked on all maps. Maps generated by mapping software usually have 20-foot intervals.

There may come a time where you need to determine the contour interval based on the map you have. To do this, simply find the difference between the two contour interval lines (the dark brown lines with the numbers) and divide that by the number of light brown contour lines (always include one of the dark brown contour interval lines). See the example. **(Fig. 9-28)**

Map Revisions

From the mid-1940s through the late 1980s the 1:24,000-scale, 7.5-minute topographic quadrangle was the primary product of the U.S. Geological Survey's (USGS) National Mapping Program (NMP). This map series includes about 53,000 map sheets for the conterminous United States and is the only uniform map series that covers this area at such a large scale. There are four main categories of map revision: minor, basic, complete, and single edition. Minor revision is done on maps that have few changes since the last revision; it includes boundary updates and corrections of previously reported errors. Basic revision updates feature from digital orthophoto quadrangles (DOQ) and aerial photographs. Complete revision of all layers is seldom performed because of the high cost. Single-edition revisions are done by the U.S. Department of Agriculture Forest Service using procedures like basic revision. Contour update is an optional part of basic and single edition revision but is not often done because of the high cost. These revision programs were not designed to do replacement mapping. Most map revision is done from remote and secondary data sources, including the following:

(Fig. 9-28) Image showing the index lines (1800 & 2000) and the individual contour lines 1820-1880). 20 feet intervals. Photo courtesy of J. Bobot

- Geometry is controlled and some feature content interpreted from DOQs.

- Most feature content is interpreted by using stereophotographs from the National Aerial Photography Program.

- Boundary and name information is collected from Federal databases, other maps, and State and local agencies.

(Fig. 9-29) Example of how new building are added to the map. The topo map at right shows the original building (in black) and then the addition as well as all the other new buildings. Image courtesy J. Bobot.

As we know, purple on a topographical map designates revisions. A topographical map is updated using aerial photographs. Every so often, planes fly over and take photographs. These semi-transparent photographs are then placed over the old topographical map and new buildings **(Fig. 9-29)**, roads or development areas are added to the map.

9.12 Finding North Without a Compass

To find North without a compass (Option #1)

You will need at least partial sun for this to work. Place a stick in the ground and mark the shadow with a stone. Wait 15 minutes and mark the shadow with a twig. Draw a line between the stone and the stick. At a 90-degree angle, you will find North.

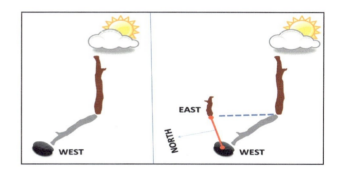

To find North without a compass (Option #2)

Take an analog watch and point the hour hand at the sun. Next, holding the watch in place, imagine an angle formed by the hour hand and a line from the 12 o'clock position to the center of the watch. Then draw an imaginary line bisecting that angle. That line indicates south in the Northern Hemisphere. During daylight saving time, create the angle from the one o'clock position instead of the 12 o'clock position.

To find North without a compass (Night Option)

You will need a clear sky and the ability to locate the Big Dipper. This constellation usually sticks out in the night sky. Draw a line from the two stars that make up the "cup". The North Star (Polaris) is 5 times that distance in a straight line from those stars. You will find the North Star in the tail of the Little Dipper.

FOOTNOTES

(1) Government of Canada (8 April 2016). "National Topographic System Maps". Earth Sciences – Geography. Natural Resources Canada. Archived from the original on 15 May 2016.

(2) A guide to coordinate systems in Great Britain (PDF), D00659 v2.3, Ordnance Survey, March 2015, archived from the original (PDF) on 24 September 2015

(3) "USGS Map Booklet". USGS. Archived from the original on 9 May 2015.

(4) Map Scales, Fact Sheet FS105-02, (February 2002)

(5) McClure, Bruce (2013). "Polaris is the North Star". Astronomy Essentials. EarthSky. Archived from the original on 2014-03-09

(6) US Army Field Manual #3-25.26.

(7) Bowditch, Nathaniel (2002). American Practical Navigator. Paradise Cay Publications. ISBN 9780939837540.

(8) "USGS Map Booklet". USGS. Archived from the original on 9 May 2015.

(9) Willemsen, Diederik. "Compass navigation". SailingIssues.

(10) "New Datums" National Geodetic Survey

(11) Carnes, John (2002). UTM: Using your GPS with the Universal Transverse Mercator Map Coordinate System. MapTools. ISBN 0-9710901-0-6.

(12) Federal Geographic Data Committee. "The US National Grid: A Simple and Powerful Geospatial Tool [FGDC USNG Info Sheet 4]" (PDF). FGDC

(13) "NSARC Designates USNG as the Land SAR Coordinate System". EPC Updates (St. Paul MN).

VITAL VOCABULARY

100,000-meter Grid: These are 100,000 meter x 100,000 meter squares within the GZD and are represented by a two-letter grid value within the Index Map.

Azimuth: This is an angular measurement in a spherical coordinate system also known as a heading or bearing.

Cardinal Points: These are the directions of north, south, east, and west, commonly denoted by their initials: N, S, E and W.

Contour Interval: This is the elevation difference between lines - on the 1:24,000 scale map, contour intervals are usually 10 or 20 feet.

Contour Lines: Lines on a topographical map that denote elevation. They are usually 20 feet apart.

Declination: Is the difference between grid north, true north, and magnetic north.

Earth's Magnetic Field: Earth is largely protected from the solar wind, a stream of energetic charged particles emanating from the sun, by its magnetic field, which deflects most of the charged particles.

Easting: Is a measurement of East-West position, within the zone, in meters.

Geoaddress: This is the identification of the real-world geographic location of an object.

Grid Zone Designation (GZD): This is the 6° wide UTM zones, numbered 1–60, and they are intersected by latitude bands that are normally 8° high.

Heading: This is the relative position of one point with respect to another point without the distance information and is also known as a bearing or azimuth.

North Pole: (Geographic North Pole) is defined as the point in the northern hemisphere where the Earth's axis of rotation meets the Earth's surface.

Northing: Is a measurement of North-South position, within the zone in meters.

Pace: This is equal to one natural step, about 30 inches long.

Planimetric Maps: These maps show both natural and man-made features such as roads, streets or other points of interest (state road map) and are usually to scale.

Quadrangle: This is an area that can be subdivided into 16 townships, and has limits generally measuring 24 miles (39 km) on each side, although this distance is not exact due to the effects of surveying and mapping the curved surface of Earth.

Ranger Beads: This is a manual counting tool used to keep track of distance travelled through a pace count.

Relief Maps: This map (or terrain model) is a three-dimensional representation, usually of terrain. When representing terrain, the elevation dimension is usually exaggerated by a factor between five and ten; this facilitates the visual recognition of terrain features.

Ridgeline: This is a geological feature that features a chain of mountains or hills that are of a continuous elevated crest for some distance.

Slope: The rate of rise or fall of a terrain feature.

Topographical Maps: These are produced by the United States Geological Survey (USGS) and are scaled in a suitable fashion for foot travel (7.5 & 15 minute maps) and depict detailed information about the terrain and other features such as elevation, roads, buildings, water and vegetation.

Universal Transverse Mercator (UTM): Is a grid-based coordinate system for specifying locations on the surface of the Earth.

US National Grid (USNG): This is a standard that established a nationally consistent grid reference system that provides a seamless plane coordinate system across jurisdictional boundaries and map scales; it enables precise position referencing with GPS, web map portals, and hardcopy maps.

The following is a step-by-step explanation of determining UTM Coordinates.

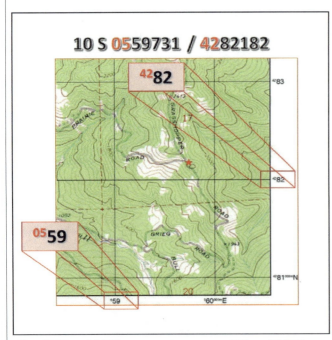

The "05" and "42" represent an area within a 10,000 x 10,000-meter location. This is way too vague to direct anyone to your location. We will continue to use the coordinate positions to get us closer and closer to our position.

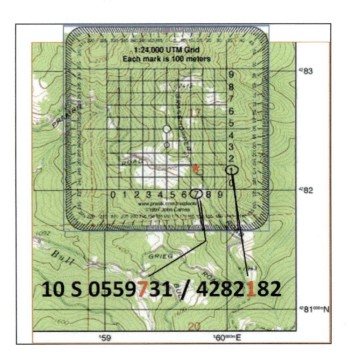

The grid overlay will need to be used to narrow the position down further. The "7" and the "1" is obtained from the grid reader by reading it from left to right and bottom to top. The small squares represent an area of 100 x 100 meters. Whereas this is narrowing down your position, it is still too vague for someone to either locate you or you to locate someone else.

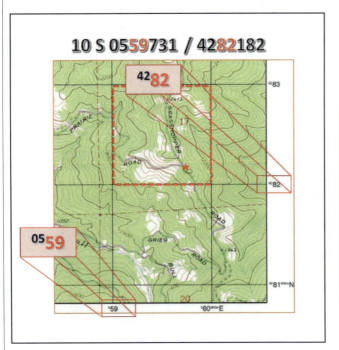

The "59" and "82" represents an area within a 1,000 x 1,000-meter location. This is closer and more precise. These numbers can be located along the margin or edge of the topographical map.

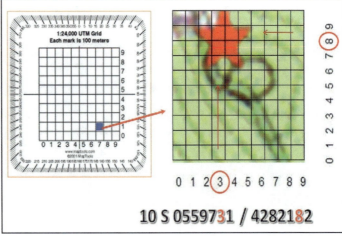

With the grid reader in place, look at the small 100 x 100-meter square. Taking that square and creating, in your mind, an equal grid to that of the grid overlay, you will be able to obtain the "3" and the "8". This will get you as close as 10 x 10 meters.

USGS Topographical Map Border (Margin) Information Guideline

UPPER LEFT CORNER

1. The Publisher (United States Department of the Interior Geological Survey)
2. Geographical Coordinate (Lat/long)
3. UTM (Easting) Coordinate
4. UTM (Northing) Coordinate

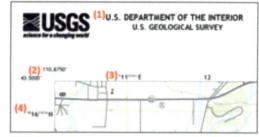

UPPER RIGHT CORNER

1. Quadrangle Map Title
2. State/County
3. Series
4. Geographical Coordinate (Lat/long)
5. UTM (Easting) Coordinate

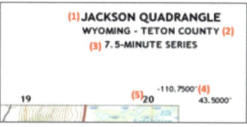

LOWER RIGHT CORNER

1. Geographical Coordinate (Lat/long)
2. UTM (Easting) Coordinate
3. UTM (Northing) Coordinate

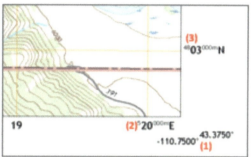

LOWER LEFT CORNER

1. Geographical Coordinate (Lat/long)
2. UTM (Easting) Coordinate
3. Datum Used
4. Revisions

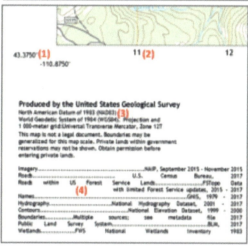

BOTTOM CENTER

1. US National Grid Location (100,000m Square ID & Grid Zone Designation)
2. UTM Grid & Magnetic North Declination
3. Scale in Feet and Meters
4. Quadrangle Map Location and Adjoining Quadrangles
5. Contour Interval

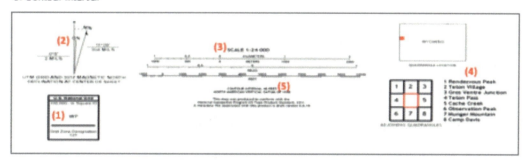

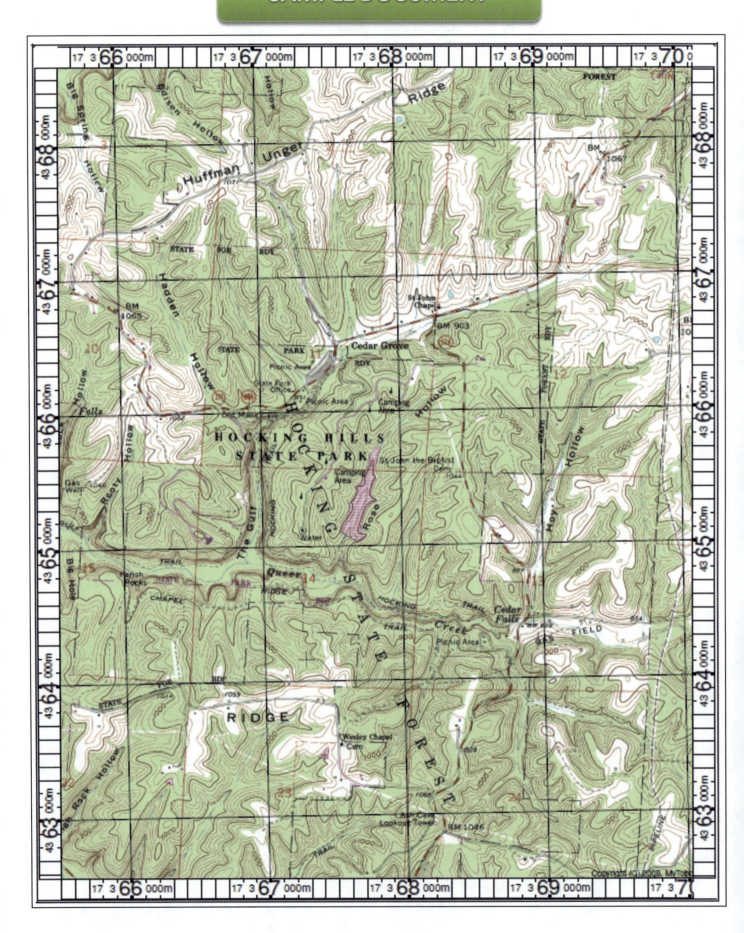

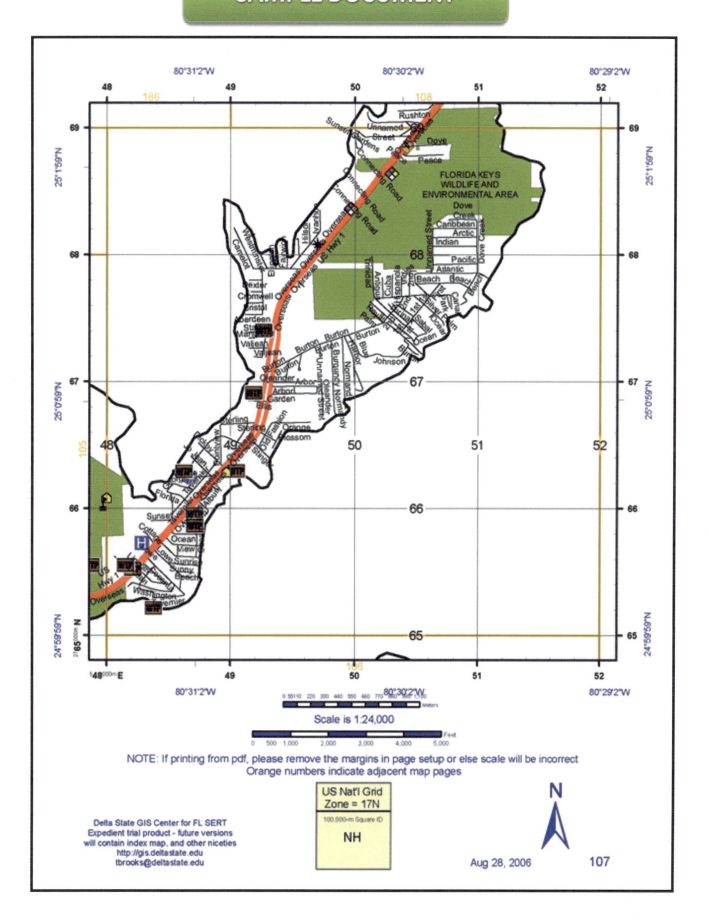

Topographic Map Symbols

What is a Topographic Map?

A map is a representation of the Earth, or part of it. The distinctive characteristic of a topographic map is that the shape of the Earth's surface is shown by contour lines. Contours are imaginary lines that join points of equal elevation on the surface of the land above or below a reference surface, such as mean sea level. Contours make it possible to measure the height of mountains, depths of the ocean bottom, and steepness of slopes.

A topographic map shows more than contours. The map includes symbols that represent such features as streets, buildings, streams, and vegetation. These symbols are constantly refined to better relate to the features they represent, improve the appearance or readability of the map, or reduce production cost.

Consequently, within the same series, maps may have slightly different symbols for the same feature. Examples of symbols that have changed include built-up areas, roads, intermittent drainage, and some lettering styles. On one type of large-scale topographic map, called provisional, some symbols and lettering are hand-drawn.

U.S. Department of the Interior
U.S. Geological Survey

Reading Topographic Maps

Interpreting the colored lines, areas, and other symbols is the first step in using topographic maps. Features are shown as points, lines, or areas, depending on their size and extent. For example, individual houses may be shown as small black squares. For larger buildings, the actual shapes are mapped. In densely built-up areas, most individual buildings are omitted and an area tint is shown. On some maps, post offices, churches, city halls, and other landmark buildings are shown within the tinted area.

The first features usually noticed on a topographic map are the area features, such as vegetation (green), water (blue), and densely built-up areas (gray or red).

Many features are shown by lines that may be straight, curved, solid, dashed, dotted, or in any combination. The colors of the lines usually indicate similar classes of information: topographic contours (brown); lakes, streams, irrigation ditches, and other hydrographic features (blue); land grids and important roads (red); and other roads and trails, railroads, boundaries, and other cultural features (black). At one time, purple was used as a revision color to show all feature changes. Currently, purple is not used in our revision program, but purple features are still present on many existing maps.

Various point symbols are used to depict features such as buildings, campgrounds, springs, water tanks, mines, survey control points, and wells. Names of places and features are shown in a color corresponding to the type of feature. Many features are identified by labels, such as "Substation" or "Golf Course."

Topographic contours are shown in brown by lines of different widths. Each contour is a line of equal elevation; therefore, contours never cross. They show the general shape of the terrain. To help the user determine elevations, index contours are wider. Elevation values are printed in several places along these lines. The narrower intermediate and supplementary contours found between the index contours help to show more details of the land surface shape. Contours that are very close together represent steep slopes. Widely spaced contours or an absence of contours means that the ground slope is relatively level. The elevation difference between adjacent contour lines, called the contour interval, is selected to best show the general shape of the terrain. A map of a relatively flat area may have a contour interval of 10 feet or less. Maps in mountainous areas may have contour intervals of 100 feet or more. The contour interval is printed in the margin of each U.S. Geological Survey (USGS) map.

Bathymetric contours are shown in blue or black, depending on their location. They show the shape and slope of the ocean bottom surface. The bathymetric contour interval may vary on each map and is explained in the map margin.

BATHYMETRIC FEATURES

- Area exposed at mean low tide; sounding datum line***
- Channel***
- Sunken rock***

BOUNDARIES

- National
- State or territorial
- County or equivalent
- Civil township or equivalent
- Incorporated city or equivalent
- Federally administered park, reservation, or monument (external)
- Federally administered park, reservation, or monument (internal)
- State forest, park, reservation, or monument and large county park
- Forest Service administrative area*
- Forest Service ranger district*
- National Forest System land status, Forest Service lands*
- National Forest System land status, non-Forest Service lands*
- Small park (county or city)

BUILDINGS AND RELATED FEATURES

- Building
- School; house of worship
- Athletic field
- Built-up area
- Forest headquarters*
- Ranger district office*
- Guard station or work center*
- Racetrack or raceway
- Airport, paved landing strip, runway, taxiway, or apron
- Unpaved landing strip
- Well (other than water), windmill or wind generator
- Tanks
- Covered reservoir
- Gaging station
- Located or landmark object (feature as labeled)
- Boat ramp or boat access*
- Roadside park or rest area
- Picnic area
- Campground
- Winter recreation area*
- Cemetery

COASTAL FEATURES

- Foreshore flat
- Coral or rock reef
- Rock, bare or awash; dangerous to navigation
- Group of rocks, bare or awash
- Exposed wreck
- Depth curve; sounding
- Breakwater, pier, jetty, or wharf
- Seawall
- Oil or gas well; platform

CONTOURS

Topographic

- Index
- Approximate or indefinite
- Intermediate
- Approximate or indefinite
- Supplementary
- Depression
- Cut
- Fill
- Continental divide

Bathymetric

- Index***
- Intermediate***
- Index primary***
- Primary***
- Supplementary***

CONTROL DATA AND MONUMENTS

- Principal point**
- U.S. mineral or location monument
- River mileage marker

Boundary monument

- Third-order or better elevation, with tablet
- Third-order or better elevation, recoverable mark, no tablet
- With number and elevation

Horizontal control

- Third-order or better, permanent mark
- With third-order or better elevation
- With checked spot elevation
- Coincident with found section corner
- Unmonumented**

CONTROL DATA AND MONUMENTS – *continued*

Vertical control

Third-order or better elevation, with tablet	BM ✕ 5280
Third-order or better elevation, recoverable mark, no tablet	✕ 528
Bench mark coincident with found section corner	BM ⊥ 5280
Spot elevation	✕ 7523

GLACIERS AND PERMANENT SNOWFIELDS

- Contours and limits
- Formlines
- Glacial advance
- Glacial retreat

LAND SURVEYS

Public land survey system

- Range or Township line
  - Location approximate
  - Location doubtful
  - Protracted
  - Protracted (AK 1:63,360-scale)
- Range or Township labels — R1E T2N R3W T4S
- Section line
  - Location approximate
  - Location doubtful
  - Protracted
  - Protracted (AK 1:63,360-scale)
- Section numbers — 1 - 36   1 - 36
- Found section corner
- Found closing corner
- Witness corner — WC
- Meander corner — MC
- Weak corner*

Other land surveys

- Range or Township line
- Section line
- Land grant, mining claim, donation land claim, or tract
- Land grant, homestead, mineral, or other special survey monument
- Fence or field lines

MARINE SHORELINES

- Shoreline
- Apparent (edge of vegetation)***
- Indefinite or unsurveyed

MINES AND CAVES

- Quarry or open pit mine
- Gravel, sand, clay, or borrow pit
- Mine tunnel or cave entrance
- Mine shaft
- Prospect
- Tailings
- Mine dump
- Former disposal site or mine

PROJECTION AND GRIDS

Neatline	39°15' / 90°37'30"
Graticule tick	55'
Graticule intersection	
Datum shift tick	

State plane coordinate systems

Primary zone tick	640 000 FEET
Secondary zone tick	247 500 METERS
Tertiary zone tick	260 000 FEET
Quaternary zone tick	98 500 METERS
Quintary zone tick	320 000 FEET

Universal transverse mercator grid

UTM grid (full grid)	273
UTM grid ticks*	269

RAILROADS AND RELATED FEATURES

- Standard guage railroad, single track
- Standard guage railroad, multiple track
- Narrow guage railroad, single track
- Narrow guage railroad, multiple track
- Railroad siding
- Railroad in highway
- Railroad in road
- Railroad in light duty road*
- Railroad underpass; overpass
- Railroad bridge; drawbridge
- Railroad tunnel
- Railroad yard
- Railroad turntable; roundhouse

RIVERS, LAKES, AND CANALS

- Perennial stream
- Perennial river
- Intermittent stream
- Intermittent river
- Disappearing stream
- Falls, small
- Falls, large
- Rapids, small
- Rapids, large
- Masonry dam
- Dam with lock
- Dam carrying road

RIVERS, LAKES, AND CANALS – *continued*

Perennial lake/pond	
Intermittent lake/pond	
Dry lake/pond	
Narrow wash	
Wide wash	
Canal, flume, or aqueduct with lock	
Elevated aqueduct, flume, or conduit	
Aqueduct tunnel	
Water well, geyser, fumarole, or mud pot	
Spring or seep	

ROADS AND RELATED FEATURES

Please note: Roads on Provisional-edition maps are not classified as primary, secondary, or light duty. These roads are all classified as improved roads and are symbolized the same as light duty roads.

Primary highway	
Secondary highway	
Light duty road	
Light duty road, paved*	
Light duty road, gravel*	
Light duty road, dirt*	
Light duty road, unspecified*	
Unimproved road	
Unimproved road*	
4WD road	
4WD road*	
Trail	
Highway or road with median strip	
Highway or road under construction	
Highway or road underpass; overpass	
Highway or road bridge; drawbridge	
Highway or road tunnel	
Road block, berm, or barrier*	
Gate on road*	
Trailhead*	

* USGS-USDA Forest Service Single-Edition Quadrangle maps only.
In August 1993, the U.S. Geological Survey and the U.S. Department of Agriculture's Forest Service signed an Interagency Agreement to begin a single-edition joint mapping program. This agreement established the coordination for producing and maintaining single-edition primary series topographic maps for quadrangles containing National Forest System lands. The joint mapping program eliminates duplication of effort by the agencies and results in a more frequent revision cycle for quadrangles containing National Forests. Maps are revised on the basis of jointly developed standards and contain normal features mapped by the USGS, as well as additional features required for efficient management of National Forest System lands. Single-edition maps look slightly different but meet the content, accuracy, and quality criteria of other USGS products.

SUBMERGED AREAS AND BOGS

Marsh or swamp	
Submerged marsh or swamp	
Wooded marsh or swamp	
Submerged wooded marsh or swamp	
Land subject to inundation	

SURFACE FEATURES

Levee	
Sand or mud	
Disturbed surface	
Gravel beach or glacial moraine	
Tailings pond	

TRANSMISSION LINES AND PIPELINES

Power transmission line; pole; tower	
Telephone line	
Aboveground pipeline	
Underground pipeline	

VEGETATION

Woodland	
Shrubland	
Orchard	
Vineyard	
Mangrove	

** Provisional-Edition maps only.
Provisional-edition maps were established to expedite completion of the remaining large-scale topographic quadrangles of the conterminous United States. They contain essentially the same level of information as the standard series maps. This series can be easily recognized by the title "Provisional Edition" in the lower right-hand corner.

*** Topographic Bathymetric maps only.

Topographic Map Information

For more information about topographic maps produced by the USGS, please call:
1-888-ASK-USGS or visit us at http://ask.usgs.gov/

ISBN 0-607-96942-3

Printed on recycled paper

UNIT 10 | CLUES & TRACKING

10.1 Clue Consciousness

10.2 The Art of Tracking

10.3 Clues, Signs and Tracks

10.4 Factors That Affect Sign

10.5 Print/Track Documentation

10.6 Tracking Equipment and Clothing

10.7 Human Remains Detection (HRD)

10.8 Lost Track Procedures

> Upon completion of this chapter and the related course activities, the student will be able to meet the following objectives:
> - Identify the qualities of a good searcher
> - Explain the "Three R's of Clue Detection"
> - Define the various clue categories
> - Explain "Wide Angle Vision" and the use of the "Searcher Cube"
> - Identify the various types of "sign"
> - Be able to "age" and document sign
> - Describe the decomposition process

10.1 CLUE CONSCIOUSNESS

What is Clue Consciousness? It is having the training and experience to understand the importance of clues to the overall search effort. We search for clues first and then the subject. There are far more clues out there than subjects. A person will leave thousands of clues in their travels. The key is to be able to find those clues and identify which clues could possibly be found that are related to the subject. Detection and recognition of clues is what separates us, the searcher, from the public or the outdoors enthusiast.

QUALTIES OF A GOOD SEARCHER

- Patience	- Curiosity	- Endurance	- Honed Senses
- Honesty	- Perseverance	- Good Observation Skills	- Inquisitive Mind
- Knowledge of Fauna and Flora	- Good Field Craft Skills	- Mental/Physical Determination	

Knowing where and how to search for clues is vital to the success of locating your missing subject. We should always remember that night searches can also yield clues if the risk does not outweigh the reward. We need to also keep in mind that a lack of clues is still a clue!

> People can't fly!
> If they were there…
> they left clues!

Searcher Mentality

It is very important that the searcher be mentally as well as physically prepared to search.
Low morale or personal issues that are adding stress can decrease a searcher's performance. The environment can not only limit your field of vision, it can have an emotional effect as well. Gloomy and dreary weather conditions, being cold and hungry or physically drained will also hinder a searcher's ability to perform.

Clue Orientation Theory is the ability to logically theorize the correlation of a clue to the specific lost subject in a methodical manner. This is learned skill and comes with training and experience. Unless searchers train to detect and recognize those subtle signs, they may see something but fail to recognize its meaning or importance.

Visual Attention

Humans pay attention visually in three different ways: [2]

- **Selective** - Attending to one task over another.

- **Divided** - Only one cognitive process occurs efficiently at a time.

- **Automatic** - Visual attention does not require focus.

When a Clue is Found

Once you have noticed something of importance and have investigated it, you will need to decide if the clue is relevant. If we reported every little bit of "trail trash," we would be searching for years. That is why it is important to categorize the clues we find.

The 3 R's When a Clue is Found

- **R**eport the find to command: They will let you know what (if anything) to do with it.

- **R**ecord: Make a note of what you found, specifically where (to the nearest detail).

- **R**esume: Get on with your search (unless command advises otherwise)
  You are looking for a person remember!

Clue Categories

Clues can be classified into four basic categories. The first are **physical clues**. These are clues that are tangible such as a footprint or a piece of the missing subject's equipment that was discarded. The next type of clues are **recorded clues**. These are clues about the subject that have been recorded in the Missing Person Questionnaire or statistical data that can be applied to the missing subject such as their medical condition or appropriate speed table.

The next type of clues are **people clues**. These are the people who have witnessed the subject or may have been in a similar situation in the same environment. The final type of clues are the **event clues**. These are events that have led up to the subject being missing. [3]

There are some general principles that can be applied to clue awareness:

- Clue awareness begins with the preplanning of searches and ends with the final debriefing of the searchers.

- All clues should have equal weight until they can be positively identified and evaluated. Do not form opinions about the search, and then look for clues to support your opinions.

- The primary skill of being "clue aware" is improved through training and practice.

- There is only one missing person, but numerous clues. Looking for the person gives us only one chance of success, while looking for clues can give hundreds of chances.

Assuming the search area contains the missing person, all the clues needed to locate him or her are also in the search area. Most unsuccessful searches are the result of clues going unnoticed or unreported. Different resources usually have different abilities to detect clues. Area searchers, including trackers, dogs, and hasty teams are generally the most successful in locating clues. Aircraft and grid searchers are usually only good for locating subjects. Grid searching is usually used only as a last resort since the nature of grid searching will destroy all clues in an area. Everywhere that you travel during your search assignments you must be looking for clues. Search managers depend on clues to give us a direction of travel.

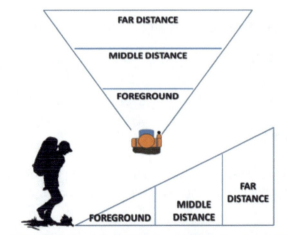

(Fig. 10-1) Example of how to split the visual area into manageable segments. Image courtesy of J. Bobot.

Wide Angle Vision

Wide Angle Vision is the ability to view your

surroundings in its entirety while keeping from getting "tunnel" vision. It is also being able to see motion, standout objects from your peripheral vision as well as your foreground vision (Fig. 10-1). The key is to divide the visual area. Take an area and divide it into three areas: foreground, middle distance and far distance. Scan each area prior to moving forward. If something of interest is seen – investigate.

The Searcher Clue Detection Aid

The searcher perceives sensory impressions indicating presence of object. You see it, hear it, touch it, smell it... it stands out as something being worthy of investigation.

A detection aid is used to help you process the images you are looking at is called the searcher cube. Imagine you are inside a glass cube. The cube has six fields of view, forward, backward, right, left, up and down. You need to search as this cube is hovering along with you.

To improve detection, keep your mind on the job while searching. Don't worry about where other teams are or what they are doing.

Have an idea (through proper investigation and interviews) what you are looking for and utilize the Searcher Cube. (Fig. 10-2) After negotiating a hazard, stop, zone back in, continue and avoid target fixation. [4]

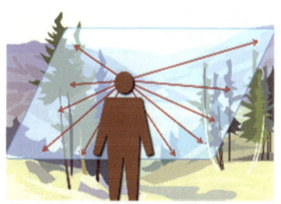

(Fig. 10-2) The Searcher Cube. Image courtesy of J. Bobot

When looking and searching in your "cube" take each direction (six in all) and direct your foveal field (snapshot gaze) and cover all aspects of the surface areas within the plane (Fig. 10-3). It helps to allow those things that "don't belong" to pop out and grab your attention. When this occurs, investigate.

(Fig. 10-3) Example of a searcher splitting up a side of the cube into near, middle, and far segments as they scan. Image courtesy of J. Bobot.

The fovea is the part of the eye that send clear, sharp images back to the brain. The foveal field of view is one to two degrees of the entire visual area. [5] In complex environments, the eye rarely detects on the first pass. Your peripheral vision detects light, color & movement well. Enhanced detection through scanning is the mark of a great SAR technician and takes practice and concentration.

Detection Variables

There are many variables that can limit or enhance a searcher's ability to detect clues. A searcher needs to be aware of these variables in order to adjust to them in the field. This is the most important task a searcher has - the ability to detect clues. [6]

Hard to See: (non-moving, low contrast & small size) means that it would be more difficult to detect.

- Mobility – Is the missing person moving?

- Color – Pink has been proven to be the most difficult color to detect in any given terrain.

- Size – Can vary from as small as a bent blade of grass to the subject themselves.

Environment: More obstructions, low visibility and difficult terrain mean that an object would be more difficult to detect.

- Terrain – How difficult is the terrain to travel over. Because the more difficult it is, the more time you'll spend concentrating on it rather than searching.

- Blinds – Trees, buildings, undulating landscapes.

- Visibility – Rain, snow, wind, or all three, or all three at night!

Sensor: A limited, poor quality and attitude sensor means that the subject would be more difficult to detect.

- Limitations – Using the right sensor for the job. Don't use dogs where there would be no scent. Don't use helicopter FLIR in dense woodland etc.

- Attitude – Remember back to our preparedness discussion and the rationalizations and attitudes we talked about?

- Skills– How well trained is your sensor? What are its best qualities?

Recognition

- Interpretations of impressions to determine their source and cause. You recognize the object as being relevant to your task. Without recognition, detection is of no value!

10.2 THE ART OF TRACKING

Tracking is the act of following someone by stringing together a continuous chain of their sign. It has been suggested that the art of tracking may have been the first implementation of science, practiced by hunter-gatherers since the evolution of modern humans. [7] Apart from knowledge based on direct observations of animals, trackers gain a detailed understanding of animal behavior through the interpretation of sign and track.

In this way, much information can be obtained that would otherwise remain unknown, especially on the behavior of rare or nocturnal animals that are not often seen. This applies to the searching of people as well. They, too, have specific behaviors and are essentially two-legged animals.

Mantracking is a term used to describe the art of following a person on foot. The use of tracking in Search and Rescue has gained popularity in the past few years for several reasons. One of those reasons is because mantracking has proven to be a valuable resource that may help shorten the search. Another reason is the increased availability of tracking certifications and training, thus making trained mantrackers more available as a resource. Reading this text will not make you a "tracker." [8]

Mantracking is an art and like any art requires hours of training and practice. This section will give you the basic skills to identify a track and document it. As searchers, our goal is to help locate a lost individual. But it's important to understand that we are not just looking for a person.

10.3 CLUES, SIGNS AND TRACKS

We should be looking for any physical indication that the lost individual has left behind. A **clue** is a piece of evidence or information used in the detection of a crime or solving of a mystery. **Sign** is any physical evidence, not limited to footfalls, of a person's passage or presence. Sign can be as easy to identify as a hat or candy wrapper; or as difficult to spot as a broken twig or foot impression. Some examples of sign:

- Sap from a bruised tree trunk or root.

- Disturbance in animal, bird, or insect life (broken spider webs are a great indicator of passage).

- Changes in color of vegetation due to disturbances.

- A lack of moisture or dew on vegetation.

- Mud, soil, or sand on vegetation.

- Bruising, breaks or cuts on vegetation.

There are a few more terms that you should be familiar with when dealing with sign.

- **Ground Litter** is the unmistakable sign of recent movement in a given area.

- **Ground Signs** are ground-level marks or disturbances like a footprint.

- **Top Sign** is defined as any sign above the ankle like bent grass. When tracking, we need to look for characteristics or patterns.

A **Sign Pattern** is the sign that serves to indicate the habits or particularities of the subject like a drag mark. Identification as either the **prime** (or conclusive) sign, also called "good" sign or the sign that is being followed or **secondary** (or substantiating) sign, which is all other sign, prints, tracks, etc. that MAY be linked to the subject.

Sign Cutting is the most efficient way of locating clues quickly. It is also one of the most difficult skills to learn. A basic description of sign cutting is the process of looking for clues a person passed through an area by cutting across his presumed or know direction of travel at right angles. The ground must be thoroughly gone over for **tracks**, a series of sign left from the passage of a person that can be positively identified, such as footprints. This should yield clues about the location of the subject. [9]

Key Identifiers of a Track

- T - Toe Digs
- R - Rock Rolls
- A - Angles, shapes

C - Compression

K - Kick Marks [heel]

With sign cutting, a series of clues can be identified that will provide the ever valuable "direction of travel" (Fig. 10-4). If no clues are found, this may indicate the subject is not in the search area, and the search area should be changed or expanded. Although sign cutting has some limitations in terms of thoroughness, the speed with which it can be done more than offsets this limitation. In most cases, time is a critical factor in locating the missing person. It is better to locate a portion of the clues that may lead to the missing person quickly than to spend all your time trying to find every clue in the search area. A few clues found can be enough to determine the subject's direction of travel.

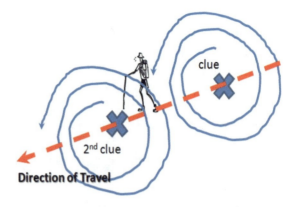

(Fig. 10-4) How sign cutting can lead to the determination of the subject's direction of travel. Image courtesy of J. Bobot.

It is important to remember that every person, even one that does not want to be found, is a clue generator. This is particularly true for tracks. Your ability to locate and identify these clues will directly affect the outcome of the search.

Sign Indicators

Visual clues lead a searcher to investigate. There are several things that can make up a visual clue. The first is the outline or outer edge of the sign. The shape or its special formation usually comes into view next. The color or hues will be noticed in the sign such as being darker or lighter compared to its surroundings. Contrast is closely related to the color and the hue allowing you to make a visual comparison. Upon closer examination, texture may be noted such as a change in the surface characteristics like the roughness or smoothness. Lastly how does the light interact with the sign. Is there a shadow or reflection in the sign? Remember that just like we look for clues and then the missing subjects, we look for sign before we look for track. [10]

(Fig. 10-5) Example of sign pointers. Image courtesy of J. Bobot.

We look for sign pointers (Fig. 10-5) that help with direction of travel or "point" to areas needing further investigation. **Sign transfer** is when material is moved from its original resting place to another location by the passage of a person or object (Fig. 10-6) and can sometimes aid in the determination of the subject's direction of travel.

(Fig. 10-6) Example of sign transfer. Image courtesy of J. Bobot.

Track traps can improve the searcher's chance of detecting a print or track in an area of ground (Fig. 10-7). These are areas of loose or sandy ground or "cuttable" areas in a segment where the searcher can cut for sign. These are also areas where you would find wet sand, mud, soft dirt, snow that can indicate that a person has passed through this area by leaving prints in the trap material. Man-made track traps are made by scraping an area clean so as to show sign easily and can be returned to at a later time.

(Fig. 10-7) Two trails merge with loose red soil. A perfect "Track Trap". Image courtesy of Daniel Case.

10.4 FACTORS THAT AFFECT SIGN

Prints and tracks depend greatly on the condition of the ground and the weather. A searcher needs to know some basics when searching for sign in various terrains and conditions. The geographical features of the terrain can help or hinder you in your search for sign. [11]

Grasslands, Fields, and Open Areas

If you know what you are looking for, grass is a great indicator of passage. The first and last 45 minutes of the day, when the sun is low or at night will give you the best chance of seeing passage through grassy areas. Higher grass, above your ankle will be pressed down and form a pointer in the direction the subject was going. Tall grass will stay down for a considerable length of time, depending on the weather. Shorter grass will "spring" back up sooner.

Grass also presents a contrast in color to the normal undergrowth when pressed down. Dew, from the night before may also be wiped off by the passage of a person. If the subject has mud on their shoes, bits may be found on top of the blades of grass.

Rocky Ground

Rocky ground sounds like it would be impossible to find a print or track. The key is to stop looking for a footprint in these conditions. If you tell yourself to search for a footprint, you will miss the signs that you can see. Sometimes there will be no print at all, but if you're using your tracking stick to find the next footfall, it may be evident by a disturbance or displacement of a rock. A flanker cutting for sign may also notice rock displacement, thereby allowing the tracking team to move ahead. A displaced rock may still be embedded in its original spot, but you might find that it's been pushed slightly away from the dirt that was once right up against it.

The location of this resulting space caused by the person pushing off as he or she walked will indicate direction of travel.

- Look for mini-track traps in the fine dust or dirt around rocks or outcroppings.
- Look at color changes in the stones.
- Look for stones that may have been overturned.
- Look for scratches or scuffs made by boots or other equipment like a trekking pole or

steel-tipped walking stick.

- Watch for any moss or lichen that have been displaced or rubbed off.

- Check for bruising on any small vegetation that has been growing up between the cracks.

Forested Areas

There are many aids and pointers in the forest from dry and damp soils, young vegetation, moss, dead and decaying wood and plants, trees, and bushes. Leaves on the ground make great pointers, especially when they are wet. Since there are more things to grab your attention, it helps if you look through the forest, not at it and make sure you split your cube sides into near, middle and far distances for better processing.

- Look at leaves that have been disturbed; they tend to show up darker compared to the ones around them.

- Broken twigs in a subtle impression can indicate the passage of a person.

- Pine needles can display a swirling pattern when walked through.

- There are also many places for sign to transfer on to other components of the forest like mud on logs and leaves.

Light

Lighting is so important when tracking - it can make the difference between seeing a very clear track and seeing no track at all. Shadows really make a track stand out. One would think that tracking would be better during the daylight hours. This is not necessarily the case. Tracking is easier at night than it is in full sun because a flashlight at a low angle to the ground can create significant shadows on any track that's in or near you (Fig. 10-8).

A lower intensity flashlight helps maintain night vision and reduce eye strain, but on a brightly moonlit night, a brighter flashlight might be necessary. An LED flashlight will "wash" a larger area with light instead of flooding a small area in the case of a standard flashlight.

(Fig. 10-8) Example of how low-angle light sources will cause shadows in impressions. Image courtesy of J. Bobot.

When tracking during the day, early morning and late afternoon are the best times to do so because the sun is at a lower angle and creates more shadows. Positioning yourself towards the sun can help you see the shadows more easily, or you can try using a wide-brim hat to shade the track and then use a flashlight or a mirror (from a compass perhaps) to redirect light onto it. It's amazing how this can make a track just pop right out when it might otherwise be invisible.

Time

Time is another factor that affects sign. Only experience and practice can help a searcher to be able to determine the age of sign. Shape and outline play an important part here. Fresh sign is usually clean and have crisp, sharp edges.

if you are able to, make a clean boot print in an area where the ground is soft and a little moist (not wet), go back and check the print in an hour, then after 12 hours and then 24 hours later. Make a new print each time you go and do side-by-side comparisons **(Fig. 10-9)**.

As time goes on, those edges and sides will start to fall back into the impression and the print will slowly fill up with the dirt, water, and debris.

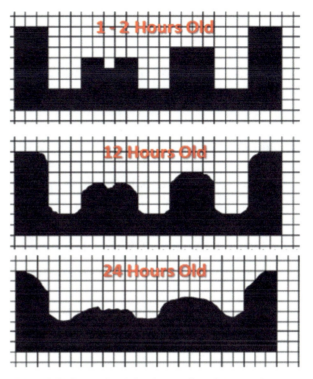

(Fig. 10-9) Example of the decay of a print over time. Image courtesy of J. Bobot.

Additional Observations

In addition to actual tracks, shine, disturbances, or rock displacements, you should always keep an eye out of additional clues. For example, if you know the person you're tracking is a smoker, watch for cigarette butts. Trail bar or candy wrappers are another type of clue. There may be blood droplets if someone has been injured.

Look for broken twigs or branches, water splashed on rocks, pieces or threads from clothing, dried mud that's fallen off someone's shoes, dew or frost trails, toilet paper or even human waste. The possibilities for clues are great, so watch for anything that "doesn't belong."

10.5 PRINT/TRACK DOCUMENTATION

The searcher will form a tracking picture of the area he/she is looking at. It should be like a story to the tracker. The tracking picture builds from one sign to the next until the searcher is able to identify the subject through the sign and can predict, to some degree, the next sign. Sign pointers aid the searcher in determining the direction of travel of the track. These pointers can be ground or top sign.

Prints refers to the marks, indentations or other sign left in the ground or material by the passage of a person or vehicle. Prints fall into one of three categories:

- **Complete Print**- The entire impression is visible.

- **Partial Print** - Not visible in its entirety.

- **Identifiable Print**- Whether complete or partial, it has at least one characteristic that differentiates it from others similar to it.

Once a print is found, the first step is to identify it on the ground. Once this is done, the print is marked in the ground by the searcher's trekking pole and the area "flagged" with flagging tape after notifying command. Next is to determine if the print is a full or partial print and marking it on the ground. The print is then checked for orientation, is it a "right" or "left" print. This is done by looking at the in-step of the print. [12]

10.6 TRACKING EQUIPMENT & CLOTHING

Like any job, you need the tools of the trade… [13]

Tracking Clothing

- Should be appropriate for the terrain and weather.
- Should be durable to withstand dense brush and rugged terrain - yet promote comfort.
- Broad-brimmed hat may protect eyes from the sun or shade tracks when the sun is high.

Tracking Equipment, Walking or Sign Cutting Stick

- A must, especially for novice trackers.
- Should be light and durable and approx. 40 inches long.
- Should have at least two "O"-rings or rubber bands on it for measuring distance and stride.

Tracking Equipment, Measuring Device

- Such as a tape measure, to measure print size or stride
- Some attach a measuring tape to their stick.
- Most simply carry a seamstress tape which is easily bent and light weight!

Tracking Equipment, Small Notepad, and Pencil

- Needed to record measurements and fill out track reports.
- A good drawing of a print will be indispensable.

Tracking Equipment, Trail Tape

- Can be carried to cordon off evidence or sign or prevent the trampling of a good track.
- Plastic surveyor's or flagging tape works well (Fig. 10-10).
- Must be retrieved after it has served its purpose.

(Fig. 10-13) Example the trail (or flagging) tape. Flagging comes in a wide-range of colors and can be tied to anything to mark a location. Image courtesy of J. Bobot.

Tracking Equipment, Flashlight

- Can be important when light is not optimum.
- Obviously, important aid to sight when on

mission.

- Good artificial light source.

Tracking Equipment, Other

- Clue Containers: Zip-Loc storage bags to keep non-scent clues safe and able to take back to base.

10.7 HUMAN REMAINS DETECTION (HRD)

This is not the most favorable task a searcher has to do; however, we need to treat these missions with the same professionalism, compassion, and effort as we would a missing child. The family of the deceased cannot continue on through the grieving process until they have closure. [14]

This means that someone needs to recover the remains of their loved one. Before we address the skills and tactics of detecting human remains, we need to have some background on how and what searchers should be searching for.

Decomposition, or rotting, is the process by which tissues of a dead organism break down into simpler forms of matter. Bodies of living organisms begin to decompose shortly after death. It is a cascade of processes that go through distinct phases. It may be categorized in two stages by the types of end products.

Most individuals do not have experience with human remains in various states of decomposition.

The first stage is characterized by the formation of liquid materials; flesh matter begins to decompose. The second stage is limited to the production of vapors. Besides the two stages mentioned above, historically the progression of decomposition of the flesh of dead organisms is viewed in phases. [15]

Phase 1: Fresh - No discoloration or insect activity.

Phase 2: Early Decomposition - Pink-white appearance with skin slippage and some hair loss as well as possible bloating and leathery appearance of the skin.

Phase 3: Active decay - This is characterized by the period of greatest mass loss, resulting from the voracious feeding of maggots, as well as from the purging of decomposition fluids into the surrounding environment. The purged fluids accumulate around the body and create a cadaver decomposition island (CDI). Liquefaction of tissues and disintegration become apparent during this time and strong odors persist.

Phase 4: Advanced Decomposition - Decomposition of tissues causes sagging flesh, caving in of the abdominal cavity, often accompanied by extensive maggot activity. There is also some bone exposure and mummification.

Phase 5: Dry/Remains - During the dry/remains stage, the resurgence of plant growth around the CDI may occur and is a sign that the nutrients present in the surrounding soil have not yet returned to their normal levels. All that remains of the cadaver at this stage is dry skin, cartilage, and bones, which will become dry and bleached if exposed to the elements. If all soft tissue is removed from the cadaver, it will be referred to as completely skeletonized, but if only portions of the bones are exposed, it will be referred to as partially skeletonized.

While it is important to understand the process of decomposition, it is equally important to understand that the rate of decomposition is affected by several variables. These variables in descending order of influence are: temperature, access by insects, burial and depth, carnivores, trauma, humidity, rainfall, body size, clothing (incomplete list). Searchers who are experienced in locating human remains understand, for example, how well human remains can blend into the baseline environment. A briefing about human decomposition, and how it may appear, may increase the chances that said remains will be detected.

The role of domestic dogs in scavenging of remains cannot be underestimated. Dogs have been observed carrying bones up to a quarter mile or more from the body, often back to their home or neighborhood. This is an important field consideration. When searching in areas adjacent to domestic dog populations, backyards should be searched for bones.

In general, the process of skeletal disarticulation by canines is generally consistent. Scavenging animals usually show the following signs:

- Early scavenging of soft tissue with no removal of the body pieces within four hours to 14 days.

- Destruction of the thorax accompanied by evisceration and removal of one or both upper extremities including the scapula within 22 days to two and half months.

- Lower extremities are fully or partially removed within two to four and a half months.

- All skeletal elements disarticulated except for segments of the vertebral column within two to 11 months.

- Total disarticulation with only the cranium and other assorted skeletal elements or fragments recovered within five to 52 months.

10.8 LOST TRACK PROCEDURES

The first thing a tracker needs to do is to locate the last known location of the person sought. This can be a sighting of the individual, or it could be the location of their last known tracks and sign. Upon arrival at the indicated area if the specific tracks and sign need to be located, the tracker should begin a search procedure. This first search procedure will give them the starting track and sign.

The tracker will first try to identify a location most likely to yield tracks or sign and then begin conducting an initial spiral (circle) search. As the tracker conducts this first search, they will look for any micro track traps and any indicators along their search path. This initial search will give the trackers their first tracks and sign and a beginning point to establish an initial likely direction of travel from that point.

Track-Following Procedure

After the tracker has found his starting point, he will then mark the track and sign on the ground and map and call in this location. The tracker will then commence his track following procedures. The tracker will follow the tracks and sign and establish the direction of travel of the person sought.

While following the line of sign the tracker will attempt to maximize the effects of light to aid in identifying and seeing tracks and sign. To do this the tracker will position himself so that the tracks are between the sunlight (light source) and their own position. The tracker will also attempt to preserve the tracks and sign he is following by staying to the side and avoiding stepping directly on the sign while tracking. While tracking the tracker will not go past his last confirmed track or sign.

The tracker will look as far ahead as possible, ideally at least 20-30 yards, to identify tracks and sign along the direction of travel to advance the tracking team along the sign as fast and accurately as possible.

If the tracker is part of a tracking team (Fig. 10-11) or duo they can work together using a cross-track procedure. This is where one tracker is following the track and the second tracker can hastily flank and attempt to "cross" or intersect the line of sign further along the direction of travel to speed up the location and following of the sign.

Special thanks to Mark Sexton of Vista Tracking for the following guidelines...

Lost Track

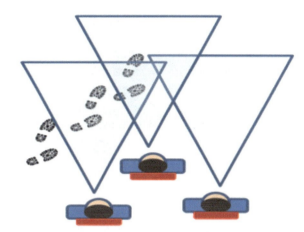

(Fig. 10-14) Example of a tracking team concept. The person in the front is on "point" with two flankers behind and off-set. This allows for multiple searchers to have the chance of detecting tracks.
Image courtesy of J. Bobot.

Step 1: Quick Scan - When the tracker can no longer see track and sign in front of him he will need to conduct a quick but thorough visual search or scan all around him to see if the subject has made a sudden turn or the tracker has accidentally gone past the last actual track or sign. If, after conducting this deliberate quick search, the tracker has not relocated the sign, the first search procedure should be conducted.

Step 2: First sign search procedure - Accordion Search Technique - The first search the tracker and tracker team will likely conduct is an individual search. The first search technique that may be employed is known as the Accordion Search Technique by SAR.

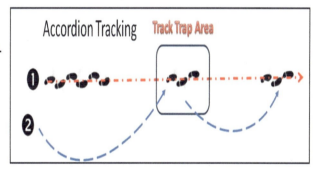

The accordion search can be particularly effective when used on or along linear terrain features such as trails and rivers. When utilized, the track or sign is temporarily marked on the ground by the tracker or team member standing next to the sign without damaging or destroying it.

The searching tracker will then determine the most likely direction of travel and move forward along the direction of travel. The tracker will ideally locate and examine any track traps during the search process.

As the tracker or team member moves forward from the last known track or sign, they will search both sides of the direction of travel. The tracker will stay alert to detect any indicators that the subject has moved off the line of travel in a new direction. If, during the search, the tracker detects sign of the subject the other team members are alerted and the tracker and team members continue the track line.

If the track is not detected, the tracker can continue their search by extending the accordion tracking technique further or they can return to their last known sign or track and implement a second track recovery procedure.

Step 3: Leap Frogging - An alternative to the Accordion Search Technique. The Leap-Frog technique is useful when the tracker does not have another team member to either mark the last known sign or to move forward to next track trap, skipping any tracks in between.

Leap frogging is generally considered more than 20 - 30 yards and out of visual sight of the area of the last known sign. The tracker, after having marked the last known track or sign, will move forward, as in the accordion method, looking for track traps and track and sign along the most likely direction travel.

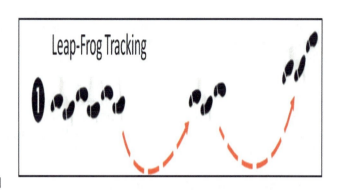

Step 4: Spiral Search - The tracker may decide to conduct the second search procedure, a spiral (circular) search. The spiral search can be done in the event the direction of travel of the subject cannot be determined. Other conditions that may indicate a circular search are areas fouled or devoid of any discernible tracks and sign. When conducting a circular search, the tracker will begin by moving back off the last known track or sign by two to three yards, looking for indicators the subject turned off the trail and the tracker had missed the turn.

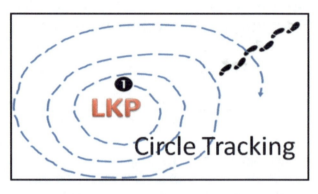

After the tracker has determined that the subject has not made a sudden turn, the next step is to begin a circular pattern search in the most likely direction of travel. The search will start small and then progressively increase in diameter with each repetition as the tracker passes the last known sign.

Another variation is to conduct the initial circle wide and then decrease the size of the circle moving progressively inward based on terrain and circumstances. With the increasing circle an ever-larger area has been covered as the tracker searches into unexamined areas. The circle search conducted by decreasing the circle area progressively inward has the advantage of going back over in more detail areas searched until near the last known track or sign.

As a tracker searches along the circular pattern, they will examine any track traps or areas that may yield confirmatory track evidence such as the outsole pattern of the subject. The key is to verify any substantiating or vegetative sign with ground sign. If the tracker relies solely on substantiating sign such as vegetation and disturbed stones or scuffs, etc., they will need to proceed carefully forward and in a cautionary mode until they confirm that the sign is that of their subject, either by finding physical evidence (such as an article of clothing or other articles) or confirmatory sign such as a full or partial track.

FOOTNOTES

(1) Bannerman, Foster, Hill, Hood, Thrasher & Wolf, (1999). Introduction to Search & Rescue. National Association for Search & Rescue.

(2) Reynolds JH, Chelazzi L, Desimone R (1999) Competitive mechanisms subserve attention in macaque areas V2 and V4. J Neurosci 19:1736–1753

(3) Bannerman, Foster, Hill, Hood, Thrasher & Wolf, (1999). Introduction to Search & Rescue. National Association for Search & Rescue.

(4) "Searching the Cube – An analysis of basic searcher scanning techniques and Training" by R "Skip" and Brett C. Stoffel.

(5) Masayuki Iwasaki and Hajime Inomara.(1986). "Investigative Ophthalmology & Visual Science" (journal), volume 27.

(6) SEBEV Search & Rescue, BERKSHIRE, UK. (2010) "LSART - Search Techniques".

(7) Robbins, R. (1977). "Mantracking: Introduction to the Step-By-Step Method", National Association For Search and Rescue.

(8) Carss, B. (2000). "The SAS Guide to Tracking".

(9) "Sign Cutting and Tracking Methods Employed by the US Border Patrol". By Jose J. Soto

(10) Carss, B. (2000). "The SAS Guide to Tracking".

(11) Liebenberg, L.W. (1990). The Art of Tracking: The Origin of Science. Cape Town: David Philip.

(12) Gilcraft's Training in Tracking, C. Arther Pearson LTD. Published by Tower House, London, 1944

(13) "Man-Tracking 101: How to Find and Follow Tracks for Search and Rescue", Equipment. Deb Kingsbury

(14) Gleason, Mark. (2008) "The Search for Human Remains in the Search and Rescue Environment". Search & Rescue Tracking Institute.

(15) Haglund, William. (1997). "Scattered Skeletal Human Remains: Search Strategy Considerations for Locating Missing Teeth, Forensic Taphonomy: The Postmortem Fate of Human Remains"

(16) Bruce Berg. (2008). "Criminal Investigation, 4th edition".

VITAL VOCABULARY

Clue Orientation Theory: This is the ability to logically theorize the correlation of a clue to the specific lost subject in a methodical manner.

Clue: This is a piece of information used in the detection of a crime or solving of a mystery.

Decomposition: (or rotting) The process by which tissues of a dead organism break down into simpler forms of matter.

Event Clues: These are events that have led up to the subject being missing.

Fovea: Is a part of the eye, located in the center of the macula region of the retina responsible for sharp central vision (also called foveal vision).

Ground Litter: This is the unmistakable signs of recent movement in a given area.

Ground Sign: These are ground-level marks or disturbances like a footprint.

Liquefaction: This often involves organic tissue turning into a more liquid state.

Mantracking: This is a term used to describe the art of following a person on foot.

People Clues: These are the people who have witnessed the subject or may have been in a similar situation in the same environment.

Physical Clues: These are clues that are tangible, such as a footprint or a piece of the missing subject's equipment that was discarded.

Prints: This refers to the marks, indentations or other sign left in the ground or material by the passage of a person or vehicle.

Recorded Clues: These are clues about the subject that have been recorded in the Missing Person Questionnaire or statistical data.

Searcher Cube: Is an imaginary cube that surrounds the searcher to aid in his scanning for clues by remembering to look up, down, left, right and forward & backward - all six planes of a cube.

Sign Cutting: Is the process of looking for clues of a person that has passed through an area by cutting across the presumed or known direction of travel at right angles.

Sign Pattern: This is the sign that serves to indicate the habits or particularities of the subject like a drag mark.

Sign: Is any physical evidence, not limited to footfalls, of a person's passage or presence.

Skeletonization: Refers to the complete decomposition of the non-bony tissues of a corpse, leading to a bare skeleton.

Top Sign: This is defined as any sign above the ankle like bent grass.

Track: Is a series of sign left from the passage of a person that can be positively identified, such as a footprint.

Tracking: Is the act of following someone by stringing together a continuous chain of their sign.

Wide Angle Vision: Is the ability to view your surroundings in it entirety while keeping from getting "tunnel" vision.

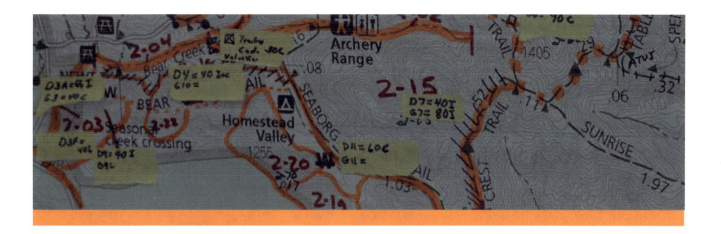

UNIT 11 | SEARCH TACTICS

11.1 Responsibilities of a Searcher

11.2 Types of Search Tactics

11.3 Search Team Types

11.4 Vehicle Search

11.5 Evidence Handling

11.6 Deceased Subjects

11.7 Searching for Bodies in Water

11.8 Urban Missing Person Search

Upon completion of this chapter and the related course activities, the student will be able to meet the following objectives:

- Define the two types of "search tactics"
- Define the various "active" Search tactics
- Explain the concept of "likely spots"
- Explain the four phases of avalanche survival
- Identify the method used in air search operations
- Identify the method of processing a vehicle
- Explain the concept of "Chain of Custody"

11.1 Responsibilities of a Searcher

The key to a successful search and rescue mission depends greatly on the searchers in the field **(Fig. 11-1)**. They must be able to apply the proper search techniques to detect and recognize clues that will lead to the missing subject. We have addressed the detecting and recognizing the clues, and in this unit, we will address tactics a search planner can deploy into the field. The search tactics can be divided into two types, active and passive. The more we can understand the concepts and tactics within these two groups, the more effective we will be as searchers.

Before a searcher deploys into the field they need to understand their responsibilities while on scene.

(Fig. 11-1) Volunteer searchers Jerry Whaley (left), Matt Thatcher (center) and Matt Evans (right). Image courtesy of J. Bobot

Required Tactical Skills

- Searcher safety is #1.
- Maintain concentration on the task at hand.
- Search for clues within YOUR assigned area.
- Maintain a positive attitude.
- Know whom you are looking for and their description.
- Know capabilities of the members of your crew.
- Have a backup plan for "what if's" and the "Murphys".

There are certainly more if we were to break every aspect down, however, these are the general responsibilities that should be understood:

- Be ready PRIOR to your callout.
- Take all necessary equipment.
- Follow all check-in procedures.
- Get your assignment & briefing.
- Ensure your radio works.
- Organize and brief subordinates.
- Complete missions as directed.
- Debrief immediately upon return.

- Be rested and ready to go back out.
- Demobilize according to plan.

11.2 Types of Search Tactics

The two types of overall search tactics that are deployed in a search are: [1]

- "searching for the subject" approach (**active search tactics**)
- "subject seeking searcher" approach (**passive search tactics**).

Passive Search Tactics

The first of these tactics and one of the most important of the passive tactics is confinement/containment. We must do everything within our ability to keep the missing subject within the search area.

Just as important, we need to deploy resources that can let the planners and IC know if and when the subject leaves the search area. Often this is where you can utilize less-trained volunteers to sit or post at typical travel or exit points and monitor these areas for the missing subject who may walk out and into view. This is also where extra law enforcement resources can be used to patrol perimeter roads.

Passive Search Tactics

- Confinement & Containment
    - Secure the perimeter with patrols
    - String and arrow deployment
- Attention getting
    - Emergency lights and sirens
    - Bonfires
    - Whistles and bullhorns
    - Missing Person Flyer
- Investigation
    - Interviews
    - Phone banks
    - Historical data

Another passive technique is to draw the attention of the missing subject. Those vehicles posted in key locations conducting containment and confinement can also use emergency siren, horns, or whistles that the subject, if nearby can hear and have something to direct them to a safe area. These audible signals need to be at a regular interval. Visual signals may include emergency lighting, a campfire at night or smoke during the day.

Investigation is the last of the passive techniques, but in no way any less important that the others. The collection of data is vital to the planner who is taking all the information gathered and putting a search plan into place. Investigation should occur both initially as well as an ongoing assignment. The National Association of Search and Rescue (NASAR) states that the lack of proper investigation continues to be a major problem during many search incidents.

One of the most important investigation tools is the Missing Person Questionnaire - This document is used to record of specific information gathered about the lost subject. This is also a chance for the search planning team to connect with the family. In addition, family support systems should be activated and part of the interview process, which could include a chaplain or a family liaison officer. During this process, we sometimes get more information than we need from the family or that is relative to the task at hand.

Active Search Tactics

These are the "boots on the ground" or "people in the field" approaches that generate clues that the planner will use to first determine a direction of travel and then use to deploy future search teams. When searchers are in the field, it is not necessary that each person walk a straight line.

When searchers are walking in a **"purposefully wandering"** fashion they are free to investigate things that grab their attention **(Fig. 11-2)**. This prevents them from focusing on walking a straight line. The only thing that is required is that they "guide" off someone or something to help them stay on course. This method of walking is called purposefully wandering where each searcher tries to maintain their sweep width.

(Fig. 11-2) Example of a searcher "purposefully wandering". Image courtesy of J. Bobot.

Active Search Deployments

There are search tactics that include several organized methods used in the search area to detect a lost subject or clues. These consist of:

- Rapid/Hasty Search
- Area Search
- Route Search
- Loose grid techniques
- Tight grid techniques
- Evidence searches

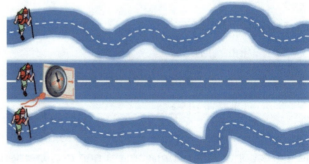

(Fig. 11-3) Example of an area search, guiding off a compass heading. Image courtesy of J. Bobot.

- Continuous Limited Search

A **rapid/hasty search** usually refers to the efforts very early on of search areas immediately surrounding the last known point.

An **area search** is a search that has been assigned to team of five to seven trained searchers. This assignment directs the team to guide along an identifiable compass heading for a defined distance **(Fig. 11-3)**.

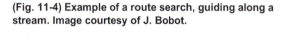

(Fig. 11-4) Example of a route search, guiding along a stream. Image courtesy of J. Bobot.

A **route search** is a search assignment that directs the team to guide along an identifiable natural or man-made landform **(Fig. 11-4)**. This is also called terrain-based searching. Natural landforms include streams, tree-line, ridge, valley, etc. Man-made landforms include roads, power/hydro-lines, fence/property lines, railroad tracks, etc.

Grid searches may help locate missing persons, find evidence **(Fig. 11-5)**, or rule out a large area (i.e. fields, forests). These are searches of last resort for missing persons when resources are limited. The reason for this is the amount of manpower required to conduct this type of search in an area.

The concept of grid searches calls for a large number of people, lined up in a straight row. The searches progress slowly and methodically with each person standing an even-spaced distance away from each other. One important key to grid searches is not to take the path of least resistance. All places must be involved such as thorny or rocky areas.

Grid searches are highly effective in discovering small clues as to the missing person's travel. Items passed over in a broader search are found by conducting a thorough grid search. Examples might include torn clothing, dropped jewelry, or equipment. Frequently, discoveries made during a grid search will lead to a location or point a direction for the next search.

(Fig. 11-5) Searchers conducting an evidence (grid) search at a dam. Image courtesy of J. Bobot.

Evidence searches are very methodical and time consuming. There usually is low urgency and are performed under the supervision of a forensic specialist. In most cases it is an "object" and not a "subject" that is being sought.

Continuous Limited Searches are those search operations that have had the physical "in the field" search suspended and are in an information-gathering phase as all possible objectives have been accomplished.

Likely spots

You, as a searcher, have an obligation to conduct the search in the segment that you are assigned. This means that if you are told to search the property and the adjoining outbuildings, and you know that the family and/or local law enforcement have done it prior, you need to search those areas again.

It is important that you "know" your subject. If the subject is a young girl who is always fishing or playing near the pond or a young boy who loves building forts in the forest, are their "likely spots" the same? Probably not.

Check drains and culverts as well as insets and caves. Look for any place your subject may take shelter **(Fig. 11-6)**. Always check the missing person's (MP's) property and home thoroughly **(Fig. 11-7)**.

(Fig. 11-6) Example of a "likely spot. A missing person would seek shelter in this hollow tree. Image courtesy of J.

11.3 Search Team Types

Search Team Types [1]

- Hasty Search Techniques (Type I Search Team)
- Loose Grid Search (Type II Search Team)
- Tight Grid Search (Type III Search Team)
- Evidence Search (Type IV Search Team)

(Fig. 11-8) Members of the Ohio Special Response Team's Hasty Team waiting for a mission at their annual FTX. Image courtesy of J. T. Bobot.

Hasty Search Techniques (Type I Search Team)

It requires that a specialized team conduct a rapid, efficient and conclusive search of an area with a high probability of producing the clues or the subject. These search teams provide a fast-initial response. They are usually four to six immediately available and very mobile searchers **(Fig. 11-8)**. They should be skilled enough to follow clues if discovered.

These are usually used early in search but may be used anytime. These teams are often used to investigate the area around a discovered clue of the initial last place the subject was seen. They may also be deployed to search high hazard locations within the search area, or a trail the subject was known to hike. These teams are made up of well-trained, self-sufficient, and very mobile searchers who deploy to likely spots that are quick and easy to search.

These would include "Points and lines" (no area) and consist of specific locations which might include:

- Camp sites & abandoned vehicles.
- Buildings (cabins, trailers, etc.).
- Trails, tracks, paths, roads.
- Thorough check of the last known point (LKP) or the point (or place) last seen (PLS).
- Follow known or suspected routes.
- Other "Likely Spots" that relate to the subject's character, likes and interests.

Last Known Point (LKP) is a physical location where you suspect the missing subject has been from the clues you have found. While Point Last Seen (PLS) is a location where someone last saw the lost subject and can change as the investigation develops.

Loose Grid Search (Type II Search Team)

The goal is to quickly cover larger areas with fewer resources **(Fig. 11-9)**. This search may use three to seven searchers, but usually just three. The amount of overlapping area scanned by searchers in adjacent search lanes should be minimal. The amount of area between adjacent search lanes scanned should be minimal.

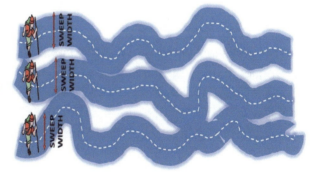

(Fig. 11-9) An illustration of a team conducting a Loose

Tight Grid Search (Type III Search Team)

The goal is conducting a very thorough, high coverage search of a segment **(Fig. 11-10)**. This search may use a crew made up of three to seven searchers, rarely more. This is a slow, highly systematic area search where unskilled searchers may be mixed with skilled searchers.

(Fig. 11-10) MISSING PICTURE

Evidence Search (Type IV Search Team)

The goal is the same as a tight grid search. This search may use a crew made up of seven to 10 or more searchers **(Fig. 11-11)**. This is a slow, highly systematic area search. Unskilled searchers should not be used. The overlapping of the search lanes is always used for increased coverage.

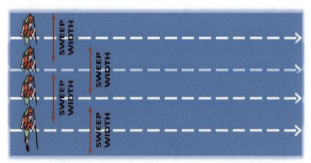

(Fig. 11-11) An illustration of a grid team conducting a thorough evidence search with overlapping lanes. Image courtesy of J. Bobot.

Route Cutting

It is important that if you suspect that the subject may have travelled on a particular trail or route, ensure that you do not walk in the center of that trail. Position the trail between you and the sun to allow the light to highlight any scuffs, tracks, prints or other marks. Make sure that you investigate all trail branches or other possible side routes for any sudden change in direction.

When sign cutting several different routes or segments of the search area, can allow the search planner to map all the clues found by the teams. This is vital in plotting the subject's direction of travel.

11.4 Vehicle Search

The subject's last known point (LKP) could have been the vehicle they leave behind at the trailhead parking lot. Evidence found in the vehicle may hold an important key to finding the missing subject. Crucially, if the vehicle is the last place a subject was known to be, preserving scent evidence for K9 handlers is the primary concern. Searchers should not enter a vehicle until a K9 handler has had a chance to retrieve a scent article. Search management should request that law enforcement also refrain from entering the vehicle until K9 handlers have arrived.

The types of evidence that may be found in the vehicle will be dependent on the person who left it. Items like alcohol or empty pill bottles (always check the name of patient, drug name, dose, when it was filled and the quantity). The date filled and quantity can lend to the amount the missing subject could have taken in the event of a possible suicide. The presence or absence of a cell phone could aid in contacting the subject or gathering information from text messages. Clothing left behind may indicate the subject's ability to deal with weather changes.

Before the searchers get to the car, like any other "likely spot" that could generate a clue, the searchers should cut for sign in a reverse fashion. Instead of circling out from a found clue, searchers should circle in toward the vehicle. This is done so that they do not contaminate the scene walking toward the vehicle from one of more directions.

Once the area around the vehicle has been adequately searched, the first phase of the vehicle search begins. The first phase of the vehicle search should include looking for prints near the doors and any discarded items or other clues that could be under the vehicle.

The second phase should be the front passenger compartment. If the vehicle is locked and inaccessible, simply peering through the windows can reveal clues. If the vehicle is unlocked and accessible, begin with the driver's side and systematically search the compartment. Make sure that you search all small cubby-holes and consoles as well as above the visors.

Once the driver's side of the front passenger compartment has been searched, continue to the passenger's side, and include the glove box.

(Fig. 11-12) A heroin needle under the driver's seat. Image courtesy of J. Bobot.

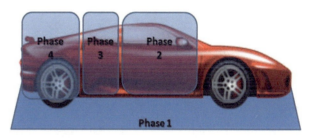

(Fig. 11-13) Example of the four phases of a vehicle search. Image courtesy J. Bobot.

⚠ CAUTION

The searcher needs to practice on the side of caution when searching under seats and hard to see areas. He-she does not want to stick their hands under a seat and risk being punctured by a contaminated needle or other item.

(Fig. 11-12)

A small mirror and flashlight will allow the investigator to check these areas without the risk of exposures or injuries.

The third phase will include the rear passenger compartment. The fourth phase of the vehicle search includes the hatch area, cargo area or trunk **(Fig. 11-13)**.

Any items found in a vehicle should be checked to help form a timeline of the last 24-48 hours. This would include receipts, documents with dates on it, medication bottles with date filled, the quantity and the dose. This can calculate how many pills should be in the bottle.

11.5 Evidence Handling

Another type of search data is evidence that is recovered during or even before the search begins. This evidence or individual objects or clues form a chain that links them to the missing subject. You may recover a boot print and a cigarette butt that matches the boot style and brand of the missing subject forming the evidence chain. [3]

In order to protect the clues that we find, we must assume that until the person is found alive and well, the search could lead to a criminal case. We must treat each clue as if it is evidence **(Fig. 11-14)** in a criminal case and protect the Chain of Custody (CoC).

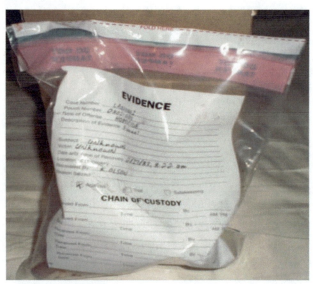

(Fig. 11-14) Example of an evidence bag. Clothing should be placed in paper bags to protect the scent. Image courtesy J. Bobot.

An example of chain of custody would be the recovery of a bloody knife at a murder scene:

- Officer Andrew collects the knife and places it into a container, then gives it to forensics technician Bill.

- Forensics technician Bill takes the knife to the lab and collects fingerprints and other evidence from the knife. Bill then gives the knife and all evidence gathered from the knife to evidence clerk Charlene.

- Charlene then stores the evidence until it is needed, documenting everyone who has accessed the original evidence (the knife, and original copies of the lifted fingerprints).

The chain of custody requires that, from the moment the evidence is collected, every transfer of evidence from person to person be documented and that it be provable that nobody else could have accessed that evidence. It is best to keep the number of transfers as low as possible.

In the courtroom, if the defendant questions the chain of custody of the evidence it can be proven that the knife in the evidence room is the same knife found at the crime scene. However, if there are discrepancies and it cannot be proven who had the knife at a particular point in time, then the chain of custody is broken, and the defendant can ask to have the resulting evidence declared inadmissible.

Chain of Custody (CoC) refers to the chronological documentation or paper trail, showing the seizure, custody, control, transfer, analysis, and disposition of evidence, physical or electronic. Because evidence can be used in court to convict persons of crimes, it must be handled in a scrupulously careful manner to avoid later allegations of tampering or misconduct which can compromise the case of the prosecution toward acquittal or to overturning a guilty verdict upon appeal. The idea behind recording the chain of custody is to establish that the alleged evidence is, in fact, related to the alleged crime, rather than having, for example, been planted fraudulently to make someone appear guilty.

Clue Processing

We don't often think we are doing anything wrong when we come across a clue when we are all trained to "find" clues, since that is what we are supposed to do. We don't just look for people, we look for clues that will lead us to the subject.

However, we need to be very cautious when dealing with clues. The problem begins when we start interacting with that clue. Every search and rescue mission involving a missing person should be considered a criminal act until proven otherwise. That is why, for most of the country, the local law enforcement agency runs search and rescue incidents.

Those clues that we handle could be used as **evidence** in a criminal case. Evidence in the broadest sense includes everything that is used to determine or demonstrate the truth of an assertion. Giving or procuring evidence is the process of using those things that are either (a) presumed to be true, or (b) were themselves proven via evidence, to demonstrate an assertion's truth. Evidence is the currency by which one fulfills the **burden of proof**. The burden of proof is often associated with the necessity of proof always lying with the person who lays charges. [4]

The first step in proper clue or evidence handling is to have a plan in place. This happens at the command or planning level and should be conveyed during the search mission or all-hands briefing. Any items that could be linked to a criminal case (bullet casing **(Fig. 11-15)** for example) should be left where it is found and the law enforcement agency with jurisdiction should be called.

(Fig. 11-15) A 9mm shell casing on the ground. Image courtesy J. Bobot.

Evidence can have many forms. We have seen that evidence can be a print that you have casted or a candy wrapper you picked up or that shirt that is being used as a scent article. If searchers are not told how to handle a clue, the searcher should start asking some important questions.

- How should the evidence be recorded? Should we bring it back to our debriefing? Sketch it, take a photo with our phone?
- How should search crews contact command? Should they use a cell phone (we all know the media monitors the radio frequencies) or use a code over the radio?
- How should the area around the clue be marked?

Handle any clue as if it were the only clue recovered and will be entered into evidence

11.6 Deceased Subjects

A missing person that is found alive is a subject. A missing person that is found deceased is evidence. Searchers must be respectful but must take certain precautions to protect the forensic evidence at the scene and on the remains.

The first team on scene with a subject should determine which team member has higher medical training (EMT, Paramedic, etc.). The team member with highest medical training should assess the subject for vital signs. If the subject requires medical assistance, the team should provide that until additional resources arrive on scene. If there are obvious signs of death, then the searcher should then leave the same way they approached. The search team should then secure the perimeter and keep everyone away from the body until the coroner/CSI personnel arrive.

Often, searchers who are not responsible for documenting the obvious death criteria can be too casual about the determination of death. They may be excited they have made a recovery, or they may decide not to try to resuscitate because the patient "looks dead" or falls within an accepted protocol for not rendering life-saving actions. But be mindful of those who may be investigating the incident and who must write the paperwork and meticulously document the physical findings that allowed them to make the determination of obvious death.

Searchers should be able to recognize the obvious signs of death that are standard protocols.

11.7 Searching for Bodies in Water

Understanding what happens to 'bodies in water' is not an exact science; the variables in every case are immense. However, there are some general 'rules of thumb', which have been learned and observed by those who have worked in this field for many years.

When someone goes into the water, whether accidentally or intentionally, it is impossible to say how long he or she will stay afloat before drowning. Factors such as clothing, injury, swimming ability, water temperatures etc., all play an important part in the eventual outcome.

When someone drowns, it is generally thought that the gasses in the body become compressed, causing the body to sink. Decomposition then sets in. After some time, gases accumulate within the body and it starts to rise to the surface again. Once on the surface, gases will eventually leave the body and it will once again sink. It is difficult to put a time scale to this, as much depends on surface temperature. There are resources that will estimate how long it takes a body to float in certain temperatures.

It is unusual for the body to resurface again for a second time. Bodies in rivers tend to get pushed to the sides. In slow-flowing waters, bodies can become trapped in deep pools and 'backwaters', (areas of water which flow up stream, usually near riverbanks). However, given time, it is usual for them to eventually get pushed out of these areas. Large rocks and sunken trees will often catch and hold bodies.

If someone arrives quickly enough at the scene, they stand a good chance of finding the person/body at or very near the point of entry. If the point of entry is known, there is a high probability that the body will remain on that side of the river for at least the first two bends downstream. In a river flowing at between one and half and three knots, a body will move down stream. Anything less and the body should remain in position. However, even in fast flowing rivers, there is a good chance that the body will remain near the point of entry.

Very often it is difficult and at times impossible to search the riverbank you are walking on because of overhangs or dense undergrowth **(Fig. 11-16)**. Searchers should have on PFDs (personal flotation devices) when 10 feet or less from water. Searchers should be placed on both riverbanks and be told to spend as much time searching the opposite bank as they do the bank they are standing on. The person on the opposite bank often has a better chance of seeing a body hung up on vegetation or tree roots than the person searching that bank.

(Fig. 11-16) Example of shoreline overhangs and dense undergrowth. Image courtesy of J. Bobot

It is always worth sending people quickly downstream to overlook the river from any vantage point, such as bridges or high embankments. This might give them the opportunity to spot the body being carried by the current. Shingle banks and shallow areas of water, downstream from the point of entry, should be given close attention as being potential catchment areas for the body. If the river has a clear flow to the sea, a body will go straight out to sea, particularly in the lower reaches of the river.

11.8 Urban Missing Person Search

This is a search in an urban setting, a city or suburb, rather than a wilderness setting. Searchers are asked to look for hiding spots and possibly be more alert to the possibility of criminal acts associated with the missing person. Dementia patients often go missing in more urban settings. Searchers must be more aware of hazards associated with urban settings to include traffic, animals, private property, industrial sites, chemicals, and confined spaces.

Small groups of three people who can quickly cover a neighborhood going door-to-door **(Fig. 11-17)**. This is both an informational gathering as well as an active search. Teams either get permission to search yards or ask that the owners search and call 911 if they find someone.

The urban setting can be set up much like that of a wilderness search **(Fig. 11-18)**. The area is broken into segments and systematically completed. It is estimated that it takes three to five minutes per house to conduct an urban interview. Segments should be sized with that consideration. Thus, about 15 houses an hour for three-person interview team.

(Fig. 11-17) The Meatpacking District neighborhood of Manhattan in New York City. Photo courtesy of GK tramrunner22

When someone is lost or missing, the more eyes out looking the better. One way to do this without putting untrained people in the field is to conduct urban interviews in the area. People may have seen the missing subject and not know it until someone asks them about it. This process is time and labor intensive and should be conducted by personnel that have the trust of the agency in charge such as the local C.E.R.T team, Red Cross, HAM Radio Group or other local volunteer group.

When you contact a landowner, you need to be courteous and friendly.

The Interview Team (Fig. 11-19)

- **Person #1** stands at the street and becomes the safety over-watch. They have radio comms to the ICP.

- **Person #2** is the greeter and introduces the group to the landowner and asks the questions like have you seen this child (shows photo).

- **Person #3** is the scribe, they document the street address, the name of the person and if they allow the team to enter the back yard or not.

(Fig. 11-18) Sections of a neighborhood set up much like a wilderness search. Photo courtesy of J. Bobot

Teams will complete the SAR-107 Urban Interview Form and return it to planning upon completion of their search. **(See SAMPLE DOCUMENT at the end of the unit)**

FOOTNOTES

(1) Bannerman, Foster, Hill, Hood, Thrasher & Wolf, (1999). Introduction to Search & Rescue. National Association for Search & Rescue.

(2) "SAR Field Search Methods - Search Techniques Used by Trained Teams in the Field", Kentucky Office of Emergency Management. Author unknown.

(3) Davis Oldham: 'Evidence' (English 101 & 102) at Shoreline Community College, shoreline.edu

(4) American College of Forensic Examiners Institute. (2016). The Certified Criminal Investigator Body of Knowledge. Boca Raton, Florida: CRC Press

VITAL VOCABULARY

Active Search Tactics: These are tactics that involve searchers entering the search area looking for subjects or clues.

Area Search: This is a search that has been assigned to team of five to seven trained searchers.

Burden of Proof: This is often associated with the necessity of proof always lying with the person who lays charges.

Chain of custody (CoC): This refers to the chronological documentation, or paper trail, showing the seizure, custody, control, transfer, analysis, and disposition of evidence, physical or electronic.

Continuous Limited Search: These are search operations that have had the physical "in the field" search suspended and are in an information-gathering phase as all possible objectives have been accomplished.

Evidence Chain: Individual clues that when linked together point to the missing subject.

Evidence Searches: These are very methodical and time consuming, usually low urgency and under the supervision of a forensic specialist.

Evidence: This, in its broadest sense, includes everything that is used to determine or demonstrate the truth of an assertion.

Grid Searches: These resource-intensive searches may help locate missing persons, find evidence, or rule out a large area (i.e. fields, forests) and should only be done after high-probability areas have been searched.

Last Known Point (LKP): This is a physical location where you suspect the missing subject has been from the clues you have found.

Passive Search Tactics: These are tactics that promote the subject seeking the searchers, keeping the subject in the search area or clues learned through investigation.

Point Last Seen (PLS): This is a location where someone actually last saw the lost subject and can change as the investigation develops.

Route Search: This is a search assignment that directs the team to guide along an identifiable natural or man-made landform. Also called a terrain-based search.

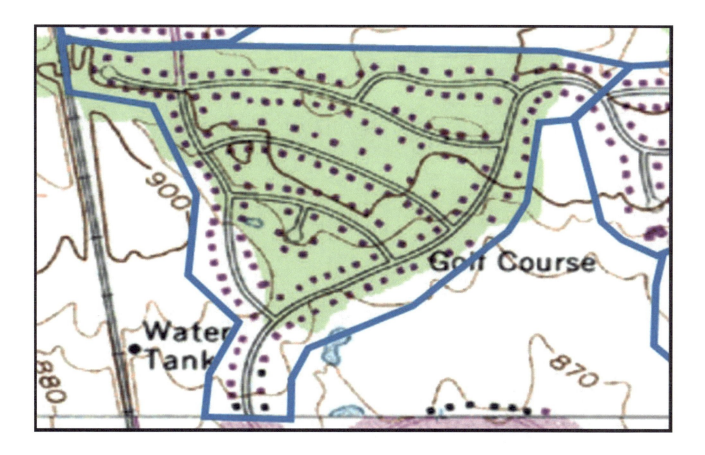

Using the map above with the street marked with a red line, we can calculate how long it should take a three person team to contact all
the homes on the road using 3-5 (4 of average) minutes it takes to
conduct an interview.

If there are 25 homes on the road and we multiply that number by 4 (minutes each). It should take about 100 minutes or one hour and
forty minutes.

It also would take a three-person team to contact 15 homes per hour.

KEEPING TRACK OF YOUR PACES WHILE CONDUCTING AN AREA SEARCH

You are tasked to conduct an area search along a compass heading for a given distance. If you were to search along the heading your search width would be greatly reduced. You would not be able to "purposely wander within your search area".

If you have a trekking pole you can pace out 10 paces and stick the pole in the ground along your heading. Then you are free to wander around to look for clues. Once you have spent a few moments looking, go back to the trekking pole, shoot another heading and pace out another 10 paces and repeat until you reach the end of your track.

"Purposely wandering" allows for investigation of the terrain around you.

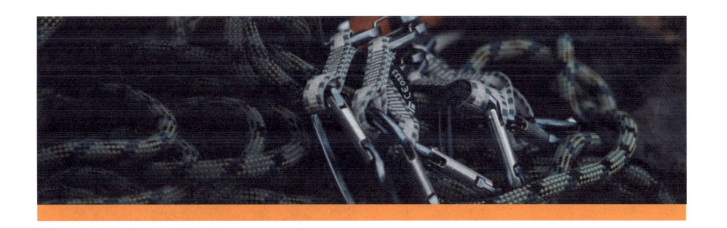

UNIT 12 | **RESCUE & RECOVERY**

12.1 The Rescue Phase
12.2 Factors Leading to Rescue
12.3 Rope Composition and Care
12.4 Knots and Hitches
12.5 Wilderness Extrication and Medical Care

Upon completion of this chapter and the related course activities, the student will be able to meet the following objectives:

- Be able to demonstrate the nine knots and hitches used in SAR
- Identify the parts of a rope and the basic care and maintenance
- Be able to assist with documentation of care
- Be able to build the hypothermic burrito

12.1 The Rescue Phase

This is the portion of LAST that consists of the last three components:[1]

Accessing... by walking up to the person or by the use of technical rescue methods such as ropes.

Stabilize... Once the subject is accessed, they must be stabilized prior to transport. For the most part, your basic first-aid skills will be enough.

Transport... Moving the subject to medical personnel. When you come across a missing subject, approach slowly and calmly! Evaluate the MP's Vital signs and stabilize any life-threatening conditions prior to transport and extrication.

Accessing the Subject

We are searching for a lost or missing person. This person is also known as the **subject**. The subject will become a **patient** once emergency care has begun.

(Fig. 12-1) OSRT Rope Rescue Team member hooked in to a stokes basket. Image courtesy of J. Bobot.

Search and rescue teams may come across terrain that is too dangerous to simply continue to walk, or they may find a subject that is in an inaccessible or dangerous location. Remember that YOUR SAFETY comes first, so don't rush to reach a patient that is in a potentially hazardous location. Take your time and assess the scene, don't let adrenaline lead you into danger or an injury. **Hazardous terrain** is any landform that requires mitigation (specialized equipment and training) in order to traverse. Crews need to have a basic understanding of how to safely traverse a hazardous crossing.

Most search and rescue volunteers have basic rope skills, and many take specialized courses to learn how to build and use complex rescue systems. Until you have received more training than is offered in this course, you should always wait for experienced personnel to arrive and assist. This unit will give an overview of the ropes, knots and equipment that is often used in the rescue of a missing person.

Some basic rope skills can aid the search team leader and crew completing their search assignment. The search team needs to have some basic rope rescue equipment in order to traverse a hazardous crossing. If the team does not have the minimum equipment or training, the crossing should never be attempted. If a team is unable to cross a portion of your search assignment, the team has two options; call for a specialized team to assist the search crew with the crossing or report this inability to search during the debriefing. Whenever technical rescue needs are a possibility, those resources should be called early and placed on stand-by. Technical rescue requires advanced training and equipment **(Fig. 12-1)**.

12.2 Factors Leading to a Rescue

Anyone, or any combination of events, may produce a situation that results in the need to be rescued, stabilized, and treated. When a person is unable to self-rescue, they will require the assistance from emergency providers.

Some of the general reasons why a person may need rescue are:

- Improper clothing or footgear and inadequate preparation for weather conditions resulting in hypo or hyperthermia.
- Fatigue due to overextension of abilities.
- Dehydration and inadequate food.
- Lack of physical conditioning, injury, illness, or exposure to an adverse environmental condition or event.
- Itinerary confusion or lack of navigational proficiency (getting lost) due to inadequate planning and leadership.
- Inadequate recognition of environmental, physical, or mental factors.
- Accidental injury that makes "walking out" impossible.

When part of a rescue team, make sure that you respond with what you will need to assess, treat, and stabilize the patient in the field. Even more importantly, is what you will need to maintain that treatment in the event that the extrication will be prolonged due to rapid weather changes or other conditions. Be prepared! It is highly recommended that those who complete any wilderness search and rescue course also be trained to at least the level of an advanced wilderness first aid (WFA) provider. The completion of a wilderness first responder (WFR) or wilderness EMT (WEMT) course is preferred.

Rope rescue is a subset of technical rescue that involves the use of static nylon kernmantle ropes **(Fig. 12-2)**, anchoring and belaying devices, friction rappel devices, various devices to utilize mechanical advantage for hauling systems, and other specialized equipment to reach subjects and safely recover them. Rescue should not be attempted by individuals who have not been formally trained. Local rescue authorities may be able to provide information on rope rescue training, practice, and equipment.

Belaying refers to a variety of techniques used in climbing to exert friction on a climbing rope so that a falling climber does not fall very far. A climbing partner typically applies the friction at the other end of the rope whenever the climber is not moving, removing the friction from the rope whenever the climber needs more rope in order to be able to continue climbing. The term **belaying** is also used to mean the place where the belayer is anchored; this would typically be a ledge, but may instead be a hanging belay, where the belayer is suspended from protection in the rock.

(Fig. 12-2) OSRT Rope Rescue Team member going over the edge of a cliff. Image courtesy of J. Bobot.

12.3 Rope Composition and Care

Kernmantle rope is rope constructed with its interior core (the kern) protected with a woven exterior sheath (mantle) that is designed to optimize strength, durability, and flexibility. The core fibers provide the tensile strength of the rope, while the sheath protects the core from abrasion during use. The name is derived from German Kernmantle which means coat protected core.[2] One or more of the rope characteristics (strength, durability, and flexibility) are often altered somewhat, depending upon the ultimate use of the rope, at the expense of the other properties.

For example, rope used in caving is generally exposed to more abrasion than other forms of recreation, so the mantle is woven more tightly than rope used in climbing or rappelling. However, the resulting rope is cumbersome and difficult to tie knots in.

Kernmantle construction **(Fig. 12-3)** may be used with both **static rope** and **dynamic rope**. Static ropes are designed to allow relatively little stretch, which is most useful for hauling, rappelling, and other applications. Dynamic rope is used to belay climbers and is designed to stretch under heavy load to absorb the shock of a fallen climber.[3]

A dynamic rope is a specially constructed, stretchable rope. This 'stretch' is what makes it dynamic, in contrast to a static rope that doesn't have any give when under load. By stretching under load, a dynamic rope will soften the impact of extreme stresses on it, such as falls, and lessens the likelihood of failure. This is particularly useful in rock climbing, where it can absorb much of the energy of a fall (referred to as a whipper amongst rock climbers).

The rope is a climber's lifeline. It must be cared for and used properly. These general guidelines should be used when handling ropes.[4]

(Fig. 12-3) Internal structure of 10.7mm dynamic kernmantle climbing rope. The rope is composed of a 40 strand "two-over-two" braided sheath and a core made from seven 3-ply yarns with a single green tracer strand running parallel to the core yarns. Note that four of the seven core yarns are S-twist (left-handed) and three are Z-twist (right-handed). In this image the three plies of the left-most core yarn are spread apart. Sample from trimmed end of a used climbing rope. Photo courtesy of David J. Fred

- Do not step on or drag ropes on the ground unnecessarily. Small particles of dirt will be ground between the inner strands and will slowly cut them.

- While in use, do not allow the rope to come into contact with sharp edges. Nylon rope is easily cut, particularly when under tension. If the rope must be used over a sharp edge, pad the edge for protection (edge pro).

- Always keep the rope as dry as possible. Should the rope become wet, hang it in large loops off the ground and allow it to dry. Never dry a rope with high heat or in direct sunlight.

- Never leave a rope knotted or tightly stretched for longer than necessary. Over time it will reduce the strength and life of the rope.

- Never allow one rope to continuously rub over or against another. Allowing rope-on-rope contact with nylon rope is extremely dangerous because the heat produced by the friction will cause the nylon to melt.

- Inspect the rope before each use for frayed or cut spots, mildew or rot, or defects in construction (new rope).

- The ends of the rope should be whipped or melted to prevent unraveling.

- Do not splice ropes for use in mountaineering.

- Do not mark ropes with paints or allow them to come in contact with oils or petroleum products. Some of these will weaken or deteriorate nylon.

- Never use a mountaineering rope for any purpose except mountaineering.

- Each rope should have a corresponding rope log, which includes date put into service, dates of inspection and any other material info.

- Never subject the rope to high heat or flame. This will significantly weaken it.

- All ropes should be washed periodically to remove dirt and grit, and rinsed thoroughly. Commercial rope washers are made from short pieces of modified pipe that connect to any faucet. Another method is to machine wash, on a gentle cycle, in cold water with a nylon safe soap - never bleach or harsh cleansers. Ensure that only front-loading washing machines are used to wash ropes.

- Ultraviolet radiation (sunlight) tends to deteriorate nylon over long periods of time. This becomes important if rope installations are left in place over a number of months.

- When not in use, ropes should be loosely coiled and hung on wooden pegs rather than nails or other metal objects. Storage areas should be relatively cool with low humidity levels to prevent mildew or rotting. Rope may also be loosely stacked and placed in a rope bag and stored on a shelf. Avoid storage in direct sunlight, as the ultraviolet radiation will deteriorate the nylon over long periods.

A rope can be cleaned by forming it into a **chain sinnet** **(Fig. 12-4)** to prevent excessive tangling and washing it in front-loading clothes washing machine with soap flakes. Strong cleansers, including bleach and detergent should not be used on life-critical nylon components. Commercial rope cleaning devices are also available. A chain sinnet, also called a daisy chain, is a method of shortening a rope or other cable while in use or for storage. It is formed by making a series of simple crochet-like loops in the line. It can also reduce tangling while a rope is being washed in a washing machine.

(Fig. 12-4) An example of the chain sinnet. This is also called a daisy chain. Image courtesy of David J. Fred.

12.4 Knots and Hitches

There are only a few **knots** and **hitches** that are needed in most rescue situations by search and rescue personnel. Every searcher should learn a few useful knots and practice them often. Bights and bends are usually used in combination with a Figure "8" knot. These can be bulky, but are effective in joining ropes together around an anchor point. When using ropes, understanding basic terminology is important. The terms explained in this section are the most commonly used in search and rescue and military mountaineering. A **bight** is any curved section of a rope while a **bend** is the joining of two pieces of rope. A **loop** is a bend of a rope in which the rope does cross itself while a **half hitch** is a loop that runs around an object in such a manner as to lock or secure itself. A **turn** wraps around an object, providing 360-degree contact **(Fig. 12-5)**.[5]

The ends of the rope have different names. The **running end** is the loose or working end of the rope while the **standing end** or part is the static, stationary, or loaded end of the rope. The pigtail is the portion of the running end of the rope between the safety knot and the end of the rope.[6]

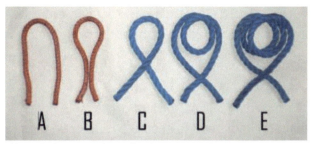

(Fig. 12-5) A: open loop, B: closed loop, C: turn, D: round turn, E: two round turns. Image courtesy of Peter Harremoës.

It is very important that a SAR technician is able to tie several basic knots. These knots not only need to be tied correctly, but every knot needs to be **dressed**. Dressing a knot is the proper arrangement of all the knot parts, removing unnecessary kinks, twists, and slack so that all rope parts of the knot make contact and it is easy to identify and safety check.

The knots and hitches that are recommended for search and rescue crews are:

- The Square Knot (Any Rope or Cord)
- The Double Fisherman's Knot
- The Figure "8" Knot
- The Figure "8" on a Bend
- Figure "8" Retrace (same as on a bend)
- The Figure "8" on a Bight
- The Prusik Knot
- The Water Knot

There are four steps to tying a good knot:

1. **DRESS...** Try to keep the ropes free of twists – with legs running side-by-side.
2. **LOAD...** Once tied, the knot should be pulled tight to avoid any accidental movement when line is loaded.
3. **TEST LOAD...** before life-loading!

4. **SAFETY...** Refers to securing any loose ends. If knot has a loose end (tail), it should be secured using another knot (a **safety knot**).

Square Knot (Fig. 12-6)

A square knot is an ancient and simple binding knot used to secure a rope or line around an object. A square knot is formed by tying a left-handed overhand knot and then a right-handed overhand knot, or vice versa. A common mnemonic for this procedure is "right over left, left over right", which is often appended with the rhyming suffix "... makes a knot both tidy and tight".

(Fig. 12-6) The Square Knot. Image courtesy of the US Army Field Manual 3-97. [7]

Tying the Knot

1. Holding one working end in each hand, place the working end in the right hand over the one in the left hand.
2. Pull it under and back over the top of the rope in the left hand.
3. Place the working end in the left hand over the one in the right hand and repeat STEP 2.
4. Dress the knot down and secure it with an overhand knot on each side of the square knot.

Checkpoints

- There are two interlocking bights.
- The running end and standing part are on the same side of the bight formed by the other rope.
- The running ends are parallel to and on the same side of the standing ends with four-inch minimum pig tails (fist-length) after the overhand safeties are tied.

Double Fisherman's Knot (Fig. 12-7)

The double fisherman's knot (also called double English or grapevine) is used to tie two ropes of the same or approximately the same diameter. It is a joining knot.

Tying the Knot

- With the working end of one rope, tie two wraps around the standing part of another rope.

- Insert the working end (STEP 1) back through the two wraps and draw it tight.

(Fig. 12-7) The Double Fisherman's Knot. Image courtesy of the US Army Field Manual 3-97.

- With the working end of the other rope, which contains the standing part (STEPS 1 and 2), tie two wraps around the standing part of the other rope (the working end in STEP 1). Insert the working end back through the two wraps and draw tight.

- Pull on the opposing ends to bring the two knots together.

Checkpoints

- Two double overhand knots securing each other as the standing parts of the rope are pulled apart.

- Four rope parts on one side of the knot form two "x" patterns, four rope parts on the other side of the knot are parallel.

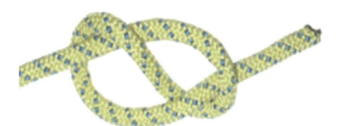

(Fig. 12-8) The In-Line Figure "8" Knot. Image courtesy of the US Army Field Manual 3-97.

- Ends of rope exit knot opposite each other with 4-inch pigtails.

In-Line Figure "8" (Fig. 12-8)

The figure eight is the most common knot used in SAR. It is very important method of stopping ropes from running out of retaining devices. Unlike the overhand knot, which will bind iron-hard under strain, often requiring the rope to be cut, the figure of eight can be easily untied after even the greatest strain.

Tying the Knot

- Grasp the top of a two-foot bight.

- With the other hand, grasp the running end (short end) and make a 360-degree turn around the standing end.

- Place the running end through the loop just formed creating an in-line figure eight.

Checkpoint

- Ensure that the knot is in a figure "8" shape and not a simple overhand knot.

(Fig. 12-9) The Figure "8" on a Bend. Image courtesy of the US Army Field Manual 3-97.

Figure "8" on a Bend (Fig. 12-9)

The figure eight on a bend is used to join the ends of two ropes of equal or unequal diameter within 5mm difference.

Tying the Knot

1. Grasp the top of a two-foot bight.

2. With the other hand, grasp the running end (short end) and make a 360-degree turn around the standing end.

3. Place the running end through the loop just formed creating an in-line figure eight.

4. Route the running end of the other ripe back through the figure eight starting from the original rope's running end. Trace the original knot to the standing end.

5. Remove all unnecessary twists and crossovers. Dress the knot down.

(Fig. 12-10) The Follow-through/retrace Figure "8". Image courtesy of the US Army Field Manual 3-97.

Checkpoints

- There is a figure eight with two ropes running side by side.

- The running ends are on opposite sides of the knot.

- There is a minimum 4-inch pigtail.

Figure "8" Retrace (Same as on a bend) (Fig. 12-10)

The figure-eight retrace knot produces the same result as a figure-eight loop. However, by tying the knot in a retrace, it can be used to fasten the rope to trees or to places where the loop cannot be used. It is also called a rerouted figure-eight and is an anchor knot.

Tying the Knot

1. Use a length of rope long enough to go around the anchor, leaving enough rope to work with.

2. Tie a figure-eight knot in the standing part of the rope, leaving enough rope to go around the anchor. To tie a figure-eight knot form a loop in the rope, wrap the working end around the standing part, and route the working end through the loop. The finished knot is dressed loosely.

3. Take the working end around the anchor point and insert the rope back through the loop of the knot in reverse.

4. Keep the original figure eight as the outside rope and retrace the knot around the wrap and back to the long-standing part.

5. Remove all unnecessary twists and crossovers; dress the knot down.

Checkpoints

- A figure eight with a doubled rope running side by side, forming a fixed loop around a fixed object or harness.

- There is a minimum four-inch pigtail.

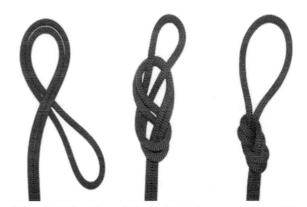

(Fig. 12-11) The Figure "8" on a bight. Image courtesy of the US Army Field Manual 3-97.

Figure "8" on a Bight (Fig. 12-11)

The figure eight on a bight is used to form a fixed loop in a rope. It is a middle or end of the rope knot commonly used in conjunction with a carabiner for a tensionless anchor.

Tying the Knot

1. Form a bight in the rope about as large as the diameter of the desired loop.

2. With the bight as the working end, form a loop in rope (standing part).

3. Wrap the working end around the standing part 360 degrees and feed the working end through the loop. Dress the knot tightly.

Checkpoints

- The loop is the desired size.
- The ropes in the loop are parallel and do not cross over each other.
- The knot is tightly dressed.

Water Knot (Fig 12-12)

The water knot is used to attach two webbing ends. It is also called a ring bend, overhand retrace, or tape knot. It is used in runners and harnesses and is a joining knot.

Tying the Knot

1. Tie an overhand knot in one of the ends.
2. Feed the other end back through the knot, following the path of the first rope in reverse.
3. Draw tight and pull all of the slack out of the knot. The remaining tails must extend at least 4" beyond the knot.

(Fig. 12-12) The Water Knot before tightening (top) and after (bottom). Image courtesy of David J. Fred.

Checkpoints

- There are two overhand knots, one retracing the other.
- There is no slack in the knot, and the working ends come out of the knot in opposite directions.
- There is a minimum four-inch pigtail to allow for safety knots to be added.

(Fig. 12-13) The Prusik Knot. Image courtesy of the US Army Field Manual 3-97.

Prusik Knot (Fig. 12-13) - Friction Hitch

A Prusik knot is a friction hitch or knot used to put a loop of cord around a rope, applied in climbing, canyoneering, mountaineering, caving, rope rescue, and by arborists. The Prusik knot (hitch) is used to put a moveable rope on a fixed rope such as a Prusik ascent or a tightening system. This knot can be tied as a middle or end of the rope Prusik. It is a specialty knot made from a section of accessory cord joined by the double fisherman's knot called a Prusik sling.

When the knot is free of a load, the knot will easily slide along the rope it is attached to. However, when a load is placed on the knot, it will lock down and prevent any further movement.

Tying the knot

1. Take the Prusik Loop (six-foot length of 6mm cord connected with a double fisherman's knot) and lay to end, opposite the knot on the working rope.

2. Reach down through the 12-inch bight. Pull up both of the working ends and lay them over the long rope. Repeat this process making sure that the working ends pass in the middle of the first two wraps. Now there are four wraps and a locking bar working across them on the long rope.

3. Dress the wraps and locking bar down to ensure they are tight and not twisted. Tying an overhand knot with both ropes will prevent the knot from slipping during periods of variable tension.

Checkpoints

- Four wraps with a locking bar.
- The locking bar faces the climber.
- The knot is dressed with no ropes twisted or crossed.
- Other than a finger Prusik, the knot should contain an overhand or bowline to prevent slipping.

(Fig. 12-14) The Clove Hitch. Image courtesy of the US Army Field Manual 3-97.

Clove Hitch (Fig. 12-14)

The clove hitch is an anchor knot that can be used in the middle of the rope as well as at the end. The knot must have constant tension on it once tied to prevent slipping. It can be used as either an anchor or middle of the rope knot, depending on how it is tied.

Tying the Knot

1. Hold rope in both hands, palms down with hands together. Slide the left hand to the left from 20 to 25 centimeters.

2. Form a loop away from and back toward the right.

3. Slide the right hand from 20 to 25 centimeters to the right. Form a loop inward and back to the left hand.

4. Place the left loop on top of the right loop. Place both loops over the anchor and pull both ends of the rope in opposite directions. The knot is tied.

Checkpoints

- The knot has two round turns around the anchor with a diagonal locking bar.
- The locking bar is facing 90 degrees from the direction of pull.
- The ends exit 180 degrees from each other.
- The knot has more than a four-inch pigtail remaining.

The Safety Knot

As an added measure of safety, use an overhand safety knot whenever tying any type of knot. Although any properly tied knot should hold, it is always desirable to provide the highest level of safety possible. Use of the overhand safety knot eliminates the danger of the end of the rope slipping back through the knot and causing the knot to fail.

12.5 Wilderness Extrication and Medical Care

This text will not cover comprehensive wilderness medical care as there are hundreds of courses, textbooks and information available to the SAR student. However, there are a few recommendations that should be considered. As for the level of medical care that should be provided in the remote wilderness setting, it is safe to say that the highest possible should be provided.

Most medical care providers are "urban" based such as basic first aid or even emergency medical technicians. It is highly recommended that all urban providers take a wilderness or remote medical course such as Wilderness First Responder (WFR) or a Wilderness EMT (WEMT). Having a member of the team who is at least a Wilderness First Aid provider is vital.

When a subject is located, they may be in need of medical assistance. Making sure that you have basic medical first aid equipment in you 24-hour pack is for you, but also for a subject that needs care. Whichever team member has the highest medical training should take the lead and immediately begin assessing the patient. Another team member can begin to request additional resources, including higher medical care or equipment, like a stretcher, or litter, which is the most commonly used means of extrication. There are several different kinds used in the backcountry - ones used in the snow are different that those used in summertime. A litter is a medical device used to carry casualties or an incapacitated person from one place to another. To prep the subject for transport when the temperature is cooler and to prevent shock and hypothermia, wrap them in a "hypothermia burrito" fashion.

"The Thermal Burrito" Hypothermia Wrap

Perhaps one of the most common and most dangerous ailments to affect the outdoor traveler is hypothermia. And though many factors may lead to hypothermia, it is most commonly the result of wet clothing, a cold environment or improper clothing.

Most climbers encounter the onset of mild hypothermia at one point or another during their careers. Many of us have certainly hung belay station, shivering, and wondering we didn't bring that extra jacket. But for most of us, things never get any worse than that. Severe hypothermia in the field requires immediate attention. Wilderness medicine providers have devised a simple treatment which relies on a variety of materials that most backcountry travelers normally carry.

(Fig. 12-15) The Hypothermia Burrito. Apply heat packs (in extreme cold) and wrap in a double (wool blanket outer and space blanket inner) layer, folding and covering the victim. The addition of a simple 8x8 plastic tarp can add a wind barrier on the outer layer. Image courtesy of the www.outdoorED.com.

They use these pieces of equipment to create a "thermal burrito" or a "hypo-wrap" **(Fig. 12-15)**.

- Lay out a tarp on the ground.
- Place 1 or 2 pads down on top of the tarp. Two pads are always better than one.
- Stack three sleeping bags on top of the pads.
- Place the victim inside the sleeping bag in the middle.
- Wrap the victim in the tarp.
- Provide the victim with hot water bottles. These should be placed under the arms and at the crotch. Additional bottles may be held or placed at the victim's feet. [8]

Documentation

While team members are assessing and requesting resources, others can be taking notes for the medical provider, so that a good hand off to higher medical care can happen when the subject is brought out, or those resources come in. Until that happens, the search team is responsible for the patient and so must document care.

When documenting the assessment, care and treatment of a wilderness patient in a remote setting, the ability to "trend" a patient is vital. Trending is the recording of patient vital signs to identify any physiological. It is recommended that any stable patient should have their vital signs taken every fifteen to thirty minutes. While an unstable patient should have their vitals taken every five to ten minutes.

While documenting your medical care there are so many different methods to do this. As with other aspects of response, this text recommends the "CHART" method of documenting patient care. In the available narrative section of your department or agency run report the CHART method is used. This method is a simple way to organize your thoughts and assessment, especially for those who are new to patient assessment and care.

CHART method

CHART narratives follow a visual layout based on the letters in the acronym to document patient care. Here is a checklist of questions medical providers should answer before submitting a patient care report (PCR):

- Are your descriptions detailed enough?
- Are the abbreviations you used appropriate and professional?
- Is your PCR free of grammar and spelling errors?
- Is the chief complaint correct?
- Is your impression specific enough?
- Are all other details in order?

C - This section is for the patient's chief complaint. This is what the patient "tells you" and not what you note. This would also be the "symptoms".

H - This section is for the history of the present injury or illness. What happened or led up to the incident.

A - This section is usually the largest and consists of your primary and secondary assessment. You would include the ABC's and any life-threatening conditions. You would include your findings from your head-to-toe secondary assessment such as broken bones or medical findings, or "signs."

R - This section is for treatment. You can use the symbol for a prescription (℞) if you would like.

T - This section is for your transport considerations and actions.

FOOTNOTES

(1) Bannerman, Foster, Hill, Hood, Thrasher & Wolf, (1999). Introduction to Search & Rescue. National Association for Search & Rescue.

(2) Andreas Unterschuetz. "All Single Rated Climbing Ropes Available".

(3) Sterling Rope Guide to Rope Engineering, Design, and Use

(4) Army Field Manual FM 5-125 (Rigging Techniques, Procedures and Applications) (PDF). Technical Manual No. 3-34.86/Marine Corps, Reference Publication 3-17.7J. The United States Army. 2012.

(5) Ashley, Clifford W. (1944), The Ashley Book of Knots, New York: Doubleday.

(6) History and Science of Knots, K&E Series on Knots and Everything, Singapore: World Scientific Publishing, pp. 181–203, ISBN 978-981-02-2469-1

(7) Field Manual FM 3-97.61 (TC 90-6-1) Military Mountaineering August 2002

(8) American Alpine Institute - Climbing Blog, August 2008. Posted by Jason D. Martin.

(10) Advanced Search And Rescue Paperback – January 2, 2006. Published by The: National Association For Search & Rescue. By Craig Banner. ISBN-10: 0986444030.

(11) Leuthäusser, Ulrich (June 17, 2016). "The physics of a climbing rope under a heavy dynamic load". Journal of SPORTS ENGINEERING AND TECHNOLOGY. doi:10.1177/1754337116651184.

(13) "How to use a chronological approach for ePCR narratives". EMS1.com. April 3, 2017.

VITAL VOCABULARY

Belaying: This refers to a variety of techniques used in climbing to exert friction on a climbing rope so that a falling climber does not fall very far.

Bend: term used to join to pieces of rope.

Bight: This is any curved section, slack part, or loop between the two ends of a rope.

Chain Sinnet: This is a method of shortening a rope or other cable while in use or for storage.

Dress: This is the proper arrangement of all the knot parts, removing unnecessary kinks, twists, and slack so that all rope parts of the knot make contact.

Dynamic Ropes: These ropes are specially constructed, stretchable rope designed to soften the impact of extreme stresses on it, such as falls, and lessen the likelihood of failure.

Fall Factor: This is the ratio of the length a climber falls before his rope begins to stretch and the amount of rope available to absorb the energy of the fall.

Half Hitch: This is a loop that runs around an object in such a manner as to lock or secure itself.

Hazardous Terrain: This is any landform that requires mitigation (specialized equipment and training) in order to traverse.

Hitch: This is a type of knot used for binding rope to an object.

Kernmantle Rope: This is a rope constructed with its interior core (the kern) protected with a woven exterior sheath (mantle) that is designed to optimize strength, durability, and flexibility.

Knot: This is a method of fastening or securing linear material such as rope by tying or interweaving.

Loop: A loop is a bend of a rope in which the rope does cross itself.

Patient: This is someone to whom you have started rendering emergency care.

Prusik Sling: This is a mechanical rope-grab that works like a ratchet, moving freely up the rope, but grabbing when a load is placed down on it.

Running End: A running end is the loose or working end of the rope.

Safety Knot: This is a simple knot used to secure the primary knot if adequate tail is remaining.

Standing End: The standing part is the static, stationary, or nonworking end of the rope.

Static Ropes: These ropes are designed to allow relatively little stretch, which is most useful for hauling, rappelling, and other use.

Subject: This is someone who is waiting for assistance and has suffered an injury or medical emergency.

Turn: This is part of the rope that wraps around an object, providing 360-degree contact.

UNIT 13 | LOST PERSON BEHAVIOR

13.1 Missing/Lost Person Research

13.2 Building a Search Plan

13.3 Dementia and Alzheimer's Disease

13.4 Additional Considerations

13.5 Reactions to Being Lost

Upon completion of this chapter and the related course activities, the student will be able to meet the following objectives:

- Explain the concept of missing person behavior and how individual characteristics are used in planning
- Understand the characteristics of a missing person with dementia
- Be aware of the possible methods of suicide and build that into your planning

13.1 Missing/Lost Person Research

Missing person behavior studies refers to the analysis of historical search data for the purpose of gaining insight into the likely actions of a lost or missing person. We use this data to draw conclusions or best guess planning on where to search. For example, lost subjects will frequently follow travel aids, such as geographical paths of least resistance or trails.[1]

Most of the current missing person behavior statistics and characteristics come from the International Search & Rescue Incident Database (ISRID). The ISRID is an ongoing research project established in 2002 by Jim Donovan. The overall goal of the project was to develop a low-cost graphical software package to assist in the planning and operations of ground SAR. Data was collected from 12 countries. As of 2008, the ISRID project had collected 50,692 SAR cases with the majority from the United States (91%), followed by New Zealand (5%), Canada (2%) and the United Kingdom (1.4%) from over 40 agencies and organizations. Missing or lost subjects are classified by either their age group, their activity, or their mental status.

It is helpful, at the onset of a search, to consider the answers to the following basic questions about subject behavior and to search accordingly: 1) is the subject mobile or immobile, and 2) is the subject responsive or unresponsive? As time elapses and intelligence or clues are obtained regarding the subject, these scenarios can become more specific regarding subject intentions, background, and the characteristics of the search area.[2]

In predicting lost person behavior, it is useful to place them into 'Subject Categories.' There has been a lot of work done on this over the years, but doesn't it make sense that a lost child at a fair is going to behave differently than a despondent adult?

SAR team members can use this to predict behavior and increase their likelihood of finding the missing person. The missing person can be placed into one of the different subject categories and then searchers can use the certain behavior traits that particular group has. They can use that knowledge to predict actions and allocate resources that reflect those predictions. A lot of these studies have come out of North America but there are also many UK sources. There are numerous excellent research, books, studies, texts, websites, and courses out there on the subject and many notable authorities.

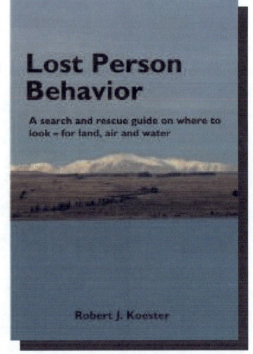

One such book is **"Missing Person Behavior" by Robert J. Koester**. This book places lost and missing persons into 41 categories from the International Search & Rescue Incident Database (ISRID) which contains over 50,000 reported SAR incidents. This data has been collected from Australia, Canada, New Zealand, South Africa, Switzerland, United Kingdom, and the USA.

Lost person behavior statistics refers to the analysis of historical search data for the purpose of gaining insight into the likely actions of persons being searched for.

13.2 Building a Search Plan

In order to manage an incident involving a search for a missing person we need a search plan. Understanding Lost Person Behavior is key to this plan. Ideally this plan will be the outcome of some organized process or procedure that will answer a few key questions such as:

- Where should we search?
- Who are we looking for? - Not just a description, but a "profile" - a psychological and physical profile.
- How do we search with the resources we have?
- What type of containment do we need?
- What additional investigation should be carried out?

When developing a search plan, we need to create a scenario that helps form the basis for the search methodology. The importance of developing a search plan is to allow the story to illuminate what the missing subject did leading up to their disappearance and using that insight to form a strategic plan.[2]

A deductive reasoning approach is a method of systematically analyzing the circumstances surrounding the subject who is lost or missing. The outcome of the analysis is then applied to the establishment of the search area. For example, realizing that a hiker is known to travel off trails will result in expanding the search area to include these areas. Knowing that a photographer had a specific destination for that day will help establish the search area in that general direction.

Why should searchers consider lost person behavior? As the primary function of a searcher is to locate clues, the ability to understand as much as we can about our missing subjects will aid in the locating of those clues.

Missing person behavior can aid searchers by:

- Knowing if this lost person falls in a group that would travel long distances or be unlikely to navigate difficult terrain.
- Knowing if the lost person would "hide" or "evade" the searchers.
- Knowing if the lost person would answer a voice call or a whistle.

Factors That Affect Missing Person Behavior:

- General state of mental and physical health of the subject and ability to cope.
- Outdoor experience/survival training.
- Effects of the environment (Terrain, vegetation and weather).
- Circumstances leading up to their disappearance.
- What were their known plans/routes?

- Knowledge of the area in which they are lost.

13.3 Dementia and Alzheimer's Disease

Dementia is a broad term that describes a group of conditions in which a person has a progressive loss of cognitive functioning and memory, and can also include personality changes and decline of social skills. The most common cause of dementia is **Alzheimer's Disease**, but they are not interchangeable.

The cause for most Alzheimer's cases is still mostly unknown except for the one to five percent of cases where genetic differences have been identified. Alzheimer's Disease is characterized by loss of neurons and synapses in the cerebral cortex and certain subcortical regions. **(Fig. 13-3)** This loss results in gross atrophy of the affected regions of the brain.

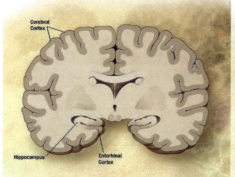
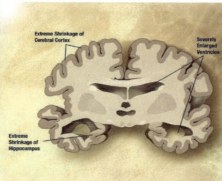

(Fig. 13-3) Comparison of a normal aged brain (left) and the brain of a person with Alzheimer's (right). Characteristics that separate the two are pointed out. Image courtesy of ADEAR: "Alzheimer's Disease Education and Referral Center, a service of the National Institute on Aging."

Alzheimer's Disease and related dementias can cause a person to act in different and unpredictable ways. Some individuals with dementia become anxious or aggressive. Others repeat certain questions or gestures, while others misinterpret what they hear.[6] These types of reactions can lead to misunderstanding, frustration and tension, particularly between the person with dementia and the caregiver. It is important to understand that the person is not acting that way on purpose. Aggressive behaviors may be verbal (shouting, name-calling) or physical (hitting, pushing). These behaviors can occur suddenly, with no apparent reason, or can result from a frustrating situation. Whatever the case, it is important to try to understand what is causing the person to become angry or upset.

The person with Alzheimer's may not recognize familiar people, places, or things. He or she may forget relationships, call family members by other names or become confused about where home is. They can get stuck in a prior time period, believing that they live someplace they moved from decades ago. The person may also forget the purpose of common items, such as a pen or fork.

Memory loss and confusion may cause the person with Alzheimer's to perceive things in new, unusual ways. Individuals may become suspicious of those around them, even accusing others of theft, infidelity or other improper behavior. It's common for a person with dementia to wander and become lost. In fact, more than 60 percent of individuals with Alzheimer's will wander at some point. They may try to go home when already there or may be attempting to recreate a familiar routine, such as going to school or work.[7]

Wandering can be caused by a number of external stimulants. This behavior may be related to:

- Physical discomfort - Illnesses or medication.
- Overstimulation - Loud noises or a busy environment.
- Unfamiliar surroundings - New places or the inability to recognize home.
- Complicated tasks - Difficulty with activities or chores.
- Frustrating interactions - Inability to communicate effectively.

Sundowning Syndrome is a psychological phenomenon associated with increased confusion and restlessness in patients with some form of **dementia**. Most associated with Alzheimer's disease, but also found in those with mixed dementia, the term "sundowning" was coined due to the timing of the patient's confusion. For patients with sundowning syndrome, a multitude of behavioral problems begin to occur in the evening or while the sun is setting. [8]

While the specific causes of sundowning have not been empirically proven, some evidence suggests that circadian rhythm disruption enhances sundowning behaviors. Sundowning seems to occur more frequently during the middle stages of Alzheimer's disease and mixed dementia. Patients are generally able to understand that this behavioral pattern is abnormal. Sundowning seems to subside with the progression of a patient's dementia. Research shows that 20 to 45 percent of Alzheimer's patients will experience some sort of sundowning confusion.

Symptoms are not limited to but may include:

- Increased general confusion as natural light begins to fade and increased shadows appear.
- Agitation and mood swings. Patients may become fairly frustrated with their own confusion as well as aggravated by noise.
- Patients found yelling and becoming increasingly upset with their caregiver or rescuer is not uncommon.
- Mental and physical fatigue increase with the setting of the sun. This fatigue can play a role in the patient's irritability.
- Tremors may increase and become uncontrollable.
- A patient may experience an increase in their restlessness while trying to sleep.
- Restlessness can often lead to pacing and or wandering which can be potentially harmful for a patient in a confused state.

13.4 Additional Considerations

Missing Children with ADHD

Children with ADHD who go missing can be at greater risk because of their condition. Attention Deficit Hyperactivity Disorder (ADHD) affects both children and adults.

The main characteristics of ADHD are hyperactive and impulsive behavior, often coupled with a very short attention span, and a difficulty forming relationships with others.[9]

Their awareness of danger is reduced, which can lead them to engage in some physically dangerous activities, such as playing near fast flowing rivers or railway lines. They can be impulsive, often acting before they think, they are easily distracted and often forgetful. Children with ADHD tend to travel further than children of a similar age who do not have ADHD. Their poor social skills may make it difficult for them to ask for help, or to engage with others. Because the effects of ADHD medication last for around four to five hours, it is imperative to establish early on in any missing person enquiry when the child last took his or her medication.

Due to the impulsive nature of their condition and their tendency to be distracted by irrelevant things, it is difficult to predict the places that they will be found. Therefore, it is extremely important to establish what their interests are, as these may provide vital clues as to the places they are likely to go to or the activities they might indulge in. Finally, remember that no label or diagnosis will give a perfect description of an individual child with ADHD. They are all different and will act in different ways. [10]

Suicidal Ideology

In some cases, enough investigative data may lead to the conclusion that a missing subject may be suicidal, or despondent. Therefore, it may be prudent to develop the 'twin-track' search strategy where one track is based on the probability that this is a conventional missing person and the other is based on the probability that the person intends to take their own life. When planning the search strategy in relation to the probable or possible suicide, the first steps are to consider the likely method used and likely location chosen **(Table 13-1)**.

Suicidal ideation is thinking about, considering, or planning suicide. The range of suicidal ideation varies from fleeting thoughts, to extensive thoughts, to detailed planning.[11] Most people who have suicidal thoughts do nogo on to make suicide attempts, but suicidal thoughts are considered a risk factor.

TABLE 13-1
Common Methods Of Suicide For Males
➢ Hanging
➢ Jumping from cliff, bridge, etc.
➢ Hit by train
➢ Car exhaust
➢ Setting fire to themselves
➢ Drug overdose
➢ Electrocution
➢ Self-inflicted gun shot
➢ Slashing neck/wrist
Data taken from "Missing Person, Understanding & Responding" By Grampian Police Department, North East Scotland.

13.5 Reactions to Being Lost

The psychology of becoming lost presents a paradox. Lost individuals can't really be studied until they are found. Then, it's too late. When you become lost, you are disoriented, and your perception is distorted. The woods no longer feel familiar, and your confidence level is greatly diminished.

Many outdoor travelers, especially hunters, believe there is some sort of shame in becoming turned around. But it happens. We have all heard the stories. They usually begin like this. "I wasn't lost; camp was lost!" or "I got turned around and twisted."

Often, the excuse blames other circumstances, as in, "It sure got dark fast!" or, "The trail was poorly marked, steeper, longer and in worse shape than expected." On occasion, the truth comes out. "I was tired and wasn't paying attention," or, "I was tracking a wounded deer and lost my bearings," or, "I forgot my map, compass, flashlight ..."

External circumstances are often blamed, and a thick swamp, a heavy blowdown or a poorly marked trail intersection takes the brunt of the blame. Rarely does the individual traveler take responsibility for becoming lost.

Possible Corrective Actions

Generally, people who find themselves "lost" will become emotional, irrational, scared or panicky. When this happens, they will attempt to correct their situation and use one or more the following methods.

Hug-A-Tree / Stay Put - This is the most successful tactic employed by those who find themselves "lost." Every woods safety program stresses the importance of "staying where you are" when becoming "lost". Very few people employ this tactic, possibly due to how passive it is. Children are the most likely to use it.

Random Walking - These subjects are totally confused, and usually very emotional, they move around in random patterns attempting to locate something that is familiar. After a while they usually change tactics or stop and stay. However, school-age children tend to continue to employ these tactics and not stop until they are exhausted.

Travel Aid Following - These subjects will attempt to follow trails, paths, drainages or other landforms that present themselves as aid to their travel. They are uncertain as to which direction they are to go, so they just continue to walk along a path of least resistance.

Direction Sampling - These people are certain that help is just over the hill or around the bend, so they simply walk in any direction until they are again reminded that they are "lost" and change direction. There have been cases where missing subjects have walked across roads, highways and railroad tracks because there were sure the direction they were going would take them home. This tactic has often placed them even deeper into areas where their chance of injury is higher.

Trail Sampling - These people are just like those who employ direction sampling but use trails and paths as their guides. They will pick a path and walk it until they reach a decision point and randomly choose a direction.

Backtracking - These people, once they get turned around, reverse their direction in order to find something that is familiar. This can be a very effective method if the lost person has the skills and patience to employ it. Unfortunately, lost persons seem reluctant to reverse their direction of travel without good reason, believing perhaps that it would just be a waste of time and safety might be over the next hill or around the next bend in the trail.

A child can be there one minute and gone the next… each person deals with being lost or missing in different ways. It is up to us, as search planners and searchers, to predict how they will react. Photo courtesy of J. Bobot

Using Folklore - This is a miscellaneous category that refers to an attempt to find themselves by stories or folklore adages on how to find their way in the woods or being lost. Some are that all water leads to civilization, or moss only grows in the north side of a tree.

When It Happens

The first step in not becoming a statistic is coming to the realization that you are lost. The very second that thought crosses through your head you need to stop. In the first hour, the panic that can set in kills. Panic is a very powerful force. As your body detects the fear it pumps out tremendous amounts of adrenaline and endorphins into your system. Both have a narcotic effect and are responsible for your increased breathing, your body feeling warm and breaking out in a sweat.

There are documented cases of people becoming lost in the woods, throwing off all of their gear and even ripping off their clothing as they run panicked through the forest. When night falls, with no gear, no water and no clothing, exposure sets in and kills of the lost hiker. The most frightening thing about being lost in the woods is you will not truly know how you will react until it happens.

FOOTNOTES

(1) Hill KA, ed. Managing the Lost Person Incident. 2nd ed. Centreville, VA: National Association of Search and Rescue; 2007.

(2) Wilderness Search Strategy and TacticsKen Phillips, BS; Maura J. Longden; Bil Vandergraff; William R. Smith, MD; David C. Weber, BS;Scott E. McIntosh, MD, MPH; Albert R. Wheeler III, MD, WILDERNESS & ENVIRONMENTAL MEDICINE,25,166–176 (2014)

(3) Missing Person Behaviour - An Aid to the Search Manager, 1st Edition, Dave Perkins and Pete Roberts Northumberland National Park SRT, Centre for Search Research Ged Feeney Penrith MRT & Mountain Rescue Council Statistics Officer.

(4) Turner, J.M. (July 2002). "From Woodcraft to 'Leave No Trace': Wilderness, Consumerism, and Environmentalism in Twentieth-Century America" (PDF). Environmental History. Environmental History, Vol. 7, No. 3. 7 (3): 462–484. doi:10.2307/3985918. JSTOR 3985918.

(5) "In Depth History of Leave No Trace". Leave No Trace. Archived from the original on 2006-07-18.

(6) Burns A, Iliffe S (February 2009). "Alzheimer's disease". BMJ. 338: b158. doi:10.1136/bmj.b158. PMID 19196745.

(7) U.S. Congress, Office of Technology Assessment (1992). Special care units for people with Alzheimer's and other dementias: Consumer education, research, regulatory, and reimbursement issues. Washington DC: Government Printing Office. ISBN 978-1-4289-2817-6.

(8) Khachiyants N, Trinkle D, Son SJ, Kim KY (2011). "Sundown syndrome in persons with dementia: an update". Psychiatry Investig. 8: 275–87. doi:10.4306/pi.2011.8.4.275. PMC 3246134. PMID 22216036.

(9) Attention Deficit Hyperactivity Disorder". National Institute of Mental Health. March 2016. Archived from the original on 23 July 2016.

(10) Dobie C (2012). "Diagnosis and management of attention deficit hyperactivity disorder in primary care for school-age children and adolescents": 79. Archived from the original on 1 March 2013.

(11) Gliatto, MF; Rai, AK (March 1999). "Evaluation and Treatment of Patients with Suicidal Ideation". American Family Physician. 59 (6): 1500–6. PMID 10193592.

VITAL VOCABULARY

Alzheimer's Disease (AD): This is an incurable, degenerative, and terminal disease and is characterized by a serious loss of cognitive ability in a previously unimpaired person, beyond what might be expected from normal aging and is the most common form of dementia.

Dementia: This is a serious loss of global cognitive ability in a previously unimpaired person, beyond what might be expected from normal aging

Folklore: This consists of legends, music, oral history, proverbs, jokes, popular beliefs, fairy tales and customs that are the traditions of a culture, subculture, or group.

Suicidal Ideation: This is the thinking about, considering, or planning suicide.

Sundowning Syndrome: This is a psychological phenomenon associated with increased confusion and restlessness in patients with some form of dementia.

Made in the USA
Columbia, SC
05 July 2025